REVOLUTION AND AUTHORITARIANISM
IN NORTH AFRICA

FRÉDÉRIC VOLPI

Revolution and Authoritarianism in North Africa

HURST & COMPANY, LONDON

First published in the United Kingdom in 2017 by
C. Hurst & Co. (Publishers) Ltd.,
41 Great Russell Street, London, WC1B 3PL
© Frédéric Volpi, 2017
All rights reserved.
Printed in India

The right of Frédéric Volpi to be identified as the author of
this publication is asserted by him in accordance with the
Copyright, Designs and Patents Act, 1988.

A Cataloguing-in-Publication data record for this book
is available from the British Library.

ISBN: 9781849046961

This book is printed using paper from registered sustainable
and managed sources.

www.hurstpublishers.com

CONTENTS

CONTENTS

ACKNOWLEDGEMENTS

I have been fortunate enough to spend my time in the collegial sur-roundings of the School of International Relations at the University of St Andrews during the writing of this book. I am grateful for all the productive exchanges that I have had with my colleagues over the last few years, and particularly with the members of the Institute of Middle East, Central Asia and Caucasus Studies. Special thanks to Ray Hinnebusch and Adham Saouli for sharing their insights about the region. My students in my courses on the Middle East and North Africa, at both undergraduate and postgraduate level, also kept the debate alive over the years. Special acknowledgement to my former PhD student Carmen Geha, with whom I had many an interesting discussion on Libya.

I wish to acknowledge the support of the Gerda Henkel Foundation, which provided funding through their programme 'Security, Society and the State' for a research project in Tunisia. The time I spent there was crucial in shaping my views about the political evolution of the country. My colleague and collaborator on this project, Fabio Merone, played a key role in introducing me to many little-known aspects of Tunisian social and political activism, and I am most grateful for his help and insights. Thanks are also due to Francesco Cavatorta for insti-gating this collaboration in the first place and for our valuable exchanges over the years.

I also wish to acknowledge the support of the LabexMed research laboratory at the Maison Méditerranéenne des Sciences de l'Homme for offering me a research fellowship at the Institut de Recherches et

ACKNOWLEDGEMENTS

d'Etudes sur le Monde Arabe et Musulman (IREMAM) in Aix-en-Provence. My stay there was highly beneficial for documentary research on the region. I am grateful to Myriam Catusse for facilitating this process, and for her research insights. I also benefited from discussions with Amin Allal during my stay.

Finally, I wish to thank the Centre for the Advanced Study of the Arab World (CASAW) for funding the research network 'People, Power and State Power', which provided a most useful context for scholarly exchanges during the time I was working on this book. A special acknowledgement to Ewan Stein who expertly co-directed the network with me and with whom I had so many interesting exchanges about the trajectories of the uprisings. Thanks to Larissa Alles, our research fellow for the network, who was most helpful in coordinating these activities. Thanks also to Emanuela Dalmasso for sharing her insights and contacts in Morocco in that context.

In the elaboration of the conceptual framework of the book I have benefited from discussions with Charles Kurzman, James Jasper and John Chalcraft. All the conceptual flaws or misrepresentations contained in the book are entirely mine. Thanks to all the colleagues who shared their views about the Arab uprisings over the last few years; some of their thoughts are to be found here in one form or another.

Thanks to Michael Dwyer and Jon de Peyer for all their efforts on the publication front.

Finally, I must give an enormous thank-you to Julia, my wife, and to Lada and Marie, my daughters, for their support and patience during all those months that I spent working on this book.

1

INTRODUCTION

UNDERSTANDING AND EXPLANING THE ARAB UPRISINGS

'In international affairs, and throughout the social world, there are two sorts of stories to tell and a range of theories to go with each. One story is an outsider's, told in the manner of a natural scientist seeking to explain the workings of nature and treating the human realm as part of nature. The other is an insider's, told so as to make us understand what the events mean, in a sense distinct from any meaning found in unearthing the laws of nature.'

Martin Hollis and Steve Smith,
Explaining and Understanding International Relations

In International relations, comparative political studies, or social movement research, we face recurrent dilemmas regarding the most appropriate way to present patterns of change. The events of the Arab uprisings in North Africa in 2011 constitute no exception. They can be described by actor-centric narratives stressing the contingency of protest episodes and their outcomes. They can also be portrayed as unfolding longer-term trends in which specific combinations of economic, military, social and political factors regularly shape the form and outcomes of change. These two 'stories', as Martin Hollis and Steve Smith call them, cannot easily be combined into a linear explanation. In effect, law-like generalizations are meant to minimize precisely those idiosyncratic factors that are crucial to an actor-centric perspective. A 'natural scientific' approach identifies those factors that constrain (or facilitate) human action in a regular fashion, so that idiosyncratic behaviours are averaged out and the process of change is more structured and predictable. This situation would reflect Marx's notion that people make history but not in circumstances of their own choosing. Agent-focused accounts, by contrast, indicate to what extent historical understandings, cultural interpretations, socio-economic constraints or institutional processes can be transformed by the skilful (or fortunate) articulation of choices and actions that people generate. In this perspective, there is no history to be made; there are just histories that people make for themselves as they experience events.

In 'explanations' we commonly combine these two 'stories'—wittingly or unwittingly—into a single narrative.[1] Sometimes one type of account is intuitively more meaningful, sometimes the other. However, the distinction highlighted by Hollis and Smith remains crucial in the sense that it makes clear that there is no way of fully reconciling these two worldviews. The more one considers in detail what made sense for specific actors—be they revolutionaries, occasional protesters, soldiers, generals or presidents—in particular circumstances, the more one unearths idiosyncratic views that cannot be neatly subsumed under a general theory of action. Conversely, the more one looks for law-like, statistically expressed generalizations, the more political transformations can be explained retrospectively on the basis of known processes of institutional change, regardless of the actors' views on the matter. There cannot be an explanation of political change that offers both the most detailed insider's perspective and the most thorough scientific account of the very same political events.

In recent years, the 'dynamics of contention' approach developed by Doug McAdam, Sidney Tarrow and Charles Tilly has been criticized precisely on this point.[2] Their account of contentious events grounded on specific mechanisms and processes ended up reintroducing through the back door a form of structural historical dependency to underpin the overall comparative framework.[3] Ultimately, it is not a case of choosing the one or the other. It is more a case of appreciating the limitations of our argument when we have to stress one aspect of change at the expense of the other. As Mounia Bennani-Chraïbi and Olivier

Fillieule have suggested regarding the Arab uprisings, what matters is to balance law-like historical processes and thick narratives of particular events without trying to subsume the one into the other.[4]

Comparatively speaking, the dominant tendency in recent decades has been to stress statistically relevant generalizations in order to provide more systemic models for different categories of interactions. Even when considering highly uncommon political transformations like revolutions, the focus remains on identifying clear patterns in hectic processes of change. Sidney Tarrow noted that while 'moments of madness—when "all is possible"—recur persistently in the history of social movements', the important question about such moments was, in his view, 'their relation to the historical development of the repertoire of contention'.[5] A dominant trend in social movement theory stresses the importance of repertoires of contentious actions that are transmitted between places and over time, and that regularly shape the form, means and outcomes of political contention. In this perspective, the specific actor-centric narratives that help activate these generic mechanisms become relatively uninteresting after the event because they are hardly more meaningful than 'moments of madness'.[6] In such a (natural scientist) explanatory perspective, what does not repeatedly make sense does not make sense.

In democratization studies the significance of actor-centric views has long been central to the debate. In the conclusion to their classic *Transitions from Authoritarian Rule*, Guillermo O'Donnell and Philippe C. Schmitter stressed that during periods of democratic transitions, 'the high degree of indeterminacy embedded in situations where unexpected events (fortuna), insufficient information, hurried and audacious choices, confusion about motives and interests, plasticity, and even lack of definition of political identities, as well as the talents of specific individuals (virtù) are frequently decisive in determining the outcomes'.[7] This emphasis was meant to set apart these episodes of political transition from institutionalized processes that entrenched established political choices and behaviours.[8] In a similar perspective in the case of revolutionary change, Charles Kurzman highlighted that what shaped the actions of the protesters at the height of the Iranian revolution was often very far removed from the putative causes for mobilization that analysts had posited.[9] In such a context, the rational choice models and cost-benefit analyses invoked to explain the event hardly took into account what a revolutionary situation was like but instead generated abstract actors who behaved according to abstract reasons in order to explain the outcome.

Scholars of democratization and revolution have tried hard to detail the factors that structure such political behaviours, especially when the main actors of change are not part of the elites. Considering mobilization among communal elites, Dan Slater warned that 'spontaneity and creativity may be quintessential traits of contentious politics, but this does not mean that collective protests are equally likely to erupt or to prevail in all times and places. Unless we do the historical work to uncover where oppositional political cultures come from, it is difficult, if not impossible, to explain why so many societies have produced neither democratic revolutions nor large-scale authoritarian crackdowns but persistent quiescence.'[10] While the endeavour to identify regularities across time and space is commendable, it is too often the case that the 'quintessential' spontaneous creativity of the actors, once acknowledged, disappears from the actual explanation. In many recent accounts of the Arab uprisings, this tension is palpable when it comes to describing the apparent unpredictability of these events. At best, as Kurzman has remarked, the importance of meaning for the participants is acknowledged in a tick-box fashion, as a set of 'independent variables' whose implications are not considered seriously in the explanatory framework.[11] Often, the temptation is simply to say that extraordinary protest behaviour is primarily the result of people being mistaken about what they could possibly achieve by revolting. In that case, analysing the pathways of reform and repression implies leaving aside the dynamics of the uprisings themselves in order to better join the dots between the political situations obtaining before and after events.[12]

Making sense of the Arab uprisings

The account that I present in this book strives to retain the implications of meaning-making in the construction of the causality and understandings of the 2011 Arab uprisings in North Africa. The argument is not merely that the idiosyncrasies introduced by multiple actors undermined the structural unfolding of revolution and transition in the region, but also that the protest episodes themselves were crucial elements in the formation of new political identities and processes. The task therefore is to generate better linkages between actor-based processes and the institutional-based dynamics of regime change and political reform. To this end, I introduce a distinction in the explanatory narrative between episodes characterized by a high degree of indeterminacy and periods characterized by institutionalized politics and routine (authoritarian) governance. Hence, rather than compare and contrast the situations of those Arab countries that experienced regime change in 2011, I map the processes of change and of resilience that followed protest episodes in two countries that witnessed dramatic political transformations (Tunisia, Libya) and in two countries that experienced only mild institutional reform (Algeria, Morocco).

In the most hectic cases of transition, the process observed is that of a political revolution which involves the fall of the old regime and the institutionalization of a new political system. In more managed processes of change, we have institutional reforms initiated in the face of protest that lead to the reassertion of the power of the ruling elites, with more or less significant concessions made to opposition actors. In my account of the Arab uprisings in North Africa, I focus on the rapid meso-level transformation of these behavioural and institutional routines. The changes considered can be relatively transient, such as the Algerian riots of January 2011, or limited in scope, such as the Moroccan 20 February Movement. They can be socially and politically more significant for longer periods of time, as with the Tunisian Revolution and democratic transition or with the recurrent armed mobilization and conflict in Libya since 2011. In all cases, protest episodes end in a formal return to institutionalized politics, usually in the shape of an electoral democracy—be it as a substantive system of governance or as a front for continuing authoritarian rule. This return to 'normality' is characterized, domestically and internationally, by an intersubjective recognition that the actions of government and opposition are once again predictable and routine.

In this perspective, analyses of the overall trajectories of stability and change in the region prior to the uprisings continue to provide useful insights into the dynamics subsequent to the uprisings. It would be misguided to discard earlier works on authoritarianism in the region simply because they did not anticipate the form and content of the 2011 uprisings. These earlier perspectives are useful not only because 'old-style' authoritarianism is still very prevalent in the Middle East, but also because they illustrate the diversity of political dynamics and explanations of the region. It is precisely the contrast between contentious politics and routine authoritarian governance that helps us to better comprehend the spectrum of politics in the region. The *explanandum* of the book, the phenomenon that is to be understood, is the shift between one form of routine governance and another in four countries affected by the 2011 wave of uprisings. This account is thus not constructed primarily to characterize regime failure or revolutionary success across the region. Instead, it proposes an analysis of the trajectories of mobilization in the four North African countries that highlights their convergences and divergences, and the linkages between protest dynamics and models of governance.

Before the uprisings, those scholars focusing on law-like generalizations in Middle East and North African politics generally came to the conclusion that no dramatic change of regime was to be expected there in the short to medium term. The 'other story', focusing on the perspective of the actors in the region did not fare particularly better. Analyses of social, religious and political activism considering a substantive transformation of the views and possibilities of political action did not suggest that a sizeable wave of anti-regime contestation was coming. Both at the institutional and the grassroots level, scholars noted how people made sense of the prevailing situation of authoritarian governance, and developed cognitive and practical strategies to cope with, avoid, benefit from or subvert the 'rules of the game'.[13] Their accounts clearly explained change and resilience during periods of routine authoritarian governance by approximating political agency under ordinary circumstances. What they were not meant to explain were situations when routines broke down and agency became more unpredictable. Kurzman argued that 'the greater the degree of deinstitutionalization, the harder it is to argue that people are falling back on an established pattern of behavior without being aware of doing so'.[14] Once protest events began to gain momentum across the region in early 2011, earlier understandings of authoritarian resilience became far less relevant in explaining the dynamics of these non-routine situations.

The narrative proposed in this book stresses how social and political actors are more than fettered to the past and guided by predictable means–ends calculations. Yes, people always and everywhere do make history in circumstances not chosen by themselves. However, neither they nor those recounting their story are fully aware of the circumstances. As such, their actions, and the consequences of these actions, are only explained intersubjectively in relation to those circumstances that each narrative finds most relevant for its own explanatory purposes.[15] In the book, I adopt a three-stage approach to narrating the processes of change during the Arab uprisings in North Africa (reflecting three sets of circumstances). While there are processes that overlap several periods, each stage is characterized by a dominant set of causal dynamics. The first stage corresponds to the implosion of the ruling authoritarian system. This period is defined by the sharp increase in the mobilization of protesters against the regime and an accompanying decrease in the capabilities of the ruling institutions. The second stage corresponds to the reconstruction of practices and discourses around the demands of the protesters and the counter-propositions of the regime to halt the process of deinstitutionalization. This period is marked by the diffusion of new consensuses and compromises that underpin a new (actual or promised) political order, and the institutionalization of new or reformed mechanisms of governance. The third stage involves the reconstruction of routinized behaviours in and by this new system of governance. This period is characterized by a formal recognition of these new arrangements at home and abroad—be they the outcome of revolutionary dynamics or of a more or less genuine reform process—and by political demobilization.

The book ahead

Chapter 2 starts with an examination of the debates about authoritarianism and democratization, and stability and change, in an 'exceptional' Middle East. I outline how mainstream accounts of Middle East politics framed stalled transition processes and authoritarian 'upgrading' as structural features of regional stability. The chapter then introduces the notion of mobilization in relation to the construction of protest events, arenas and actors. I make an analytical distinction between political causality and causal explanations during periods of rapid deinstitutionalization, and during periods of routine (authoritarian) governance. Processes of institutional and extra-institutional changes are thus understood in terms of the (re)production of specific set of interactions. This perspective diverges from earlier structural accounts of regional politics explaining regime stability through an analysis of the factors constraining institutionalized processes of change or protest mobilization. The framework departs from conventional notions of political opportunity structure by proposing an explanatory narrative of protest episodes grounded on the interactions between acts, arenas, and agents of contention (in that specific order).

Chapter 3 presents the longer-term factors that have been known to shape routine authoritarian governance prior to the Arab uprisings. The notion of routine authoritarian governance emphasizes the ideational and material importance of sequences of interactions regularly followed by both government and opposition over time. Among these interactions I focus particularly on the role that legitimacy, coercion and cooptation played in the entrenchment of specific patterns of political behaviours ('authoritarian bargains'). As a counter-weight to this narrative, I highlight how 'protest costs' were repeatedly overcome at different historical junctures, and how regimes had to adapt in response to these (unsuccessful) challenges from below or from counter-elites. Authoritarianism in the pre-Arab uprisings period is thus narrated as an ever-changing combination of identities and practices that has been maintained at equilibrium by ruling elites for several decades

Chapter 4 introduces the 'eventful sociology' that characterizes the emergence of protest episodes in the four country cases. Events are non-routine sequences of actions that reshape the routine forms of governance (and opposition) structuring everyday social and political life. Transformative events initiate a transformation of behaviours, which is both strategic and reactive, reshaping social and political life first at the local level. In this chapter, I describe the emergence of new causal processes and their interaction with pre-existing practices of governance. To this end I place side by side the views and strategies of different pro- and anti-regime actors in the face of unexpected events and consequences. The narrative outlines how sequences of events produced new practices, arenas and actors of contestations, often as unintended consequences. This event-centric account of protest episodes highlights the transformative role of protest as protest in the construction of newly effective forms of political behaviours.

Chapter 5 focuses on the routinization of the interpretative and behavioural changes initiated by these protest episodes. I detail the rearticulations of protest mobilization and their implications for preexisting practices of governance. The analysis illustrates how the self-reflective construction of 'revolutionary' practices fundamentally reframed government and opposition interactions. The modalities of mobilization and the role played by violence are flagged as the factors that most decisively shaped the strategic choices of the protesters at that stage of the uprisings. A rising protest momentum is only one of the possible outcomes of the protests. The counter-narrative illustrates how the routinization of protest can lead instead to the entrenchment of non-system-challenging forms of mobilization. In those cases, the interactions between actors progressively reaffirm the repertoires of contention and techniques of governance already established in the polities.

Chapter 6 returns to the issue of routine governance in North Africa in the post-uprisings context. Here I detail the processes of reinstitutionalization of new or reformed models of governance in each of the four country cases. These processes indicate the construction of revised political consensuses which become embodied in the institutional reorganizations of the immediate post-uprisings period. As a counterweight to this narrative, I highlight the continuities in mobilization that keep challenging the authority of the post-revolutionary state or the reformed authoritarian system. The narrative is articulated around key events that signal a new acknowledgement of routine, institutionalized forms of governance instead of protest behaviours. In this context, the construction of 'revolutionary' and 'reformist' narratives serves to produce post-uprisings actors by breaching the gaps between the many understandings and experiences of the uprisings. The interactions between these revised repertoires and identities structure the politics of the post-uprising states by entrenching a new combination of democratic and authoritarian routines.

2

ACTS, ARENAS AND ACTORS

FRAMING THE UPRISINGS

The 'exceptionalism' of the Middle East

Just before the Arab uprisings, Asef Bayat noted that 'the idea that "everywhere the world has changed except for the Middle East" has assumed a renewed prominence, with different domestic and international constituencies expressing different expectations as to how to instigate change in this region'.[1] Just as Bayat echoed a long-standing frustration about the lack of political progress in the Middle East, scholars and policy-makers alike were about to be utterly surprised by the sudden turn of events in the region. Not only would there be change in a region that previously had been characterized by decades of authoritarian resilience, but the form that those challenges to authoritarianism took during the Arab uprisings was also unexpected. This book investigates the form and content of these uprisings. It is about the shape of those particular 'democratic revolutions' and models of authoritarian resilience that prevailed in North Africa in the second decade of the 21st century. The argument elucidates some crucial features of the processes of revolutionary change and authoritarian governance that produced successful and unsuccessful cases of regime change in four North African countries—Tunisia, Libya, Algeria and Morocco.

My contention throughout this book is that the events witnessed recently in the Middle East and North Africa (MENA), and the causal dynamics underpinning them, are not 'exceptional'. While such revolutionary political transformations are uncommon—like the regional political context that produced them—they are located on the same spectrum of political causality as other political processes. The notion of 'exceptionalism', which has a long, infamous pedigree in Middle East politics, is more often than not an indication of intellectual capitulation rather than an element of political explanation. 'Exceptionalism' is merely an avoidance strategy in the face of evidence that requires a serious rethinking of those theoretical and analytical perspectives commonly used to explain routine political governance and change.

Before the Arab uprisings, the issue of a supposed regional exceptionalism to democratization was duly criticized by both comparativists and area specialists. Scholars commonly stressed that generic models of democratization were too simplistic and did not consider sufficiently the causal processes shaping political order (and change) in different sets of circumstances.[2] While sophisticated comparative and specialist accounts all envisioned the possibility of democratic change in the MENA region, they highlighted the practical impediments that constrained such development in the 2000s.[3] As the academic and policy debate increasingly focused on the practical obstacles to political democratization, a dominant narrative emerged by the end of the decade that stressed that change would be most unlikely in the short to medium term in the region.[4]

This partial blindness to the possibility of rapid and dramatic change in the MENA countries contributed in a roundabout way to the implicit return of the idea of regional exceptionalism and created many of the subsequent explanatory conundrums regarding the Arab uprisings. This fallacy was usually not grounded on essentialist arguments derived from an older Orientalist vision of the Middle East that stressed that the political and religious culture there was fundamentally different from a 'Western' one. This type of narrative was already largely discredited by the 2000s, even though lingering stereotypes continued to underpin representations of the Middle East, particularly in relation to political Islam.[5] Instead, scholarly debates generated a form of conjectural exceptionalism grounded on empirical observations of recent political developments in the region that emphasized the circumstantial production (and reproduction) of strong authoritarian systems and weak democratic opposition forces. Such a perspective helped to naturalize the presence of authoritarianism in the region by highlighting the multiple mechanisms by which authoritarian regimes could maintain the status quo.[6] Scholars of comparative politics thus noted that, relative to other regions, the Middle East displayed a reduced propensity towards democratization.[7] Steven Heydemann's notion of authoritarian upgrading, based on the instrumentalization by ruling elites of civil and political society, of economic reform, of communication technology and of international linkages, captured well the causal underpinnings of this circumstantial 'exceptionalism'.[8]

These perspectives on institutionalized authoritarianism and routine authoritarian governance contributed to the portrayal of a growing depoliticization of social and political movements in the region. In this particular context, Bayat coined the term 'nonmovements' to refer to the 'collective actions of noncollective actors'. To account for the possibility of change, he argued that nonmovements embodied 'shared practices of large numbers of ordinary people whose fragmented but similar activities trigger much social change, even though these practices are rarely guided by an ideology or recognizable leaderships and organizations'.[9] The specialized literature on the MENA prior to the Arab uprisings thus emphasized a pattern of authoritarian normality in the region that gave a certain coherence and meaningfulness to the situation, as well as generating particular expectations framed by this understanding.[10] Questions and answers were thus neatly matched in explanations that highlighted the short- to medium-term stability of the system.

It has been common since the Arab uprisings, just as it was common after September 11, to criticize specialists of the region for their flawed approach to the issues that mattered.[11] Yet, this is not an exceptional problem of Middle East studies, but a more general limitation of the social sciences when it comes to explaining and understanding particular types of events. In his thought-provoking book *Black Swan*, Nassim Taleb illustrates well how social scientists, economists, policy-makers and indeed almost everyone else routinely use explanations that discard statistically small occurrences precisely because they are uncommon, even though they may have large consequences.[12] Like other narratives, the accounts proposed by Middle East specialists were explanatory devices deployed to tie together an array of data in order to infuse them with a specific meaning.[13] Far from being a simple issue of misrepresentation of Middle East politics, the construction of these narratives illustrated a far more common predicament with organizing and interpreting data.

Acts, arenas and actors

The challenge for understanding the Arab uprisings resides precisely in avoiding easy notions of exceptionalism to account for the agency of the actors and the contingency of these events. A related danger is to rely on overarching structuralist explanations of change that tend to explain away contingent behaviours altogether. Hence, what I seek to provide for the Arab uprisings is a narrative that details the contentious interactions that shaped protest events and processes of deinstitutionalization (and reinstitutionalization). Regarding these episodes of contention, I take my cue from James Jasper that it is best not to posit notions of political opportunities but instead to address directly what the actors do.[14] Accordingly, I position the actions of the people involved in these events not only at the centre of my analysis but also at the start of it. Instead of trying to reconstruct the structural opportunities and set of factors that led to particular protest dynamics, I develop the explanation first of all in relation to the initial act of transgression—the 'event', as described in Sewell's account of an 'eventful sociology'.[15]

The explanatory model proposed in this work goes against the grain of much scholarly analysis. It is not constructed according to long- and short-term trends leading up to a particular event which constitutes the 'spark' that ignites long-dormant conflicts. It does not assume long-overdue rearticulations of power that explain subsequent trajectories of protest or a failure to mobilize effectively against the regime. Instead, the explanation places the protest event, as a potentially 'transformative event', first in the causal narrative. This is not to say that everything happens in a void. The act comes first because its 'antecedents', be they social, economic, political or religious, are only understood as antecedents holding a particular relevance once the act has taken place. In typical counterfactual reasoning, had the event not taken place, the narration of the same social, economic, political or, religious 'antecedents' would have been different and offered an explanation for stability instead of change. Importantly, I am not arguing that all the factors at play before a potential 'transformative event' are to be discarded or ignored. They are pertinent because they shape the arena of contestation in which the event will unfold at a particular time. However, by emphasizing the protest act itself, I stress that the significance of these pre-existing factors cannot be established a priori; nor can it be reconstructed a posteriori. This point is a rejoinder to Charles Kurzman's notion of an anti-explanation.[16] To explain what it must have been like before a protest for a protest to take place in this way, and what kind of reasons must have been important for the actors to act as they did, is to rationalize events in a way that we find convincing for our own purposes.

The second procedural element of the explanation concerns the notion of arena of contestation.[17] An act of protest becomes an event, and potentially a transformative event, by redefining an arena of contestation, locally, nationally, regionally and internationally. The boundaries of these arenas of contestation are defined by the interactions between the different protagonists involved in the initial event.[18] These changing interactions place in a different light the institutionalized logic of those pre-existing arenas of contestation which structure access to resources, positions of authority, discursive repertoires and so on. The relevance of the protest event is precisely to challenge pre-existing governance routines and articulations of power. Whatever structures may be in place to constrain, enable and channel societal actions (including protests), the powers that be are forced to respond to a non-routine challenge that undermines the dominant *habitus*.[19] The new set of extraordinary interactions generated by the event and the response that it elicits modifies the boundaries of the arena of contestation, with revised articulations of power, distribution of resources, discursive formations and so on. The more momentum these new interactions gather and the more the boundaries of the arenas of contestation are redrawn, the more the explanation will centre on how a transformative event has produced a revolutionary dynamic. By contrast, when interactions revert to old routines and arenas of contestations are subsumed under pre-existing structures, public (including scholarly) accounts of the event will re-emphasize the structural basis of the authoritarian status quo.

The final element of explanation is the actors involved in these events. The perspective advocated in this book de-emphasizes the impact of longer-term structural factors on the mechanisms of political change or stability. In particular, I downplay the notion that actors are characterized primarily by the ideas, discourses, practices and positions that they articulated prior to the episode of contestation—a point that is typically salient in analyses of the role of the military in the region. Instead, I define far more the actors in relation to the views, discourses, practices and positions that they acquire in relation to protest events and new arenas of contestation. To put it bluntly, revolutions create actors.[20] Quite evidently I am overstating the point in order to highlight an important difference in the conceptualization of agency. It is clear that individual and collective actors are not created *ex nihilo* by a transformative event. Their past views, words, actions and roles in older structures of governance and opposition influence the way in which they can recast themselves in relation to new events. However, this acknowledgement of the past should not obscure what is 'new' during or after a transformative event.[21] Hence, the identity of the actors is also—and sometimes, for some of them, primarily—a product of these new circumstances. Placing the actors procedurally last in the chain of causation is also a means to avoid the recurrent question about the relative weight of intentionality and unintended consequences. While what actors think they are doing is evidently important in shaping their actions, what defines them is their actions. Because the acts and the arenas of contestation come first, it is protest situations that shape revolutionary behaviours.

Interactions between actors are nonetheless crucial in understanding the process and mechanisms of change (or stability).[22] From a phenomenological perspective, as actions generate other actions and events generate other events, 'new' actors are increasingly defined by what they say and do in these contexts. At the same time, acts do not mechanically produce other acts according to a billiard-ball model of causation. Ontologically and semantically, acts and arenas of contestation are given their particular meaning and shape through the interpretations of the actors involved. Paying careful attention to the meaning that actors give to their words and acts remains important, even though the intentionality of the actors cannot directly explain causal dynamics beyond very short sequences of actions.[23] In this perspective, intentionality primarily enables actors—including those not directly involved in these processes—to attribute meaning to protest acts and arenas.

The reasons that are invoked to frame the agency of the actors, be it by the actors themselves or by external observers, provide the cognitive glue that maintains a causal narrative in a particular shape. By presenting the relation between acts and arenas in a specific light—i.e. by highlighting some economic or political trends and demands for redistribution or participation—specific categories of actors are empowered in a causal narrative (such as the 'poor' or 'political opponents'). Such a narrative can then explain multiple instances of agency by invoking rational calculations, biased perceptions of events, miscalculation caused by insufficient information, emotional responses on the spur of the moment, and so on. However, the process of change as a whole cannot be explained directly as an aggregation of these particular incidences—mainly due to the lack of systemic empirical evidence. The best that can be offered is a narrative that frames particular causal relations within a believable whole; but this is not wholly a causal explanation.

The analysis I propose presents the dynamics of the Arab uprisings in terms of evolving interactions between actors in particular arenas of contestations. Instead of talking of social movements, I follow Jasper in focusing on individual and collective actors (or 'players').[24] Instead of talking of political opportunities, I focus on the actions of these players and their consequences for other players and for the arenas of contestation in which they are active. This shift in emphasis implies that what lies at the heart of my explanation is not particular structures (political, social, economic and so on) but patterns of interactions. Institutional actors, such as 'the regime' or 'the military', are thus a set of entrenched practices of governance that repeatedly shape interactions in a particular way.[25] The process of describing particular practices is not a by-product of political change; it is also causal inasmuch as these narratives are invoked as causes for actions (regardless of their relevance outside particular arenas of contestation). In this context, processes of (rapid) deinstitutionalization and of reinstitutionalization qualify the changing interactions between the various participants act-ing individually and collectively to reshape an arena of (institutional) contestation. As one set of routine practices of governance replaces another, a new arena of formal political contestation is created—more democratic than the previous one, or less so.

'Democratic revolutions': naming events

In recent years there has been much debate among specialists about the future form of revolutions. Their arguments stressed the greater likeli-hood of 'political' rather than 'social' revolutions characterized, in their democratic variants, by mass mobilization that succeeds in changing an authoritarian regime into a (procedurally) democratic one.[26] These democratic variants have become particularly relevant after the 'velvet revolutions' and other 'democratic revolutions' in Eastern Europe in 1989 and the early 1990s that marked the collapse of the Communist bloc. As many analysts of the communist cases remarked, the 'demo-cratic' agendas proposed at the time also indicated a wariness of 'revo-lutionary' projects. They could even be seen as 'anti-revolutionary revolutions', as Richard Sakwa noted, in the sense that the democratic solution that was proposed offered no grand new ideal but simply looked at the more functional western European models of governance to replace dysfunctional socialist programmes.[27] Donatella Della Porta underscored this connection between the mechanisms of 'velvet revo-lutions' and 'eventful democratization' in her comparison between the 1989 and the 2011 waves of sudden political changes in Eastern Europe and the Arab world.[28]

In this book I consider the transformations initiated by the 2011 Arab uprisings in the MENA region as a series of successful or failed cases of political revolution, and more precisely as situations of democratic revo-lution. Using the distinction outlined by Charles Tilly between revolu-tionary situations and revolutionary outcomes, I argue that the term 'democratic revolutionary situation' is useful to describe these chal-lenges to the authoritarian regimes of the region, regardless of their outcomes.[29] In her work on the 2011 uprisings, Della Porta distin-guishes between 'eventful democratization', in cases of successful demo-cratic transition, and 'participatory pacts', in cases where the protest movement is co-opted within reforming authoritarian structures.[30] While I am in agreement with Della Porta on the usefulness of Sewell's 'eventful sociology' model to analyse these episodes of mobilization and to link up social agency and political structures, I am wary of the typology of 'mobilizations for democracy' that she proposes. Adopting a path dependency approach with set outcomes necessarily constrains any explanation of the dynamics of mobilization. A situation of democratic revolution does not presume the successful consolidation of a democratic political system, even though it indicates that a popular uprising is instrumental in the implementation of a genuine electoral democratic model.[31] The perspective advocated in this book stresses the changing causal dynamics of protest episodes rather than their final institutional outcomes. I characterize situations of democratic revolution in terms of specific shifts in routine social and political agency (corresponding to the dominant *habitus* in Bourdieu's terminology). These shifts amount, first of all, to a rapid empowerment of the citizenry, an illustration of an older model of democratic order grounded—albeit briefly—on the people (*demos*) and its power (*kratos*), or 'people's power', in a more ideologically charged contemporary representation. Secondly, these shifts may (or may not) correspond at a later stage to a normatively driven process of institutionalization that seeks to implement a particular model of liberal democracy.[32]

I argue that the processes of democratic revolution symbolizing the Arab uprisings are best positioned on a single spectrum of contentious politics, starting from the more mundane demands of social movements and ending with the more politically significant transformations produced by revolutionary changes of regime. In their argument for an integrated perspective on social activism and revolutionary change, Doug McAdam, Sidney Tarrow and Charles Tilly take a position against those who argue 'for the distinctiveness of movement politics and revolutionary politics and for the separation of both from routine contention'. They suggest instead that 'social movement cycles and revolutions fall on the same continuum, the difference in position being to what extent challenges put the existing structure of power at risk'.[33] Looking at the issue from a social movement perspective, they do not see the need to develop a particular typology of revolutionary situations located at the end of that continuum. They simply indicate that 'revolutionary situations resemble extreme cases of social movement cycles'.[34] There is indeed much to say in favour of a spectrum of political mobilization as opposed to substantive definitions of particular sequences of political change that produce a very specific teleology of their own (such as 'revolution' or 'democratic transition'). Jack Goldstone is correct to remark that the proposition that revolutionary situations are just 'extreme cases' may not be analytically useful.[35] However, Goldstone's alternative approach, built on a set typology of protest mobilization, creates a similar problem to Della Porta's. The use of empirically predefined categories of contention to analyse protest movements can certainly be useful to classify cases after the event and make projections, but it is unduly constraining as a model for tracking trajectories of mobilization.

Here, I use a modified version of the continuum argument that presents 'extreme' points of cycles of contestation as shifts in modes of mobilization (both institutionalized and non-institutionalized). In this perspective, end points correspond to the beginning of a decrease in protest mobilization caused either by the formal deinstitutionalization of the old regime (e.g. the death or departure of the ruling autocrat) or by the increasingly successful repression or cooptation of the protesters by the regime. When these turning points have been reached, protest mobilization may, and usually does, continue, but the momentum shifts away from anti-regime revolutionary protests and towards institutional political reconstruction. In short, 'revolutionary' mobilization declines and social and political activism is increasingly expressed through more institutionalized channels, such as political parties. While the fate of the ruling autocrat is commonly used to symbolize regime change, the changing tide of mobilization and the process of regime deinstitutionalization do not correspond exactly. As I will illustrate in the case of Tunisia, the protest tide turned well after the departure of Ben Ali; while in the case of Libya it did so well before the death of Gaddafi. Similarly, new social and political routines become established both before the turning point of the protest (e.g. armed mobilization and militarization in Libya) and after it (e.g. party and electoral mobilization in Tunisia). In this context, as Arthur Stinchcombe stressed, the ending of a revolutionary situation and the creation of certainty in rapidly changing circumstances are as crucial as the beginning of uncertainty.[36] In particular, at the end point of the spectrum of contestation, the decline in protest mobilization heightens the importance of the process of remobilization via more institutionalized practices (such as party politics).[37] While I am not addressing the issue of post-uprising political incorporation here, it is clear that such endgames are shaped by the trajectories and dynamics of the protest as much as by pre-existing political configurations and trends.

For Tilly, a revolution corresponds to 'a forcible transfer of power over a state in the course of which at least two distinct blocs of contenders make incompatible claims to control the state, and some significant portion of the population subject to the state's jurisdiction acquiesces in the claims of each bloc'.[38] This perspective stresses the importance of having a mass movement—as opposed to 'revolutions from above' and other 'palace revolutions'—that generates a new institutionalization of power which the ruling elite cannot suppress or co-opt. This view dovetails with Jeff Goodwin's 'broad' definition of political revolutions as 'instances in which a state or political regime is overthrown and thereby transformed by a popular movement in an irregular, extraconstitutional, and/or violent fashion'.[39] The tail end of a (democratic) revolutionary situation is thus unlike institutionalized reform processes in the sense that the transfer and practice of political power are characterised by their extra-institutional, extraordinary character. As Kurzman stressed in particular, what characterizes the revolutionary moment is that period of rapid deinstitutionalization during which the formal and informal mechanisms that ordinarily structure people's views and behaviour in the public sphere are increasingly no longer what they used to be.[40] In these circumstances, protest mobilization can enable not only a transfer of political authority (governing elites, institutions and so on) but also a change in practices of governance (and of resistance). In Sewell's eventful sociology, such 'transformative events' facilitate a swift transformation of the structures of governance, not least through the framing of these protest actions, in particular political narratives.[41]

Causality and narratives of change

Reflecting on the 'velvet revolutions' in Eastern Europe in the late 1980s and early 1990s, Timur Kuran asked: 'why does a revolution that in hindsight seems to be the inevitable outcome of powerful social forces surprise so many of its leaders, participants, victims, and observers?' Criticizing the literature for leaving unanswered the question why hindsight and foresight diverge, Kuran proposed a solution grounded in rational choice theory, viz the 'collective choice model that distinguishes between individuals' privately held political preferences and those they espouse in public'. He argued:

> A privately hated regime may enjoy widespread public support because of people's reluctance to take the lead in publicizing their opposition. The regime may, therefore, seem unshakeable, even if its support would crumble at the most minor shock. A suitable shock would put in motion a bandwagon process that exposes a panoply of social conflicts, until then largely hidden. From these newly revealed conflicts, almost any writer with a modicum of imagination will be able to construct an elaborate explanation, consistent with almost any social theory, as to why the observed revolution took place.[42]

Kuran's 'preference falsification' argument does not say that we cannot predict revolutions because we cannot know that people do not support an authoritarian regime—usually we do. Instead, it indicates that it is particularly difficult to identify the point or points at which people would join in a (would-be) revolution when unrest emerges in the country—or, in Kuran's terms, 'the precise distribution of individual revolutionary thresholds'.[43] In this respect, Kuran noted that those historians of revolution who paid proper attention to agency 'have systematically overestimated what revolutionary actors could have known'; a bias that Kuran attributed to their tendency to 'project into the past trends that later developments have revealed'.[44]

Understanding the contingency of the implicit and explicit choices that different actors made at different times during the Arab uprisings is one of the keys to understanding the dynamics and trajectories of these protests. Whilst Kuran's cautionary remarks about evaluating people's choices are useful, his preference falsification model also runs the risk of overdetermining the preferences of the actors. In particular, people may not have set preferences beforehand, at least not in an articulated strategic view that would enable them to chose a particular course of action when confronted with a new situation. Analysing the events of the 1979 Iranian Revolution, Kurzman stressed how people's estimates of the size of the unrest, and therefore their willingness to engage in protest, shifted drastically 'from moment to moment on the basis of amorphous rumors, heightened emotions, and conflicting senses of duty … Even the most thorough survey would not have predicted very far into the future.'[45] He showed that people did not actually 'know' if or when they would engage in anti-regime protests until the protest was upon them. In this perspective, protest 'thresholds' cannot be estimated in advance because they are not only based on pre-existing preferences, but on new preferences generated as the protests unfold and as people reinterpret what is happening around them and to them. Kurzman argued that during periods of political deinstitutionalization, the social and political routines providing the foundation upon which people could make 'rational', 'cost-benefit' calculations about what to do and not do repeatedly floundered. In these new circumstances, not only do new preferences and choices come to the fore, but they interact in a more haphazard process than in routine circumstances.[46] Kurt Weyland noted in particular how repeated 'deviations' induced by cognitive shortcuts, such as availability heuristic (the tendency to be impressed by recent events more than by older ones) and representativeness heuristic (the tendency to take surface similarities as objective evidence), reshaped the workings of bounded rationality in everyday calculations of risks, costs and benefits.[47]

The element of contigency in making predictions about behaviour, as Jeff Goodwin indicates, 'applies not only to people who might join a revolutionary movement but also to those whose job it is to suppress revolutions, namely, military officers and soldiers'.[48] Commenting on analyses of the 2011 Arab uprisings, Goodwin took aim at the more structurally minded and rational choice explanations of these events that suggested, a posteriori, that the structure and role of the military largely explained the trajectories of these protests. Such common explanations produced in the immediate aftermath of the uprisings fall broadly within a transitologist perspective. They generally consider that regime change or stability where the actions of the military are involved can be explained in terms of the officers' collective interests.[49] Building on her earlier account of the role of the security apparatus in Middle Eastern regimes, Eva Bellin has stated that understanding the choices of the military once again was key to understanding the outcomes of these events. After briefly mentioning the contingency of the Egyptian uprisings, she concluded that 'the logic driving these calculations was never in question. In the end, the military elites decided not to shoot and Hosni Mubarak was forced to depart the scene.'[50] In Bellin's account, the situation is mainly contingent upon the role of the military; and the (rational) choices of the leadership are predictable because they are made within a known and stable cognitive framework. Yet it is one thing to say that there are objective parameters and factors that structure the cost-benefit analyses that military actors commonly make, and another to say that this is what directly led them to make the choices they did in the circumstances. As Goodwin noted:

> The more professional and institutionalized armies in Tunisia and Egypt calculated that they could best safeguard their interests by abandoning dictators … But who at the time could predict how any particular army would react to mass protest? Who could have predicted that the Tunisian army would refuse to fight for Ben Ali? Who could say with confidence that the Egyptian army would abandon Mubarak? The structural characteristics and dispositions of armies often become apparent only after they begin to fight for their survival.[51]

From an organizational perspective, Steven Levitsky and Lucan Way, who link the likelihood of regime change to state coercive capacity more specifically, noted that while the cohesion of the security apparatus was crucial in time of crisis when high-intensity coercion needed to be employed, it was particularly problematic to evaluate such cohesion then, precisely because of the crisis context.[52] There is a particular difficulty in linking up everyday repressive calculations and mechanisms to the behaviour of specific security actors (such as the military) during periods of mass protest. This is because the security institutions dealing with an insurrectional situation are not acting within the usual parameters of routine authoritarianism, and as such the (rational choice) calculations they ordinarily make are not necessarily relevant.[53] What makes the usefulness of these rational choice arguments even more doubtful is what lies outside the means-ends aspect of choices, such as emotions in particularly charged situations.[54] Detailing the circumstances of the Arab uprisings helps us understand the frailty of the choices and decisions taken at the time, and how easily they could be reversed when circumstances demanded it or, alternatively, how easily they could be portrayed as the right solution when they were endorsed by other actors.

Only in a stable environment populated by unwavering, fully rational agents—or agents whose deviation from rational norms is measurable—would we expect set preferences and standard calculations to produce outcomes that are repeatedly predictable. In a less perfect social world, generic observations about the behaviour of the armed forces could still be made. As Sharon Nepstad noted in her studies of recent non-violent revolutions, it is common for soldiers to be less reliable if 'a) they share a common ethnic or religious identity with civil resisters but not with regime leaders; b) they know others who are defecting; c) if resisters remain nonviolent, thereby making repression difficult to justify; and d) if troops do not derive any direct benefits from the regime'.[55] Although both opposition and government are mindful of these factors in times of crisis, such trends do not constitute iron laws of military control (or collapse). In addition, Nepstad's categories are not just boxes to be ticked, but encapsulate a spectrum of interactions—i.e. the imagined identity is more or less common, defections are relative, protesters are more or less non-violent, security actors derive relative benefits from the regime. As Goodwin hinted, it is only when security forces are put to the test that the relative weight of these different factors in deciding the strategy of security actors can be known.

In *States and Revolutionary Movements*, Goodwin stressed that 'states structures and practices invariably matter, in other words, for the very *formation* of revolutionaries movements, not just for their success or failure—and they generally do so in quite unintended ways'.[56] In his analysis, Goodwin concentrated particularly on the relationship between the formation of effective revolutionary movements and the presence of organizationally incoherent and militarily weak states. For the Arab uprisings, such a relationship appeared to be directly relevant to the Libyan scenario, particularly once the uprising had started. However, other states of the region which were not particularly 'weak' also witnessed the emergence of powerful protest movements, albeit of the leaderless/leaderful variety. In these situations of democratic revolution, loosely coordinated movements based on a multiplicity of local counter-powers were the type of 'organization' that resulted from

MENA practices of authoritarian governance. In this perspective, the classification of states as 'weak' or 'strong' loses further relevance for the diffusion of protest waves, as leaderless/leaderfull movements were successful precisely in situations where the efficiency of the security apparatus prevented a more organized challenge to the regime. Beyond the role of security forces, notions of regime strength or weakness during the Arab uprisings revolved around the ability to co-opt opposition forces in favour of 'reform' in times of regime crisis.

The difficulties of pinning down behavioural contingency concern as much the domestic aspects of protest mobilization and regime responses as the wider regional and international sphere. Regarding the diffusion of revolutionary waves, Weyland stresses the importance of heuristics for everyone involved:

> recent events in neighboring countries that make a striking, vivid impression have a disproportionate impact and grab people's attention; and facile judgments of similarity fuel much stronger contagion than cautious rational learning justifies. The bounded-rationality approach thus predicts waves of diffusion that sweep beyond the limited range of similar political-institutional settings. In fact, cognitive shortcuts inspire fairly rash challenges of established regimes; therefore, aborted efforts and failures should be frequent. [57]

The difficulty in evaluating where and when it 'makes sense' for people to join in a protest wave underpins the difficulty of identifying countries that are most likely to be affected by movements attempting to replicate what they see happening nearby. The 'demonstrative' effect that has already been shown in analyses of democratic as well as revolutionary waves is clearly pertinent to the Arab uprisings. [58] Some of the structural factors identified by the literature on diffusion—such as the regional dimension (or geographical proximity) or an overlapping public sphere (in terms of linguistic and media networks)—retained their relevance for this wave of protests. [59] Others, like the institutional characteristics of regimes (or regime 'types'), proved to be less straightforwardly pertinent. [60] This unpredictability produced dilemmas not only for regimes and opposition in MENA countries, but also for policy-makers in the wider international community. [61] Confronted by such situations of democratic revolution, foreign governments had to guesstimate the likelihood that a protest might topple a regime and position themselves accordingly—a process that was particularly salient in 2011 in relation to the international intervention against the Libyan regime, as we will see later. Guesstimation is the only realistic political option during such episodes, as structurally determined causal outcomes come too late in the day—e.g., in the Libyan case, probably only when Gaddafi was hiding away in Sirte with a few loyal troops left around him. Such estimates can be portrayed subsequently through retroactive prediction as accurate evaluations of a given situation, even though people often end up being right for the wrong reasons. Unpacking the dynamics of the Arab uprisings helps us elucidate how this came to be.

Mobilization (and demobilization) in extraordinary circumstances

Traditionally, the scholarship on social movements and social mobilization in situations of revolution and democratic transition has been far better at dealing with the structural aspects of regime change than with the contingency of the event itself. In explaining extraordinary mobilization, the main task of the analyst has been to find rhyme and reason for these 'moments of madness', as Sidney Tarrow called them in a reappropriation of Aristide Zolberg's interpretation.[62] In these contexts, the challenge is to identify mechanisms of contention that predictably shape collective action in different socio-historical contexts. What matters most is not the exceptional behaviours that seem hard to replicate—the 'rich tapestry of collective action', as Tarrow put it—but those forms of contention that are assimilated by social movements and then reproduced through institutionalized processes. As Tarrow argues, 'the new forms of collective action invented in the enthusiasm of the moment of madness become modular ... Not the new invention itself, but its distilled, refined, and often routinized products become part of a more lasting practice of collective action.'[63] From a democratization studies perspective, Dan Slater made a very similar point when he stressed that 'spontaneity and creativity may be quintessential traits of contentious politics, but this does not mean that collective protests are equally likely to erupt or to prevail in all times and places. Unless we do the historical work to uncover where oppositional political cultures come from, it is difficult, if not impossible, to explain why so many societies have produced neither democratic revolutions nor large-scale authoritarian crackdowns but persistent quiescence.'[64] In the context of the democratic revolutions of Southeast Asia which he investigated, Slater reintroduced stability in processes of mobilization by stressing the use of nationalist and religious repertoires by established 'communal elites'.

In the MENA region, the role of authoritarian elites has also been crucial in structuring narratives that explain the inability of the political opposition to make effective anti-regime coalitions in the face of statist strategies of cooptation and repression.[65] The Arab uprisings were thus exceptional events from this perspective, as they enabled, albeit briefly, a coming together of different opposition movements.[66] In addition, as Merouan Mekouar noted, (opposition) political elites also played an important role in the diffusion of the protest movement across the region.[67] While the Arab uprisings were not directly initiated by social movements or organized revolutionaries, structured opposition movements were active throughout the protests and channelled at least some of the contentious politics. In this respect, the dynamics of protests could be explained, using Tarrow's approach, by an analysis of the strategies and choices that opposition forces make when they seek to mobilize resources in favour of change and take advantage of the political opportunities offered.[68] In the Arab uprisings as elsewhere, it could also be shown, as Doug McAdam, John McCarthy and Mayer Zald explained, the degree to which these efforts are consciously strategic changes (that is, increases) during the period of mobilization, starting out as rather inchoate at the beginning of the protest and becoming more articulate at the end.[69] Ultimately, the hectic wave of unrest that spread across the MENA countries in 2011 could be analysed as a fairly traditional instance of mobilization by social movements, in Tilly's terms, as 'an organized, sustained, self-conscious challenge to existing authorities'.[70]

In so far as the focus of the analysis remains on structured movements, then conventional social movement theory perspectives can help us understand the issue of mobilization. The way in which movements and individuals are positioned in the social and economic system—their assets, economic function, expertise and connections with various elites inside and outside the polity—provides them with a range of resources (or a shortages of them) and options. The strategic interactions shaping protests are thus a function of how groups and individuals make sense of political opportunities and mobilize their resources in order to achieve specific objectives. Ruud Koopmans defends the value of these mainstream approaches by arguing that 'the idea of political opportunity structure involves not more (and not less) than the claim that not all of the variation in levels and forms of collective action is due to the strategic wit, courage, imagination, or plain luck (or the lack of those) of the different actors involved in conflict situations, but that an important part of it is shaped by structural characteristics of the political context in which social movements, willingly or unwillingly, have to act'.[71] He recognizes, nonetheless, that protests are quite distinct from more routine avenues for mobilization, and that explanations based on political opportunity structures are more meaningful for transnational comparisons than for an account of variations within countries.[72] While it stands to reason than across polities and under routine governance, structural characteristics routinely shape conventional practices of mobilization, it remains unclear how far such characteristics help us understand less conventional forms of protest mobilization and their consequences.

The debate over the notion of 'political opportunity' is central to the analysis of the Arab uprisings precisely because there was supposed to be none before the event, according to most regional experts at the time. Mainstream social movement theory approaches have long been criticized for having an overdeterministic structural approach to the notion of opportunity and too simplistic a model of rational choice.[73] A principal challenge even before the 2011 uprisings was to account for the subjective framing of such political opportunities by the actors themselves. As William Gamson and David Meyer remark, 'an opportunity unrecognized is no opportunity at all'.[74] They stress that an opportunity is a social construction based at least in part on the perception of possible change. Some of the main contributors to the framing debate repeatedly note the tension between the notion of structural opportunity and the idea of framing opportunities. Robert Benford and David Snow argue that 'the degree or extent of political opportunity in any society is seldom, if ever, a clear and easily read structural entity. Rather, its existence and openness is subject to debate and interpretation and can thus be framed by movement actors as well as by others.'

However, they insist that political opportunities are not purely socially constructed entities; but instead 'the extent to which they constrain or facilitate collective action is partly contingent on how they are framed by movement actors as well as others'.[75] This approach is well encapsulated in McAdam, McCarthy and Zald's notion of framing as 'the collective processes of interpretation, attribution and social construction that mediate between opportunity and action'.[76] In this perspective, the framing process only acts as a link between a predefined political opportunity structure and social mobilization. Framing in itself does not constitute a cause or starting point for mobilization.

Hank Johnston and John Noakes concede that, occasionally, framing can 'trump political structure' or 'generate its own political opportunities'. However, they are quick to add that 'cases where framing activities by themselves alter institutional political structures directly are relatively rare'.[77] In this perspective, 'a movement can either unintentionally misread or strategically ignore the political context and mobilize in the absence of objective opportunities such as state weakness or shifts in power relations'. Pointing to the issue of the 'optimism' of activists, Gamson and Meyer concur that 'since movement action can sometimes create political opportunity, this lack of realism can produce a self-fulfilling prophecy'.[78] These arguments nonetheless remain problematic, as the only opportunities that can be identified with certainty are the ones that are realized, and are thus only identified after the event. To talk about the optimistic views of activists in contrast with a more objective, rational baseline for action is somewhat hazardous. As the Arab uprisings illustrated, if a collective action is successful, in what sense did its initiators lack realism? It could be said that the protesters misread the level of mobilization, of resources, of struggle required to bring this opportunity for change to fruition; and they ended up being right but for the wrong reasons. Yet, at the same time, analyses of the countries in which the uprisings took place equally lacked realism in their assessment of the opportunities that could be relevant.

In the countries of the Arab uprisings, since there were no 'objective' structural opportunities to challenge the regime, it was to be expected that people would not mobilize under ordinary circumstances. Political demobilization had been well analysed by regional specialists before 2011 and presented as one of the factors underpinning the stability of the MENA regimes. As Bayat noted just before the uprisings, 'since there is slight or no agency to challenge the ossified status quo, the argument goes, change should come from outside, by way of economic, political, and even military pressure'.[79] Once mobilization occurred successfully despite an apparent lack of political opportunity, the role of framing became more troublesome for structural accounts of politics in the region. A common answer to the framing predicament has been for structural-minded analyses to discount the agents of change as being somewhat delusional. Brownlee, Masoud and Reynolds thus suggested that people 'may have perceived a structural opportunity where one did not exist', and that mobilization succeeded 'partly because of a misperception that regimes were vulnerable'.[80]

A major criticism of these approaches above-mentioned, is well summarised by Jasper, who stresses that they 'ignored actors' choices, desires, and points of view: potential participants were taken for granted as already formed, just waiting for opportunities to act'.[81] The situational dimension of protest actions and of the actors involved always infuses protest trajectories with multiple potentialities. In the context of the Arab uprisings, consider the case of a protesting crowd occupying the central square of a town who hear word of a column of military vehicles coming down the road to repress them. Among other possibilities, we can easily identify 'situation 1': upon hearing the 'news', most of the people leave the square before the arrival of the soldiers to avoid the impending repression. In this context, when the military column arrive (option A), the usual suspects are rounded up and the unrest ends there and then. Alternatively, only four police cars turn up in place of the anticipated military column (option B), but, as most people went home, they are also able to round up the usual suspects and the unrest ends there and then. In this situation, what is relevant is the belief in the represive capabilities of the regime more than the repressive capabilities themselves.

Now consider 'situation 2' in which, upon hearing the 'news', most people decide to stay put for multiple reasons—they do not believe it, they are emotionally impressed by their own show of force, they miscalculate the timing of the arrival of the security forces, and so on. Option A, the military column arrive, people are shot at and flee for their lives; the unrest ends there and then. Option B, the soldiers arrive, people are shot at, but the unrest starts more forcefully in other towns as news of the massacre spreads. Option C, the military column arrives, protesters and soldiers fraternize, and the unrest gains in strength. Option D, only four police cars turn up instead of the anticipated military column; the police are overwhelmed and the unrest gains in strength. Beyond participant observation, one can best evaluate the likelihood of these different framing processes (and of their outcomes) taking place through aggregation; but aggregation only makes sense once a protest has begun and only in relation to more routine processes.

Criticizing the tendency of mainstream comparative democratization studies to focus on the macro-structural aspects of repression, Vincent Boudreau outlines how the interpenetration of repression and revolt produces particular patterns of interaction and modes of contention.[82] The formation of new choices, strategies and actors is commonly a direct outcome of protest events and of the state response, particularly when repression appears extraordinary. In more routine or semi-routine situations, protests and repression can be portrayed as a give-and-take process.[83] Protesters adapt their forms of protest and mobilization to what appears to produce the best results with the regime. They will choose more or less violent tactics depending on the positive (or negative) response of the state to these different approaches. Considering revolutionary situations, Goodwin stresses that people commonly conclude that revolution is the only way out of their predicaments 'when they confront certain types of states that respond to political dissent with repression, typically of a violent and indiscriminate nature'.[84] Short of a revolution, Ronald Francisco pointed to multiple instances of a popular 'backlash' against dictatorial regimes after cases of exceedingly high repression or a massacre; even though before the event, mobilization was limited.[85] The role of pro-regime actors, and particularly the security forces, ought not to be narrowly conceived simply in terms of active support for the ruling authoritarian elite or withdrawal of this support (and support for the protesters). These actors may also unintentionally contribute directly to the dynamics of anti-regime mobilization—a situation that, as we will see, occurred in both Tunisia and Libya in 2011.[86] Pro- and anti-regime actors strategically interact with each other, as well as deal with the unintended consequences of their action, and in so doing produce particular trajectories of regime change or resilience.[87]

The 2011 Arab uprisings provide another illustration of the argument that there is no finite number of trajectories of protests, just patterns of interaction. From an institutional perspective, highlighting the meaningfulness of particular strategic interactions between pro- and anti-regime actors is a practical way to structure the larger debates about the stability of states.[88] However, to note the repeated relevance of specific sets of interactions for institutions is quite different from assessing the predictability of these interactions, let alone of their outcomes. These are rules of thumb, not political laws. After the Arab uprisings, there has often been a temptation to argue that what happened just had to happen. In seeking for institutional regularities, there has been a tendency to revisit and rationalize the choices of the relevant actors in retrospect, once the outcomes of particular events are known. When the dust has settled and participants are asked to reflect on the events, they commonly impart new meaning to the actions they took at the time. In their turn, these post hoc reflections by the actors of the uprisings contribute further to putting a rationalistic gloss on a set of disparate events—e.g. making it a revolt for 'dignity', 'freedom', 'justice' and so on. Writing about the events, analysts in their turn use the actors' own rationalizations to further rationalize the trajectories of the uprisings; thereby making them part of a more structured and predictable evolution of these polities.[89]

The next chapter highlights the 'naturalness' of such narratives, and their inconsistencies, in four North African countries before the 2011 uprisings. Subsequently, I deliberately avoid using accounts given by the actors of the uprising outside the immediate situations in which they were active. While this approach necessarily limits the scope of interviews to factual or technical issues—that is, where, when, with whom, how, etc.—it does bring out better the heterogeneous views and perceptions that existed during the uprisings. The point of producing such an account of the uprisings is to provide a counterbalance to those explanations that naturalize the transformations that took place. By focusing on the different perspectives of multiple actors at different times in the uprisings, this account illustrates the plurality of pathways of change that were created during the uprisings, even though only one scenario could ultimately be realized in each country.

I realize that those readers endorsing a different theoretical perspective might consider that what I present here as contingent outcomes of revolutionary situations are in fact outcomes of the longer-terms development of these countries and their communities. While the next chapter retains a recognizable historical sociological dimension that stresses such long-term trends interspaced with episodes of political contingency, the ensuing analysis of the 2011 uprisings does not. The specific political breakdowns, reforms and rearticulations that I explain in terms of the contingency of the protest actions and the reconfigurations of arenas of contention and of actors' identity could be presented in this longer-term perspective as epiphenomena. They could be said to be peculiar embodiments of institutional, political, socio-economic or ideological realignments that were bound to occur at some point in those states and in that region. In this perspective, the interactions between the different events, arenas and actors that I present as the engine of change (or stability) in each country's case could be seen as symptoms of deeper social, economic, political or ideational forces. Assuming that such an analysis is able to establish causation between macro- and micro-processes, it remains possible to investigate how these structural responses may override more immanent responses to unexpected events. Still, the point remains that, even as epiphenomena, the contingent dynamics of deinstitutionalization and reinstitutionalization remain important in terms of providing a political explanation of the institutional transformations that did in fact take place. They may be mere variations on a larger theme, but, for the people who live through them, they are important variations.

3

ROUTINE AUTHORITARIAN GOVERNANCE BEFORE THE ARAB UPRISINGS

STRUCTURING THE OPTIONS FOR CHANGE

Political resilience and the appearance of stability

In the post-colonial period, studies of politics in the Middle East and North Africa (MENA) highlighted some common features that were deemed to underpin the stability of authoritarian regimes in the region (as well as generate continuing weaknesses and problems of governance). While the general characteristics of authoritarianism were analysed at length, less attention was usually paid to how different rearticulations of authoritarian governance shaped the opportunities for mass protest. Undoubtedly, this issue was not investigated in much detail because it appeared less relevant in a regional context characterized by stable, 'hard' regimes. Prior to the Arab uprisings, if the answer to how different opportunities for mass mobilization could lead to regime change remained elusive, it was mainly because the question was not asked.

The account of MENA politics proposed here highlights the qualitative variations in the mechanisms of authoritarian governance that produced political 'stability' through slightly different means. However, the main objective of this narrative is not to outline an overarching framework that would better explain how particular variations in authoritarian governance led to a revolution in some countries and not in others. With the benefit of hindsight, it is easy to say that analysts previously missed crucial causal factors, which we can now identify to produce more authoritative accounts of politics in the region. Yet, 'black swans', as Nassim Taleb and Mark Blyth describe the 2011 Arab uprisings, remain unpredictable, system-challenging events that repeatedly occur in the social world because actors do not and cannot know enough of their social environment always to have full mastery of it.[1]

Taleb and Blyth point to the misguided confidence that analysts and policy-makers gain from their ability most of the time to predict a given political situation. Certainly, it is perfectly understandable that one should focus on predicting the predictable. This focus on past successes is in practice correct for most political purposes, most of the time. What is misguided is the belief that the ability to predict or influence routine politics is directly relevant for non-routine events and processes. Mastering routine politics is meaningful up to the point where a 'black swan' turns up, at which moment it suddenly becomes far less relevant or, even worse, counterproductive. And yet, analyses of MENA politics before 2011 cannot be blamed for failing to predict what they were not meant to predict.

Contrary to Gregory Gause, there is little to be gained by criticizing Middle East experts for 'underestimating the hidden forces driving change'.[2] How could they not underestimate them if they were indeed hidden? It is precisely because analysts and policy-makers are not able to predict and control all aspects of social life that revolutions can take place and are not killed in the bud by ruling elites. The focus on actors and factors of stability in the region prior to the 2011 uprisings is constitutive of a situation in which such dramatic political changes are possible. In its turn the 'myth of authoritarian stability', as Gause names the preceding mistaken narrative, can only be replaced by another political myth.

Scholarship on the MENA prior to the Arab uprisings provides important insights into routine political governance in the region. Even after revolutions and democratic transitions, 'old' actors and practices remain visibly part of the social and political landscape.[3] While new normative, institutional, security and socio-economic practices generated by the uprisings modified routine governance to some degree in all these polities, it would be naïve to assume that earlier authoritarian strategies became mainly redundant. As this wave of contentious politics evolved towards institutionalized processes, structural explanations based on long-term trends re-established themselves as an effective way of understanding restabilized political systems.[4] While some of the authoritarian mechanisms that were previously crucial may have been superseded by new models of governance, others remain very much unchallenged. These continuities are most evident in those countries, like Morocco and Algeria, that have not experienced regime change but have implemented (very) limited reforms to ensure the continuing effectiveness of their authoritarian rule.[5]

Before the Arab uprisings, analyses of authoritarianism commonly accounted for stasis in the polities of the region mainly through three sets of interrelated factors. Firstly, they stressed the particular balance of ideological legitimation and force underpinning these authoritarian systems. Secondly, they highlighted how socio-economic constraints and opportunities were structured by patron–client relations and redistributive networks. Thirdly, and increasingly, they noted how the institutionalized political opportunities provided by the regimes were used to co-opt opposition actors. These three components combined differently to produce specific articulations of opportunities and dilemmas for authoritarian governance.[6] However, even without regime change, the countries of the region went through episodes of crisis and of system reconfiguration repeatedly in the post-colonial period. Generally, these contingencies in the continuation of authoritarian rule are not included in typologies of authoritarianism. Barbara Geddes's classic model of trajectories of authoritarianism, for example, does not describe successful power transitions within the same regime type.[7] Yet, as leaders and regimes continue in power, the changing balance of ideology and repression, and of economic and political options, modifies the dynamics of authoritarian rule.

In this chapter, I focus on the notion of regime as a particular set of codified interactions between the state and the citizens—a political regimen in the old sense of the term. This means a form of governance that is relatively independent from the personalities of those in power and that can last regardless of changes of leadership.[8] In this sense, it is possible to have situations of elite change without regime change, and of regime change without elite change (such as the democratization process orchestrated by President Chadli Bendjedid in Algeria in 1989–91).[9] In this perspective, too, the role of the repressive apparatus remains important in shaping the options for change. However, while the military may well have the will and capacity to 'save' particular elites, the very use of a military option to suppress dissent may ensure that a particular political regimen (in the sense of a model for routine interaction between the state and citizens) cannot survive. In effect, the political costs for a regime of a pyrrhic military victory against its own citizens or subjects have been well known in the region since at least the period of decolonization. Conversely, as the recent political vagaries of Egypt illustrate, the departure of particular authoritarian elites does not necessarily translate into a change of regime type.

Part of the rationale of this chapter is to present in the North African context what many scholars have already convincingly argued more broadly, namely that authoritarianism is always dynamic (à la Levitsky and Way) and upgrading (à la Heydemann).[10] The other, more pertinent intention is to stress that what may look from a broad comparative perspective like a seamless process of evolution of regimes is riddled with spur-of-the-moment responses to crises that lead regimes into new directions. The chapter thus retraces how regimes withstood challenges to the three pillars of their routine authoritarian governance through ad hoc adaptations in non-routine situations before 2011. In the same way as the extraordinariness of the 2011 uprisings is retrospectively woven into ordinary political processes and narratives about the region, the extraordinary character of past crises had also been integrated into routine understandings of authoritarian resilience in these regimes. The 'normalcy' of authoritarian rule erased over time the circumstances of its genesis and led both actors and observers to forget about the contingency of these earlier rearticulations. In effect, the actors and practices that were prevalent before the Arab uprisings were themselves the contingent outcomes of extraordinary political episodes that became normalized over time. While this chapter does not detail the precise interactions between contentious events, practices and actors in each case because of space constraints, it is certainly an endeavour that would be worth undertaking to better understand such political contingencies.

Political legitimacy and authoritarian control

Authoritarian legitimacy in early post-colonial regimes

How does the state manage to appear sufficiently legitimate to a large enough proportion of the population so that governance is actually achievable without an inordinate amount of resources being spent on repressing an unruly people? The 'legitimacy crises' that repeatedly destabilized the early post-colonial state in the MENA have long been debated in the political science and area studies literature. In the mid-1970s Michael Hudson highlighted some the dilemmas and features that would become a staple diet for analyses of regime stability.[11] They included the processes of modernization of traditional models of governance, an issue that remains particularly pertinent for the monarchies of the region. The continuing relevance of 'traditional' authority is predicated upon a constant 'invention of tradition' that makes traditional leaders politically legitimate in new socio-historical contexts. For instance, the continuing relevance of tribal allegiances since the colonial period has much to do with the adaptation of tribal actors, structures and practices to new political situations not initially defined by tribalism.[12] Post-colonial models of regime legitimacy are shaped by the different trajectories of state institutionalization initiated during the colonial period, as well as by the positioning of the new regimes vis-à-vis different notions of modern statehood.[13] These dilemmas also involved the adaptation of ideological and institutional models of state governance to support the modernist orientations of the new Arab republics—with Arabism and Arab socialism being two noticeable regional productions.

Hudson's Weberian typology provided a handy way to recognize different models of state authority in post-colonial North Africa. In the neo-traditional monarchies of Morocco and Libya, King Mohammed V and King Idris could be portrayed as using a mixture of traditional authority and charisma to buttress their political leadership. In the Arab republics of Algeria and of Tunisia, charisma was clearly a key element in Bourguiba's and Ben Bella's political leadership, as were more mundane rational-legal types of authority. During the period of decolonization most blatantly, new and old actors and practices of governance competed with each other for control of the new state. At the time of independence, King Idris in Libya and King Mohammed V in Morocco outma-noeuvred other nationalist political actors to position themselves as the main beneficiaries of national sovereignty. Idris benefited most from the external process of recognition by Britain, France and the United States, at a time when his acceptance by the population outside Cyrenaica was limited. In Morocco, by contrast, the sultan (then turned king) played a subtle political game against both the French administration and the nationalist parties to boost his popular legitimacy and leadership claims. In Tunisia, the Bey of Tunis, despite being named king at the time of the handover of power from France in 1956, could not outplay the main nationalist movement, the Neo-Destour party of Habib Bourguiba, and was swiftly deposed after independence.

In all these cases, the extraordinary set of interactions that crucially shaped the legitimacy of the new regimes was the decolonization process. This context produced particular challenges and opportunities for social and political actors that would not be easily reproduced after-wards. Decolonization and independence generated particular notions of legitimacy and practices of legitimation which contained in-built problems regarding the transmission of state authority. In time, the practices and actors of the independence struggle eventually lost their relevance. Ideationally, a principal difficulty for these post-colonial regimes was the institutionalization of an authority, acquired during a very uncommon historical episode, in the routine politics of a working post-colonial state.

In Morocco, the legitimacy boost to the authority of the monarchy gained from the anti-colonial struggle helped create what Clifford Geertz called a new 'maraboutic king'.[14] Through his calculated oppo-sition to French colonial rule during the period of pro-independence mobilization, the Sultan of Morocco was able to carve for himself a new role and legitimacy. Becoming King Mohammed V in 1957, he used his symbolic capital to place himself at the head of a parliamentary monarchy and then employed his prerogatives to outmanoeuvre the political parties. The sudden death of Mohammed V in 1961 was fol-lowed by a formal reaffirmation of the 'traditional' (including religious) authority of the monarchy among the Moroccan population to boost the position of Mohammed V's son, Hassan II.[15] The 1962 Moroccan constitution formally enshrined the prerogatives of the new king, a year after his accession to the throne. This rearticulation of the sources of legitimacy of the monarchy was increasingly supplemented by a legal-administrative form of authority backed by repression. In the 1960s, the monarchy centralized state power by building support among the rural notables to counter the challenges of the urban elites and emerging middle class. During the period of the 'years of lead' (mid-1960s to mid-1980s), the strengthening of the Moroccan security apparatus helped buttress the authority of the monarchy against internal and external challenges.[16]

A common outcome of this type of securitarian reconfiguration is the emergence of military challengers within the regime and the need for countering the possibility of coups. Hassan II narrowly escaped with his life during two coups attempts in 1971 and 1972. In 1975 the king sought to boost his 'traditional' and 'charismatic' authority, as well as move potentially troublesome military actors away from the centre of power, by annexing the Western Sahara region just as Spain was leaving its former colony. The 'Green March' into the Western Sahara bolstered the nationalist rhetoric and credentials of the monarchy and provided the army with a new fiefdom in the recently occupied territories.[17] During that decade, Hassan II revived a new nationalist charismatic leadership to deal with the limitations of legal-administrative legitimation and the issue of the loyalty of the security apparatus.

In Libya, the Senussi monarchy faced similar problems of entrenchment and transmission of its rule in the aftermath of independence. These challenges were compounded by the regional basis of support for King Idris (and the Senussi brotherhood) in Cyrenaica, in a context of rapid socio-economic changes induced by the oil boom of the 1960s.[18] As in Morocco, the monarchy had to rely on the legal-administrative authority of a growing state apparatus—including the security apparatus in order to reaffirm its rule over an increasingly complex society. The constitutional revision of 1963 that turned the federal state of Libya into a unitary state illustrated this centralization of power by the monarchy. As in Morocco, this repositioning of the Libyan monarch further away from traditional authority, and the institutionalization of the legal-rational authority of the state backed by the security apparatus, provoked challenges from the modernizing armed forces. Directly inspired by the rise to power of Nasser in Egypt, young Libyan officers began to organize themselves in revolutionary committees in the mid-1960s to orchestrate a challenge to the monarchy. In 1969, the coup by Captain Muammar Gaddafi and the Revolutionary Command Council (RCC) attempted to duplicate what Nasser had done earlier against the Egyptian monarchy.[19] This successful and nearly bloodless coup illustrated how much the traditional authority of the monarchy had lost its appeal among both the elites and the general population. The king had retained little loyalty in and control over the military, as the process of modernizing the security apparatus had unfolded with limited attention paid to the dangers of a coup.

As Gaddafi, now promoted to colonel, entrenched the revolutionary rule of the RCC using a mixture of charismatic authority, legal-rational redistributive methods and traditional authority through the cooptation of tribal leaders, he also had to contend with the neo-praetorian trend that he himself initiated. Gaddafi narrowly avoided being deposed in coups organized by his co-conspirators in the RCC in 1970 and in 1975. In response, he put in place a coup-proofing strategy based on political supervision of the military by 'revolutionary committees' which led in practice to the disorganization of the country's armed forces.[20] Particularly after the formalization of Gaddafi's revolutionary political ideology in the *Green Book* (1976) and the reform of state institutions to create the 'state of the masses' (*Jamahiriya*) (1977), this strategy of disempowering the military expanded to include all the institutionalized bodies that could constitute a counter-power to his authority. To avoid internal challenges, Gaddafi strategically chose to limit the rational-legal authority of the country's institutions by repeatedly modifying the hierarchies of power through the introduction of multiple 'revolutionary' channels of command. Behind the 'Arab socialist' rhetoric of the regime (later supplemented by an Islamic one), Gaddafi's rule in the 1980s increasingly became a form of neo-sultanistic governance in which weak institutional structures constituted an empty shell for personalistic and neo-traditional (tribal-based) patronage networks.[21]

In Algeria, the legitimacy of the political role of the military constructed during the war of decolonization was rearticulated on new rational-legal sources of authority as the Algerian revolution became institutionalized and the rule of the Front de Libération Nationale (FLN) became normalized.[22] In the process, the charismatic leadership of Ben Bella, who came to power with the support of the military, began to show its limitations as his autocratic style of governance generated ever more opposition. Ben Bella had been elected president in uncontested elections in 1963 and had tried to establish the primacy of his authority and that of the party over the army. Less than two years later, in 1965, he was toppled by his defence minister, Colonel Houari Boumedienne, in a bloodless coup. In an increasingly autocratic approach to governance, the support for Boumedienne within the military proved more decisive than the political leadership of one of main figures of the independence movement.[23] The direct involvement of military actors in governing the country ensured continuing tensions within the military elite, as illustrated by the failed 1967 coup by Tahar Zbiri, the chief of staff. Subsequently, Boumedienne monopolized the functions of president, defence minister and chief of staff.[24] Under Boumedienne, the scramble for power between the different factions involved in the war of independence generated a more unitary political and military structure in which the main task of the regime was to maintain order by allocating resources and by socializing citizens and soldiers through the party and army. The endorsement of an Arab Socialist model facilitated the merging of developmentalist and nationalist claims to legitimacy and the prioritization of a corporatist form of economic governance (until the failure of the import-substitution development strategy became clear in the second half of the 1970s).

The sudden death of Boumedienne in 1978 highlighted the difficulties of the continuing dominance of the army over the party, in a context of the military's diminishing legitimacy after independence. The nomination of Colonel Chadli Bendjedid to the Algerian presidency took place at the national congress of the FLN in the face of a challenge by the party to nominate its preferred candidate, the foreign minister, Abdelaziz Bouteflika. This episode pointed to the continuing reinvention of the tradition of the military as the country's saviour and the informal institutionalization of its influence in the state system.[25] While over time the continuing involvement of the military in politics helped entrench a particular form of neo-praetorianism, different political circumstances created at various moments different categories of neo-praetorian actors and practices.[26] By the early 1980s, internal challenges from the elites of the war of independence were euphemized, as contestation became one of relative winners and losers within a stable system of governance and not about the model of governance itself.

In Tunisia, the traditional authority of the bey-turned-king at the time of independence was weakly established and repeatedly challenged by the political activism of the main nationalist party. In 1957, a year after negotiating independence from France, the leadership of the Neo-Destour party manoeuvred to evict the king and replace the constitutional monarchy with a constitutional republic. The minimal role played by the armed forces during the process of decolonization and the building of state institutions in the early Tunisian republic was less conducive to the emergence of neo-praetorianism (even though an ill-organized coup did occur in 1962).[27] The strengthening of the country's institutional framework and of the legal-administrative authority of the regime led by the Neo-Destour party, the clear winner of the 1959 parliamentary elections, was facilitated by this lack of strong contenders for state power at the time. The charismatic leadership of President Habib Bourguiba helped buttress this system of governance and deflect challenges from the opposition. Bourguiba was particularly instrumental in curtailing the growing influence of leftist movements and the Tunisian General Workers Union (Union Générale des Travailleurs Tunisiens, UGTT) in the early 1960s. Having managed to evict Ahmed Ben Salah, the UGTT president, from his post, Bourguiba subsequently co-opted him into government in order to boost the regime's legitimacy and popularity. After Ben Salah became finance minister and minister for the 'plan' in 1961, the Tunisian regime veered increasingly towards Arab socialism. In the aftermath of the failed 1962 coup, the regime banned the communist party, and the Neo-Destour party, now renamed the Destourian Socialist Party (Parti Socialiste Destourien, PSD), became de facto a state-party.

The political legitimacy of the PSD rested at the time on the developmentalist promises of the Arab socialist experiment, an experiment which, by the end of that decade, increasingly failed to deliver. To regain some popularity, Bourguiba placed the blame for the regime's developmentalist failures on the shoulders of Ben Salah and the Left. In 1970 he reconstructed the legitimacy of the regime by denouncing Arab socialism and by turning towards economic liberalism. By co-opting liberal political actors and reorienting the economic policies of the regime, Bourguiba rebuffed a growing wave of discontent against his rule, but at the cost of growing political opposition from the left. In 1975, the formal transformation of the Tunisian regime into a right-wing authoritarian system based on economic liberalization was signalled by the reform of the constitution, which made Bourguiba president for life. Writing in 1976, Hudson observed that 'Tunisia too has its legitimacy problem; but compared to the hidden, simmering politics of the monarchies, the volatile, bitter and tragic politics in the pan-Arab core, and the unformed, often capricious and praetorian politics in the peripheral states, Bourguiba's republic appears as a relatively well legitimized political system'.[28] Yet, in 1978, one of the main legitimacy crises of the regime occurred as a result of a confrontation with the UGTT over the state's new socio-economic policies. A wave of concerted strike actions by the union culminated in nation-wide unrest, and Bourguiba had to call in the army to restore order and remain in power. This protest episode initiated another sequence of reconfiguring of the Tunisian regime—i.e. partial political liberalization—which would have significant implications in the 1980s.[29]

Changing political challenges and responses to delegitimization in the 1980s and 1990s

In North Africa, challenges to the new state authorities in the early post-colonial period came mainly from leftist movements and military coups. A couple of decades later, by contrast, these challenges centered mainly on the activities of Islamist movements. From the 1980s onwards, narratives emphasizing the 'revenge of God' (to borrow Gilles Kepel's imagery of religious politics) have been ripe in political analyses of the region.[30] In Algeria, during the war of decolonization the main Islamic reformist movement, the Association des Oulamas, had been co-opted into the FLN. After independence, the leaders of this Islamizing current would recurrently head the ministry of religious affairs in successive governments from Ben Bella to Chadli Bendjedid. While at the time Islamist networks were active in the social and cultural fields, they did not position themselves as a political opposition to the FLN. Their overt opposition to the regime would mainly manifest itself in the publishing activities of the al-Qiyyam network in the mid-

1960s. In the early to mid-1970s preachers like Sheikh Sahnoun and Sheikh Abdellatif Soltani condemned Boumedienne's socialist policies in their sermons, but with limited echo among the population.[31]

In Morocco, during the 'years of lead', the most notable act of the Islamist militants of Chabiba Islamiya (Islamic Youth), created by Abdelkrim Moutii in 1969, was the assassination of the general secretary of the socialist party Union Socialiste des Forces Populaires (Socialist Union of Popular Forces, USFP), Omar Benjelloun, in 1975. A more substantive ideational challenge to the idea of a traditional religious allegiance to the king as 'commander of the faithful' was expressed in Sheikh Abdessalam Yassine's 1973 open letter to the king, which urged a return to a 'proper' form of Islamic governance. Yassine was promptly put into jail, but his actions gave the impetus for the creation of the Justice and Charity association (al-Adl wal-Ihsane), which became the main Islamist movement in the country in the ensuing decades.[32] In Tunisia and in Libya, movements influenced by the Egyptian Muslim Brotherhood were also active during the early postcolonial period, but they limited their activities primarily to sociocultural and educational issues.

In the 1980s, a combination of external political changes and internal economic failures repositioned more centrally the relevance of Islamism in these countries. This renewed visibility was facilitated by an emerging democratization discourse promoted by international actors as the Cold War drew to end.[33] New policies promoting democracy, unhindered by the 'communist threat', modified the realpolitik calculus and introduced new criteria for judging the regimes of the region. This new international context was particularly relevant for regimes whose economic situation was increasingly characterized by the failures of Arab socialism and other forms of state *dirigisme*. The economic liberalism promoted by organizations like the International Monetary Fund (IMF), which were called upon by regimes to help resolve their financial difficulties, directly contributed to the rolling back of the welfare state in the region. The privatization of social services led to the growth of the welfare provision of Islamist organizations, which stepped in to replace state provisions. These dynamics involving the expansion of Islamist social activities into spaces where the state administration was once the main provider and source of authority have been explored in detail in the political science and area studies literature from the 1990s onwards.[34] The turn towards a neo-liberal model of economic governance and the weakening of the welfare state not only put a strain on earlier authoritarian bargains that had promised socio-economic development in exchange for political quiescence, but also reduced the appeal of secularized left-wing movements that had relied on state support to promote their views among the more traditional sectors of society. This new political and socio-economic context facilitated the (re)mobilization of Islamist movements first through *dawa* (proselytizing), then social welfare activities, and finally a more explicit political agenda for governance.

In Tunisia, weakened by his confrontation with the UGTT, Bourguiba sought to boost the legitimacy of the regime by reviving a liberal-democratic discourse. This move resulted in the formal re-establishment of multipartyism in the country ahead of the 1981 parliamentary elections. In practice, however, the political opposition remained very tightly controlled by the security services and barely managed to score 6 per cent in these elections. During this very partial opening, the secularist national discourse promoted by Bourguiba ensured that the emerging Islamist movement did not gain even token recognition from the regime. Instead, as soon as the Movement of Islamic Tendency (MIT) of Rachid Ghannouchi declared its political ambitions publicly, its leadership was arrested and jailed.[35] The continuing socio-economic difficulties experienced by the population in the 1980s ensured, however, that multiple oppositions to the regime, Islamists included, continued to mobilize disgruntled citizens outside the formal political sphere. Social discontent erupted in spectacular fashion during the 'food riots' of 1984 when the regime had to call upon the army once more to restore order. As before, the knee-jerk political reaction that followed the 1984 riots was another attempt by Bourguiba at restoring the legitimacy of his rule by making ad hoc changes to the system of governance.[36] During this period of partial political liberalization, the MIT leaders were freed and allowed to resume their social activism. Soon this period of mild political tolerance gave way to increasing state repression ahead of the 1986 parliamentary election, as the regime feared the emergence of a stronger political opposition. This repression eventually led to a boycott of the elections by the political parties. Increasingly, the charismatic and traditional legitimacy of Bourguiba as the founder of modern Tunisia began to fail because of these repeated changes of political direction and the apparent erratic behaviour of the president.

Bourguiba's strategy of frontal confrontation with the MIT led to the sentencing to death of a dozen of their members in 1987 for alleged participation in an assassination attempt against the president. This new repressive episode triggered further popular unrest and led to a decision by members of the ruling elite to push Bourguiba aside to stabilize the situation. On 7 November 1987, Prime Minister Ben Ali (who had been interior minister up to the previous month) produced a medical certificate that declared Bourguiba unable to govern. Through this 'medical coup', Ben Ali deposed the president and put himself in charge of the country, in accordance with the constitution, without generating any significant opposition.[37] The rise to power of Ben Ali, though not a textbook case of a military coup, remains linked all the same to the repeated reliance of the Bourguiba regime on the security apparatus in times of crisis. Ben Ali made a name for himself in the early 1970s as head of military security, before becoming head of internal security (that is, the police apparatus) in 1978 during the confrontation between the regime and the UGTT. After being sidelined in the early 1980s, he was recalled to help quell the 1984 riots and was rewarded with the position of interior minister. After his coup, Ben Ali initially sought to accommodate the Islamists and other opposition forces in a formal political process in order to consolidate his own legitimacy as head of state.[38] However, after organizing the partially free parliamentary elections of 1989, Ben Ali began to roll back the democratic reforms he had initiated once he reckoned that he could rule singlehandedly with the support of his new political party, the Rassemblement Constitutionnel Démocratique (the Constitutional Democratic Rally, RCD). Although both democratic and Islamist political discourses had been validated by the regime (and the population) at the end of the 1980s, the beginning of the 1990s saw the return of cruder forms of authoritarian governance. The direction taken by the Ben Ali regime would be consistent throughout this decade: increasing economic liberalization and development, alongside increasing social and political repression. At the time, Michele Angrist commented that 'as long as the economy performs reasonably well, regime stability is

assured. But in the event of a downturn, the lack of peaceful mechanisms for public, popular articulation of dissent means that over the
medium to long term instability could loom on Tunisia's horizon.'[39]

In the late 1980s, political validation of Islamism and democratization was also highly visible in Algeria during a hectic process of political
reform. Economic failure stirred social unrest in the mid- to late 1980s
and undermined the rule of the FLN. Islamist actors had already made
a notable appearance in the early 1980s, in the form of a small guerrilla
cum social bandit movement that used low-intensity political violence
to squeeze more Islamic and economic concessions from the regime.
In 1982, Mustapha Bouyali, a former military commander of the
National Liberation Army (Armée de Libération Nationale, ALN), the
armed wing of the FLN, declared jihad against the regime and led the
resistance in his home region at the head of the Mouvement Islamique
Armé (MIA). He was able to remain active for several years due to a
network of local supporters, but was eventually ambushed and killed
alongside most of his troops in 1987.[40] At the same time, independently of Bouyali, the 'free mosques' movement—an illegal network
of mosques not controlled by the ministry of religious affairs—spurred
a growth in Islamist social activism throughout Algeria. As in other
countries of the region during times of economic liberalization, the
welfare activities of the free mosques filled the gaps left by a retreating
state and gave Islamists a new popular legitimacy.[41] The increasingly
dense network of Islamist associations forming this decentralized
movement played a crucial role at the local level to validate Islamic
perspectives on governance in the place of the earlier developmentalist
discourse of Arab socialism.

The wave of nation-wide unrest of October 1988 and its brutal
repression by the Algerian army seriously damaged the legitimacy of
the FLN and the ALN. The nationalist and anti-imperialist image of the
FLN had already begun to be replaced, particularly after the economic
reforms initiated under President Chadli Bendjedid, by that of a corrupt party based primarily on patron–client relations. The brutal military repression of the October riots also contributed to a change in the
perception of the ALN, from builder and defender of the nation to that
of a ruthless internal repressive apparatus. The tensions between and
within the FLN and the ALN were heightened by this protest episode,

and the regime appeared openly divided over the political direction of the country. Under the impulse of Chadli, reformers within the regime initiated a political opening and authorized multipartyism in order to reduce social unrest.[42] This ad hoc reconfiguration of governance was designed to strengthen the rational-legal legitimacy of the regime by institutionalizing an electoral democracy. While reforming authoritarian elites aimed at the kind of weak parliamentary system that already existed in neighbouring Morocco at the time, they had little experience with multipartyism. In the early 1990s, the Islamic Salvation Front (Front Islamique du Salut, FIS) became the dominant political party of the Algerian democratic transition by building its party apparatus from the ground up, using pre-existing networks of Islamic charities and mosques. The FIS leaders were not experienced political players either, and they ended up overestimating their charismatic authority over the Islamist voting constituency as well as the rational-legal legitimacy given by elections.

As the FIS political rhetoric antagonized both secularized segments of the population and regime hardliners, particularly inside the military, Islamist activism ended up triggering a military coup in 1992 when it became clear that the FIS was about to obtain a large majority in the parliamentary elections.[43] This coup was the defining moment for the repositioning of the military in politics during the 1990s and beyond. The military leaders who evicted Chadli from office and halted the electoral process reverted to advocating the traditional legitimacy of the army as protector of the nation, this time against Islamist 'extremism'. This strategy was subsequently boosted by the drift towards indiscriminate political violence by some of the Islamist guerrilla groups that formed after the coup. Throughout the 1990s, direct military rule and military coercion were common, if only partially effective, answers to the challenges directed at the Algerian regime. The military elite sought nonetheless to keep the rational-legal mode of legitimation of electoral democracy by formally retaining elections and a multiparty system, albeit under strict surveillance. This strategy initiated a trend towards co-opting non-system-challenging Islamist actors in a pseudo-democratic institutional system in which electoral processes did not introduce uncertainty regarding the (lack of) rotation of elites.[44]

In Morocco, al-Adl wal-Ihsane's initial religious challenge to the legitimacy of the regime centred on the traditional authority of the monarch as 'commander of the faithful'. Secular political actors, by contrast, focused their criticisms on the rational-legal character of the constitutional monarchy and the associated parliamentary system. In the 1980s, in a context of socio-economic unrest ('food riots' in Casablanca (1981), Marrakesh (1984), Fez (1990)), the king sought to reduce his reliance on the repressive apparatus by orchestrating a controlled political opening that would give a greater role to opposition parties in the parliamentary system. This process gained momentum at the end of the decade and was formalized in the 1990s by means of constitutional reforms (1992 and 1996). At that time, the monarchy reached an agreement with the main opposition forces—the USFP, the Party of Progress and Socialism (PPS), and the Independence Party (Istiqlal)—which became a 'loyal' opposition to the king in the sense that they did not challenge his constitutional prerogatives. This process produced the so-called '*alternance*' (rotation of power) in 1998 when the USFP leader, Abderrahman el-Youssoufi, became prime minister. This partial political opening also provided the monarchy with an opportunity to set the terms for the inclusion of a legal Islamist party in this revamped parliamentary system.[45]

In 1996 Driss Basri, the interior minister, arranged the merging of a small political party, the Popular Democratic and Constitutional Movement (PDCM), with a non-legally recognized Islamist association, the Movement for Unity and Reform (MUR), to enable the participation of the Islamists in electoral politics—they would obtain nine seats in the 1997 parliamentary elections.[46] The MUR was viewed by the monarchy as a candidate for a 'loyal' Islamist opposition that could act as a counterweight to the popular Justice and Charity movement of Sheikh Yassine, who had long voiced his opposition to the principle of monarchical governance. In 1998, the PDCM-MUR would change its name to the Justice and Development Party (Parti de la Justice et du Développement, PJD). As this process of controlled political liberalization was unfolding, King Hassan II unexpectedly died in 1999 and was replaced on the throne by his son, King Mohammed VI. The new monarch chose to fully endorse the partial opening then associated with his father, thereby presenting change as continuity. The monarchy renewed in this way its (rational-legal) institutional legitimacy by continuing to negotiate a system of power-sharing with previously excluded social and political forces, while trying to maintain a weak parliamentary system in support of the status quo.[47]

The socio-economic and political challenges of the 1980s led the regimes of Tunisia, Algeria and Morocco to make changes to their model of governance in order to retain what they saw as the required minimum of popular legitimacy. The Libyan regime of Colonel Gaddafi, by contrast appeared less affected by such challenges during the same period. While discursive legitimation based on Arab socialism and the *Green Book* faded away in the 1980s, Gaddafi's 'no-party' system and never-ending reconfiguration of revolutionary structures and policies worked to prevent institutionalized opposition to his rule.[48] Anti-imperialist discourses continued to be used to legitimize the actions of the regime, particularly as Libya provided active support to multiple resistance movements and armed or terrorist organizations across the world. In effect, Gaddafi's adventurous foreign policy directly increased the political isolation of the regime in the 1980s and 1990s. In this context, the pressure applied by Western democracies and international financial organizations in favour of partial economic and political liberalization was hardly effective as the regime's oil revenues cushioned the economic impact of international sanctions.[49] The neo-sultanistic rule of Gaddafi in Libya was equally inimical to all forms of political opposition, and repression occasionally spurred violent conflict, in the 1990s particularly. Besides the attempted coup by military officers linked to the Warfallah tribe in 1993, the most serious violent challenge to the regime came from the Libyan Islamic Fighting Group (LIFG) from 1995 until the end of the decade.[50] Particularly strong in Cyrenaica, a region that had received limited benefits from the oil rent as the regime sought to weaken the traditional support there for the former monarchy, the LIFG was able to organize a guerrilla campaign that challenged the authority of the regime for several years, as well as stretching its repressive capabilities. Over time, however, like their Algerian counterparts, the LIFG, confronted by a financially and militarily stronger opponent, could not sustain its insurrection. While the perceived legitimacy of the regime during this military campaign remained low, the equally weak legitimacy of the Islamists in the eyes of many Libyans—a consequence of the narrow ideological basis of the movement—worked against the possibility of the LIFG creating a united front against the regime with other tribal or regional opposition forces.[51]

The 'War on Terror' and regime hardening

In the mid-1990s, Olivier Roy could legitimately talk about 'the failure of political Islam', considering the lack of success of revolutionist Islamists seeking state power in the region.[52] However, his analysis—and particularly subsequent interpretations of this argument—somewhat downplayed the relevance of other trends in contemporary Islamism.[53] While in the 1980s and 1990s those Islamist organizations hoping to emulate the Iranian Revolution had not fared particularly well, the more reformist-minded Islamists advocating a transformation of political and cultural norms and practices positioned themselves as legitimate contenders for state governance. Yet, the dominant narrative for both ruling elites in the region and international actors was that a measure of authoritarian control was needed precisely to avoid an Iranian (or Afghan or Algerian) scenario. This general policy orientation was reaffirmed in the aftermath of the 11 September 2001 al-Qaeda attacks in the United States.[54] The post-9/11 reorientation of US security policies did not, however, change dramatically the legitimacy challenges facing the authoritarian regimes of North Africa. The quest by these regimes for external political validation and accompanying financial and security rewards during the decade of the 'War on Terror' underscored the reduced ability of ruling elites to respond to the challenges facing them, and mobilize citizens around a domestic political agenda.

Throughout the 2000s, what characterized these regimes was not so much new articulations of governance linked to a changing international context, as the greater integration of authoritarian claims to legitimacy in a global security discourse. Domestically, the opportunities for political change were seriously constrained by the instrumentalization of the Islamist threat by ruling elites more than by Islamism per se. As Saad Eddin Ibrahim summarized this purported difficulty: 'we find Egypt's President Hosni Mubarak and Tunisia's President Ben Ali telling their Western interlocutors, in effect, "It is either us or Bin Laden." If that is the choice, of course Westerners—whatever their love for democracy—will opt for the autocrats over the theocrats.'[55] The Bush administration's agenda for democracy in the Middle East, particularly after the US intervention in Iraq, showed, nonetheless, a recognition that authoritarianism also fuelled a violent global Islamist militancy. This interplay between normative ideals and realpolitik calculations was well illustrated by the WikiLeaks documents revealing the assessments of US embassies throughout the region at the time.[56] It may well have been the case, as Tamara Wittes then remarked, that the capabilities of the authoritarian regimes of the region were weakening and that it made sense for the US and other international actors to reposition themselves in favour of change.[57] In practice, however, as the timing of these 'upcoming' political changes was unknown, policies promoting democracy remained focused by default on a rather limited set of liberal and secular opposition actors and on regime 'reformers'. This remained the case even if it was clear that, as Eberhard Kienle noted, 'the only conclusion that can safely be drawn is that standard recipes for democracy engineering contribute to the reconfiguration of authoritarian rule rather than to democratization'.[58]

During the decade of the 'War on Terror', North African regimes principally articulated two distinct strategies for the securitization of Islamism. In Libya and in Tunisia, the discourse on terrorism was used as a justification for the repression of all Islamist social and political activities. It was also used more broadly against other opposition actors when expedient. In Libya, Gaddafi jettisoned the Islamist propaganda that the regime had used earlier on in aid of its interventionist foreign policy—from the creation of the Islamic Legion in the 1970s to support for multiple Islamist guerrilla movements in the 1980s and early 1990s. Instead, the Libyan regime recast itself as the guarantor of non-violent Islamic practices, and even opened the door to a possible liberalization through Gaddafi's son Saif al-Islam's civil society initiatives.[59] Prior Libyan support for armed Islamist organizations ensured that the Libyan leadership had some useful intelligence to trade with the US and other European powers when Gaddafi engineered a rapprochement with his former 'imperialist' adversaries. The events of 11 September 2001 effectively provided the Libyan regime with an opportunity to normalize its position on the international scene.[60] Increased external recognition facilitated the suppression of dissent at home under the pretence of fighting 'terrorism' and ensuring 'security' in the region. As international sanctions were lifted, this external support also brought concrete rewards for the repressive apparatus, such as the acquisition of modern security equipment (for 'policing' the southern border of the European Union) or the handing over of opponents based abroad.[61]

In Tunisia, too, the regime used the narrative of the 'War on Terror' to enshrine the authority of a secular state system that was meant to be the opposite of an Islamist political order. 'Fundamentalism gives birth to terrorism,' Ben Ali declared.[62] The modernist and secularist rhetoric of the regime stressed the link between Islamism and insecurity to justify a clampdown on any form of political contestation from Islamist movements, as well as to strictly control religious social activism. The 2002 Ghriba synagogue bombing by a cell of al-Qaeda provided additional justification for the regime's position, even though violent Islamist activism was always rare in the country. The new securitarian measures, developed in line with international security concerns, further amplified the repressive tendencies of the Tunisian regime towards not only Islamists but the opposition generally.[63] The generalization of repressive techniques dressed up as anti-terrorism measures would be illustrated over the years by the regime's clampdown on the activities of the Bar Association, the Tunisian League of Human Rights and the branches of the local workers' union (particularly during the 2008 Gafsa strikes).[64] The permissiveness of the international community towards the regime after 2001 provided Ben Ali with new ideational and material resources to deal with his domestic legitimacy deficit. 'The first human right is to eat,' responded French President Jacques Chirac when questioned about France's response to the poor human rights record of Tunisia.[65] The leverage provided by cooperation on 'security' issues even facilitated the start of negotiations on the country's 'advanced' status in the EU Mediterranean Partnership programme in 2010.

In Morocco and in Algeria, the regimes constructed their securitization strategies on a more subtle distinction between anti-system and pro-status quo Islamist movements. They generally sought to repress the activities of the former, but allowed the latter to operate in the social and political fields under strict conditions. This position enabled the regimes to continue to ground their legitimacy on the rational-legal framework of democracy and strengthened their role as arbiter between 'legitimate' and 'illegitimate' political activism.[66] Organizationally, these regimes benefited from the indirect support that the opposition forces gave to this pseudo-democratic system when they agreed to 'play by the rules'. They were also able to deflect more effectively criticisms regarding poor governance by placing the blame on the country's entire political class.

In Algeria, the regime refined its system of controlled multipartyism at the end of the main period of civil conflict in the 1990s—a shift marked by the 2000 general amnesty ('law on civil concord') instigated by newly elected President Bouteflika.[67] The cooptation of the Muslim Brotherhood-inspired Movement for Peace (previously Hamas) initiated in the mid-1990s, when they participated in the ruling coalition of President Zéroual, became a staple feature of the Bouteflika presidency in the 2000s. The inclusion of 'good' Islamists in the political system ensured that the regime retained some degree of legitimacy among Islamic-minded constituencies, at the same time as it kept repressing the 'bad' Islamists who did not want to 'play by the rules'. The new securitarian concerns of the international community after 2001 facilitated the reintegration of the Algerian elites linked to the 1992 coup into regional security cooperation agreements. As a result, by 2009 Algeria had become the largest weapons importer in North Africa and had the highest military expenditure in the whole of Africa.[68] By stressing the importance of the fight against terrorism for national and international security, the Algerian regime ensured that its dubious democratic legitimacy was not a main object of international criticism or sanction.[69] In that respect, the rebranding of the guerrillas of Groupe Salafiste pour la Prédication et le Combat (GSPC) as al-Qaeda in the Islamic Maghreb (AQIM) in 2007 played into the hands of the regime.

In Morocco, the steady electoral gains made by the Party of Justice and Development (PJD) since its creation ensured that the Islamist party stuck to its strategy of accommodation with the monarchy. By 2002, it had become the third largest group in the parliament, and by 2007 the second largest group and the leading opposition party.[70] This process of mutual accommodation was not without costs for the actors involved. During the decade of the 'War on Terror', and especially after the Casablanca suicide bombings of 2003, many secular political actors as well as parts of the regime pushed for a more repressive stance against the PJD. The monarchy resisted the idea of an overall ban, which would have jeopardized its strategy of institutional legitimation based on controlled multipartyism. For the king, the PJD constituted a useful political entity that contributed to keeping alive ideological divisions and mutual defiance inside the parliament, as well as drawing some popular support away from the Justice and Charity movement.[71] The regime did, however, place enough pressure on the PJD to ensure that at its 2004 party conference a candidate with strong accommodationist views, Saâdeddine el-Othmani, won the contest to become the new PJD party leader. Institutionally, Moroccan political pluralism was identified by the international community as an example of progressive democratization that kept Islamist actors 'moderate'. Domestically, however, Moroccan voters became increasingly uninvolved in electoral processes which they perceived did not have any significant impact on governance. Similarly, among Islamist activists, the more oppositional stance of the Justice and Charity movement, which questioned the legitimacy of monarchical governance, gained in popularity whenever the political effectiveness of the PJD was doubted by voters.[72]

Structuring patronage and clientelism

The changing legitimacy claims and mechanisms of legitimation of the North African regimes were accompanied by a transformation of the 'social contract' between ruling elites, subaltern elites and the citizenry. These were based primarily on the material incentives that the regimes provided to groups and individuals to encourage them to explicitly support their rule or, at the very least, not to openly challenge the status quo. In the early post-colonial period, both monarchies and republics commonly endorsed state interventionism in the economic sector and made it a 'duty' for the ruling elites to cater for the developmental needs of the population, since they 'knew better' what was best for the country. For these regimes, the economic problems generated by various forms of state *dirigisme* usually justified a turn towards more neoliberal economic models inspired by the 'Washington consensus'.[73] In the region, rentier theory initially stressed how the developmental and governance dilemmas of oil-rich, rent-supported regimes differed from those of countries where the economy was not primarily based on wealth redistribution by the state.[74] Yet, by the 2000s, the strategies of those rentier states seeking to diversify their economy (Libya, Algeria) and those oil-poor countries seeking to develop a more competitive market economy (Tunisia, Morocco) had led the regimes to make similar-looking compromises.[75]

Commonly, the continuation of authoritarian rule in a liberalized global economy meant the endorsement of some 'free-market' reforms in order to co-opt emerging economic and political elites in state networks of governance.[76] Crony capitalism and redistributive policies were linked up with a view to tying the interests of new economic entrepreneurs to those of the ruling elites, making economic liberalization a factor of the deeper institutionalization of the regimes.[77] By passing on some of the state's responsibility for socio-economic development to private actors, the regimes of the region sought to reduce the political responsibility of the state in the everyday management of domestic economic issues. In addition, ruling elites saw these reforms as an opportunity to transfer state assets to private ownership in a way that personally benefited them.[78] Opportunities for personal enrichment, either directly or through the sponsoring of crony capitalists, varied according to the types of economic opportunities available in each polity. The mechanisms that different regimes used to harness these neo-liberal reforms to the defense of the political status quo fluctuated on a spectrum from high to low cooptation in North Africa.[79]

In the early post-colonial period, the Moroccan monarchy could largely finance state policies though the rent it received from the export of its phosphate deposits—the main source of foreign currency and of revenue for the state at the time. While these revenues were sufficient to allow the development of the Moroccan state administration and civil service, as well as some well-publicized developmental projects, they only marginally enabled the regime to raise living standards in the country (particularly in the poorer peripheral regions such as the Rif). Increasingly in the 1970s, with the fall in the price of phosphates on the world markets and the implications of the oil glut for emerging economies, the Moroccan regime faced a more difficult economic and financial situation. This predicament eventually led the monarchy to ask for the help of the IMF and the World Bank in the early 1980s. After the signing of a structural adjustment programme in 1983, the mechanisms of state intervention in the social sphere had to be rethought dramatically, as state capacity to spearhead economic growth directly became very limited.[80] New avenues for social mobility had to be created through private sector incentives as employment opportunities in the public sector decreased dramatically. After the start of the IMF programme, job offers in the public sector decreased by 80 per cent during the 1984–5 financial exercise.[81] During the same period, food subsidies were sharply reduced, increasing the legitimacy deficit of the regime, especially among the urban poor. As episodes of social unrest (e.g. the 1984 Marrakesh riots) were met by repression, the monarchy sought to depoliticize economic issues in order to implement its programme of privatization.[82]

As elsewhere in the region, this process favoured crony capitalism and political entrepreneurs close to the regime. Traditionally, the monarchy had relied on rural notables as transmission belts for its rule. In the 1980s, neo-traditional forms of patrimonialism particularly present in the countryside were strengthened through the process of economic liberalization, as pro-monarchy local notables were made to benefit from partial market reforms. In their turn, the notables elected to parliament contributed to the continuing dominance of the pro-monarchy parties in the freer and more pluralistic parliamentary system of the 1990s.[83] The monarchy itself used the economic restructuring programme to accumulate wealth in its private capacity. The strengthening of powerful business groups in which the king became the major shareholder, such as the Omnium Nord Africain (ONA), was indicative of the way in which the monarchy used privatization to bolster its financial capacities and its control over the business community. By instrumentalizing the competition between different economic and political actors seeking to be the main beneficiaries of royal support (e.g. new crony capitalist groups versus older mercantile networks), the monarchy retained or increased its influence over the urban bourgeoisie.[84] Under Mohammed VI, the emergence of a new group of business actors close to the palace also enabled the regime to recast its networks of influence in the liberalized economic context of the 2000s. The creation of a new pro-monarchy party by one of the king's close associates, the Party of Authenticity and Modernity (PAM), in 2008 also illustrated the formalization of business politics by the regime.[85]

In Tunisia, the turn towards market reform was initiated in the 1970s as the regime backtracked on its contested socialist policies. As well as being financially quite costly for the state, collectivization had generated resistance and resentment among the urban bourgeoisie and the landowners. The transition to a more liberal form of capitalism meant that the regime came to rely more on the traditional bourgeoisie and business elites.[86] Leftist activism and particularly union activism became, in this context, a major cause of concern for the ruling elite at a time of rather mediocre domestic economic performance. The ill-fated project of creating an Arab union with Libya in 1974 was mainly an attempt by Bourguiba to obtain financial rewards from its oil-rich neighbour. Domestically, the worsening of the social situation in the second half of the 1970s incited the UGTT union to take an increasingly confrontational stance in order to maximize concessions from the regime. UGTT-led strikes and protests generated a political crisis in January 1978, and Bourguiba had to call in the army to end a protest situation that was destabilizing the regime. In the aftermath of this confrontation, Bourguiba sought to boost the economic capabilities of the regime by involving more business elites in the ruling circles. While the process of economic liberalization eventually enabled the Tunisian economy to become more productive, the social costs of these policies remained very high in the 1980s, when the regime had to embark on an IMF structural adjustment programme.[87] In 1984, the Tunisian regime was confronted once again by a wave of nation-wide unrest, induced this time by price liberalization. Unlike in 1978, however, the involvement of the UGTT in the protest was minimal and pointed to the decreasing capacities of the union for mobilization. In practice, the process of economic liberalization had undermined the negotiating power of intermediary bodies like the unions by favouring an atomization of the workforce.[88]

The replacement of Bourguiba by Ben Ali in 1987, and the tentative political opening that ensued to enable the new president to co-opt established elites to his cause, did not modify the system of governance. The tendency to use privatization in order to favour crony capitalists connected to the ruling elite, which had started under Bourguiba, continued and intensified under Ben Ali in the 1990s.[89] Beatrice Hibou's Foucauldian analysis of governmentality in the polity at that time provides a detailed illustration of the way in which the institutions of the state and the policies of the regime sustained an authoritarian bargain from which the population could not easily opt out.[90] Although the regime's modernist orientation was meant to favour the urban middle class, by the end of the 1990s the increasingly kleptocratic system put in place began to erode the confidence of those very segments of population that had initially acquiesced in this authoritarian pact.[91] Illustrative of this trend was the regime's utilization of the National Solidarity Fund ('26/26'), an 'optional' contribution for enterprises and higher earners to support the poorest in society, which became in practice a compulsory tax for anyone seeking favourable treatment from the administration, while the funds themselves were siphoned off by the ruling elite.[92] In the 2000s, the increasing resentment towards the perceived greed of the ruling elite and the reluctance of the regime to open the political field undermined over time the effectiveness of this neo-liberal authoritarianism. In particular, the regime's ability to pass on the responsibility for economic mismanagement to private actors was reduced. A regime upheld as a good example of neo-liberal economic governance by international organizations was thus increasingly rendered responsible by Tunisian citizens for the dire socio-economic implications of a 'successful' macroeconomic integration.[93]

In Algeria, to kickstart the economic recovery of a country coming out of a destructive war of independence, the regimes of Ben Bella and Boumedienne opted for a state-led socialist model of development. For most of the 1960s and 1970s the Boumedienne regime pushed aggressively a policy of import-substitution to develop a heavy industry base, as well as embarking on an ambitious programme of land nationalization and redistribution. Paid for by the oil rent, this 'socialist' strategy ultimately proved unable to develop a competitive industrial or agricultural sector. It did, nonetheless, lay the foundations for those state patronage networks that served to redistribute the oil and gas rent among the general population and the regime's supporters in particular. When oil revenues declined in the 1980s, the regime of Chadli Bendjedid increasingly redirected its economic policy away from an import-substitution strategy and towards more neo-liberal, market-based initiatives. The regime tried to use an emergent group of private entrepreneurs to supplement the state redistributive networks. At the same time, this reorientation of socio-economic policies transferred into the open the opposition between leftist and liberal trends inside the FLN.[94] As elsewhere in the region, the process of economic liberalization increased socio-economic disparities in the country, even though Algeria did not have to implement an IMF structural adjustment programme in the 1980s. This situation facilitated the growth of Islamist networks critical of the policies of the regime and addressing developmental issues by using different ideological referents. The increasingly difficult socio-economic situation caused by declining oil revenues, and the accompanying reduction of subsidies, led to the nation-wide riots of October 1988—a protest event triggered by a sudden increase in the price of staple foods.

While the October riots underscored a serious failure by the regime to use redistributive policies effectively to obtain social peace, the bloody repression of the unrest further undermined its legitimacy and heightened divisions inside the ruling elite. Without immediate answers to redress the economy, Chadli and his allies proposed a political opening in order to share the responsibility for (mis)governing the country and to demote those military actors blamed for the repression. The introduction of multipartyism and electoral democracy as a means to redirect violent opposition to the regime towards more institutionalized practices successfully sidelined economic problems, but it also created a serious confrontation between the FLN and the new Islamist opposition. The 1992 military coup and ensuing civil conflict meant that economic reforms throughout the 1990s remained subservient to the immediate security needs of the military-backed regime.[95] Economic choices and policies reflected the regime's strategy of rewarding or punishing specific segments of the population, as well as seeking financial support from international creditors. The economic orientation of the regime thus kept changing over the years, from *dirigisme* in 1992–4, to liberalization and privatization under the impulse of the IMF structural adjustment plan in 1994–8, to a return towards more state interventionism after 1999 under Bouteflika. In the 2000s, although the regime occasionally tried to develop a more competitive market economy to supplement its redistributive networks, the revenues obtained from buoyant oil and gas markets ensured that the state could meet a significant part of its population's need without having to implement painful economic reforms. The regime made full use of the redistribution of the rent to strengthen its patron–client networks. In addition, the ruling elite continued to allow political spaces for crony capitalists doubling up as political entrepreneurs to complement older clientelist networks with business politics.[96]

Libya was one of the last regimes of the region to consider a turn towards a neo-liberal model of economic governance because the exploitation of the oil and gas resources of the country from the 1960s onwards made it easier for the regime to behave like a rentier state. The failure of the Senussi monarchy to harness these new resources to state institutions and to redistribute effectively this newly acquired wealth had caused its downfall in 1969. From the 1970s onwards, the main task of the new Libyan regime was to keep social tensions under control by redistributing enough of the oil rent to enough constituencies, despite its limited technical and administrative expertise. The attempts to create a socialist system—including the banning of private retail businesses and industries at the end of the 1970s—ensured that the Libyan domestic economy remained particularly weak. As in Algeria, the badly thought-through import-substitution policies proposed by the Gaddafi regime failed to give a new impulse to the industrial sector. In this context, a lack of thorough economic planning and the limited capabilities of the Libyan administration also meant an entrenchment of patron–client relations—whether through new state-sponsored ('revolutionary') networks or through older tribal networks. The US economic sanctions imposed on Libya in the mid-1980s as a result of Gaddafi's adventurist foreign policy, combined with dwindling oil revenues, led to a shrinking of these patronage networks. In response, the Libyan regime introduced a partial reform of its 'Arab socialist' model in 1987 and reauthorized small private businesses as a way to supplement the state-run economic sector by crony entrepreneurship. However, the increased economic sanctions imposed by the UN in the early 1990s in response to the Lockerbie bombing contributed overall to a greater concentration of resources in the hands of the Gaddafi family and their close associates.[97]

Competition for access to reduced state resources was one of the main factors behind the different challenges facing the regime in the 1990s. At the end of the decade, another process of partial economic liberalization, commonly associated with the rise of a younger generation within the ruling elite, notably Gaddafi's son Saif al-Islam, was initiated to address these failings. In the early 2000s, this process was accompanied on the international stage by an attempt to normalize the regime policies with a view to removing the economic sanctions targeting the country. Domestically, the partial economic liberalization process led to an increase in black market activities and crony capitalism, which contributed to growing socio-economic disparities between different segments of the population, as well as between Libyan regions.[98] However, unlike in the other North African countries, Gaddafi did not allow these economic entrepreneurs to become (co-opted) political actors who could take responsibility for developmental failures.

Political mobilization and institutionalized politics

Politically and institutionally, controlled electoralism became an increasingly important characteristic of pseudo-democratic governance in the post-Cold War period.[99] Commenting on the evolution of Arab regimes over the decades, Burhan Ghalioun notes that in the 2000s they had lost the early post-colonial legitimacy that ensured that 'their authoritarianism was almost hidden by their popularity'.[100] The populist policies that had underpinned various forms of Arab socialism and that had empowered the middle and lower middle classes after independence were no longer affordable. Nationalist and anti-imperialist forms of popular mobilization had run out of steam, while economic liberalization had created new inequalities among the citizens. In the end, these once populist regimes appeared to be serving mainly the interests of the selected few and to rely on coercion to survive.[101] In this context, some of the authoritarian elites of the region sought to institutionalize a pseudo-democratic system of political representation to provide mitigating circumstances for their rule. Others, by contrast, estimated that the costs of changing their methods of control of the opposition were greater than the benefits they could derive from it. New pseudo-democratic models generally reflected the new opportunities for regime consolidation provided by neo-liberal economic reforms. In effect, they could function as formal relays for newly empowered economic actors seeking to engage in business politics. Ellen Lust suggests that viewing electoral processes as business opportunities helps us to understand better the dynamics of controlled electoralism in the region.[102] In this perspective, we can identify in North Africa, at one end of the pseudo-democratic spectrum, the complex networks of royal influence permeating Morocco's fragmented multiparty system and, at the other end, the crude reward mechanisms of Tunisia's ultra-dominant party system; with Algeria maintaining uneasily a halfway compromise, and Libya opting out of business politics altogether.

In the 2000s, the Moroccan political system provided one of the best illustrations of these complex pseudo-democratic arrangements. The monarchy could already rely on the traditional system of patronage of rural notables to co-opt regional elites. In the 1990s, the entrenchment of a working multiparty system that included Islamists complexified the system of governance in the face of domestic and external pressures for political liberalization. A first attempt to have opposition parties support the monarchy-led process of power-sharing ahead of the 1993 elections failed when the leader of the USFP chose voluntary exile to protest against electoral fraud. As opposition forces were given more assurances, their participation in the 1997 elections permitted the nomination of the USFP leader, Abderrahman el-Youssoufi, to the post of prime minister in 1998—a process known as *alternance*.[103] In this process, authoritarian rule is recast in a more open parliamentary system in which the palace limits the prerogatives of the elected representatives and retains a network of royal appointees to oversee the administration and policy implementation without having to rely directly on repression. The creation of electoral laws working against the possibility of a strong parliamentary majority enabled the monarchy to widen political participation without handing over a significant amount of control.[104] The process of mutual accommodation of the monarchy and the opposition parties in the legislature and in the executive was underpinned by the growth of more diverse socio-economic constituencies through economic liberalization.[105] In this context, by enabling the Islamists of the PJD to have a say in formal politics, from local councils to the parliamentary system, the monarchy encouraged them to remain within a reformist approach and not to become system-challenging actors. By accepting to operate within the limits imposed by the monarchy in exchange for an opportunity to shape some aspects of governance, the legal opposition parties generally contributed to the entrenchment of the (euphemized) authority of a near-absolute monarch.[106]

In Algeria, the pseudo-democratic political system that emerged in the 1990s and became consolidated in the 2000s was the outcome of a more hectic process of political reinstitutionalization after a failed transition. In part, it was the outcome of a 'standard' democratic transition of the late 1980s, when multipartyism and electoral democracy replaced a 'socialist' state-party system. After the 1992 military coup, the new regime leaders chose to retain this formal electoral democracy model as an institutionalized mechanism to co-opt social and political actors and channel popular discontent (as well as deal with the remonstrations of the international community). In part, the Algerian pseudo-democratic system was also an outcome of the civil conflict and the process of accommodation of different political forces by the military-backed regime. From the time of the Zéroual presidency (1995–9) onwards, the regime began strategically to include in successive governmental coalitions a wide array of actors, from the Islamists of Hamas/MSP to the Berber secularists of the Rally for Culture and Democracy (RCD). Increased freedom of expression and of organization as well as a limited stake in governance was offered to political parties to obtain their participation in a weak electoral and parliamentary system. At the same time, increased competition for state patronage, as well as deep ideological divisions, kept alive the tensions between and within the political parties. The model perfected during the Bouteflika presidency (1999 onwards) produced a parliamentary system controlled by a strong presidential institution.[107] The regime also controlled the multiparty system by strengthening the two pro-regime parties, the FLN and its spinoff, the National Rally for Democracy (Rassemblement National Démocratique, RND), as well as using a strategy of divide and rule towards the opposition—playing off Islamists versus secularists, Berbers versus Arabs, socialists versus liberals. Unlike in Morocco, however, where the regime created a fragmented system in which even large opposition parties needed to build political coalitions to govern effectively, the Algerian regime did not move far away from an ultra-dominant party system. The continuing dominance of the two pro-regime parties (FLN and RND) was repeatedly obtained by electoral fraud, disqualification of opposition candidates, control of the media, vote buying and so on.[108] In this context, coalition building remained more a public display of support for the ruling elite in exchange for a stake in the redistributive networks than a process designed to ensure the formation of a stable government. While it proved effective at sharing the blame for misgoverning the country, this pseudo-democratic system produced a level of political acceptance only barely sufficient to prevent violent conflict.

The model of authoritarian governance found in Tunisia was from the start a personalistic system centred on the party led by Bourguiba. The control exercised by Bourguiba over the Neo-Destour party, and the quasi-hegemonic control of the Neo-Destour and its successor, the PSD, over institutionalized politics were what characterized the very superficially democratic Tunisian system.[109] In the late 1980s, following the eviction of Bourguiba by Ben Ali, there were new opportunities to validate multipartyism and electoral democracy, as the new president sought to co-opt opposition actors to consolidate his authority as head of state. The period of political liberalization that culminated in the campaign for the 1989 parliamentary elections (re)legitimized actors across the entire political spectrum, from the communists to the Islamists. As Ben Ali asserted his control over the regime, he dropped the democratic rhetoric at election time for fear of an opposition groundswell. Ben Ali reverted to ruling through an ultra-dominant party system, dominated by the RCD, which he had created in 1988 to replace the PSD.[110] The new president also made good use of the failures of the democratic transition and the violence in neighbouring Algeria to defer any political opening and to repress the opposition. Behind a 'modernist' agenda well promoted on the international scene, the RCD system acted even more than the FLN in Algeria as the only relevant relay between the regime and the citizens.[111]

Throughout the 1990s, reasonably efficient state management of the socio-economic demands of the population, a ruthlessly effective repression of the political opposition, and weak external pressures led the ruling elite to decide that there was no need to institutionalize a more credible multiparty system. Ben Ali would only make a token democratic gesture in 1999 when he allowed (selected) political opponents to run against him in the presidential election—a decision without any real practical consequences for the opposition, considering the administrative, economic and media hurdles confronting any would-be candidate. During the decade of the 'War on Terror', the regime saw no pressing reason to modify significantly its model of governance despite an increase in sectoral protests in the second half of the 2000s. Instead, the ruling elite continued to concentrate all decision-making powers within RCD party networks and, even more so, within Ben Ali's extended family.[112] Indicative of this continuing closure of the political field, in 2009 Ben Ali was re-elected president with 89 per cent of the vote, while the RCD obtained 84 per cent of the vote in parliamentary elections.

In Libya, Gaddafi had also set up a very personal model of 'governance of the masses' (*Jamahiriya*), which practically meant the disqualification of any organized political force in the country. This situation led to a de facto concentration of all state prerogatives in the Gaddafi family and among their allies. The 'revolutionary' methods of governance of the Libyan regime through people's committees effectively and permanently undermined the institutional capabilities of the state.[113] This strategy of control, supplemented by redistributive policies, maintained tribal allegiances as meaningful avenues of mobilization in the polity.[114] By contrast, the 'neo-sultanistic' approach of Gaddafi ensured a low level of formal political institutionalization in the country, which rendered mainly irrelevant the strategies of partial political liberalization found in other North African countries from the 1980s onwards. Owing to a lack of clearly defined political institutions and roles, pseudo-democratic political processes based on co-opting opposition movements were mostly redundant in Libya. In the 2000s, the quest for international respectability through a rearticulation of Libya's foreign policy did not have a direct impact on the domestic political scene. As the country initiated some (modest) neo-liberal economic reforms, the regime sought to silence the voices of those who were losing out in the process of economic liberalization or who were demanding political liberalization to follow. Instead, Gaddafi appeared to be moving in the direction of a 'republican dynasty' that would enable the transmission of power from father to son.[115] Yet, even the rise of a new group of more outward-looking political and economic actors, mainly associated with Saif al-Islam, did not lead to a formal political recognition of these co-opted elites through pseudo-democratic institutional arrangements.

Overstating the authoritarian Arab state

Before the 2011 Arab uprisings, it was common for scholarly analyses to focus on the successes of competitive authoritarianism in MENA polities. Accounts of 'upgrading authoritarianism' complexified the issue of resilience in the 2000s, but remained centred on the mechanisms of routine authoritarian governance. Taken individually, such analyses of authoritarianism in the countries of the region highlighted important mechanisms and factors of stability and change. Collectively, however, they inadvertently helped naturalize a narrative of authoritarian resilience that made grassroots resistance appear largely irrelevant for generic accounts of politics in the region. As scholarly narratives fed into policy discourses, the *explanandum* became part of the *explanans*, and contributed to the continuation of institutional dispositions towards the status quo.

Social and political actors from the top of the international community all the way down to the local level came to acquire certain expectations about politics in the region. These included the assessment that dissent would be effectively repressed, that the opposition would be co-opted, that electoral processes would be corrupted, that protesters would be bought off, and so on. In their turn, these expectations reinforced particular behaviours—not participating in elections, not participating in political demonstrations, not overtly voicing opposition to the regime, turning to patronage to obtain favours, and so on. Over time it was unavoidable that a gap would open up between the material factors underpinning routine authoritarian rule and the causal beliefs about regime strength that helped to stabilize these regimes.

The changing patterns of legitimacy, clientelism and political cooptation outlined in this chapter are all indications of transformations occurring within 'stable' regimes. The crises of varying intensity that led to the institutional rearticulations discussed here revealed particular social and political dynamics generated in situations where ruling elites temporarily lost control. It would be simplistic to interpret the

2011 uprisings in an unreconstructed structuralist fashion as conjunctures that resolved known pre-existing tensions that had long undermined these authoritarian systems.[116] During the Arab uprisings, just as in earlier episodes of change within regimes, political, military and socio-economic reorganizations were also shaped by the actors' perception of what was possible and worth doing in the circumstances.

Although the cognitive dissonances produced by the evolution of authoritarianism were known or could be predicted, their significance for the stability of individual regimes could not be assessed until a new crisis emerged.[117] The longer-term relevance of the structures and processes in place before 2011 for the trajectories of protest witnessed in these polities are undeniable, but it can only be part of the explanation. The rest depends of the specific social and political rearticulations that actors make as a crisis unfolds. It is precisely to the articulation of new interpretations of and behaviours towards the regimes at the outset of unrest that we turn in the next chapter.

4

CONSTRUCTING IMPOSSIBLE UPRISINGS

Causing an uprising to start sometime in 2010 in North Africa

This chapter deals with the emergence of protest and the representation of protest events. Rather than seeking to identify 'revolutionary' actors, the analysis focuses on how particular behavioural changes produced new arenas and dynamics of contestation. The narrative does not primarily seek to explain where the actors of the uprisings come from but, instead, it highlights the sequences of events that created new behaviours which appeared so effective that individuals and groups would then define themselves (and be defined) in relation to these new roles. These dynamics are explored through a chronological account of the cycles of actions and reactions that constituted the uprisings in Tunisia, Algeria, Libya and Morocco during approximately the first two weeks of unrest. More specifically, I consider particular combinations of intended and unintended consequences of these early protests. In doing so, I outline how the uprisings first appeared to different actors, and how they related what was happening to their previous experiences of protest and of authoritarian governance.

The focus of the analysis is on the early days of unrest when protest events began to be constructed as specific challenges or opportunities by government and opposition, and on the policy and behavioural adjustments that followed from this. The analysis of early protest dynamics serves to illustrate the contingency of different pathways of contestation, and their relation with established forms of protest of repression and of cooptation. At this stage, independently of the intentions of the actors, ad hoc interactions during protest events shaped new arenas and practices of contestation, which in turn began to generate new dynamics and identities. In late 2010, Tunisia provided the first indication of how the practices of governance that constituted 'normality' in the authoritarian systems of the region could be dramatically transformed.

As unrest started, the actions of the local elites and of the international community were visibly informed by the past strengths and weaknesses of the ruling regimes. In such situations, not only political control, but the image of political control was an important trope of routine authoritarian governance. In Tunisia, over the years, the regime had shaped particular expectations for ordinary citizens about the kind of social and political interactions that were permissible in the polity.[1] It is worth noting that while mass expressions of political discontent were very unusual during Ben Ali's rule, they did take place on occasion.[2] The strength of the Tunisian regime and of the other regimes in the region up to that point was to ensure that such incidents did not have widespread repercussions at home or abroad. This narrative of normality was important for the self-confidence of the ruling elites, for the image of the regimes on the international scene, and to foster the acquiescence of the population in their rule.[3]

When the Arab uprisings began, early scholarly explanations commonly pointed to this gap between the claims and the reality of governance in the countries affected by unrest. There was a discernible tendency among early accounts to argue that we 'ought to' have foreseen better the likelihood of these kinds of events happening in those circumstances.[4] Such arguments stressed that the longer-term evolution of the political, economic and securitarian situation in the region that those regimes were at risk of collapse. A major difficulty with post hoc arguments implying that the authoritarian systems were near breaking point remains how to identify such a breaking point until it has demonstrably been reached.[5] The imagery of revolutionary upsurges in terms of 'sparks' and 'powder kegs' reflects this rather mechanistic approach to events. At its heart, what is being said is that while there may be a multiplicity of explanations to account for what produced a particular 'spark', once something is identified as such, its mere presence near something else seen as a 'powder keg' will mechanically produce an explosion.

In this vein, Peter Schraeder and Hamadi Redissi argued that in the Tunisian case, 'declining socioeconomic conditions and rising authoritarian caprice provided ample fuel for the conflagration that consumed Ben Ali's rule but the combustion was not spontaneous. Several other factors were important. First was the literal and figurative spark of Bouazizi's fatal self-immolation.'[6] What remains moot in such an account is how much rationalization is involved in the assessment that pre-existing loci of resistance and inbuilt tensions within the system are directly relevant to, let alone precursors of, an actual protest. As Charles Kurzman remarked in the case of the 1979 Iranian Revolution, what looked to external observers like plausible and even convincing reasons for actions were often in practice not the reasons invoked by the protesters at the time.[7]

To avoid recasting the actions of the protesters as a direct outcome of pre-existing trends in the polity, I emphasize here in the first instance the immediate impact of the protest events on discourses and practices. Hence, from this event-centric perspective, the starting point of the Tunisian uprising was the self-immolation of Mohamed Bouazizi and the ensuing riots in his home town of Sidi Bouzid. This sequence of events initially generated at the local level a shift from known and predictable to less known and less predictable patterns of social and political behaviour. Retrospectively, Bouazizi's death and the Sidi Bouzid riots have been posited as transformative events due to the successes of the Tunisian Revolution and democratic transition. However, as William Sewell illustrated in the case of the French Revolution, transformative events are not usually immediately seen as transformative.[8] In the French case, many days passed by before the taking of the Bastille began to be viewed and presented as the crucial event of a revolt that was only then beginning to be framed as a revolution. Similarly, in Tunisia, Bouazizi's death and the Sidi Bouzid riots were only identified as the starting point of the Tunisian Revolution several weeks after the event.[9] Later on, the Tunisian uprising itself became a transformative event for other uprisings across the MENA region. A transformative event refers to a crucial stage in the political process when the level of mobilization increases significantly and when new political dynamics and interpretations are successfully set in motion.

While it is important for explanatory purposes to separate analytically the dynamics of the protests from the narrative of the 'Revolution' or the 'Arab Spring', transformative events are precisely situations that modify both political dynamics and interpretations. To reuse the example of the French Revolution: that the Parisian crowds benefited from the unexpected defensive blunders of the defenders of what had become an ill-equipped fortress and near-empty jail did not significantly affect the relevance of 'the taking of the Bastille' as a crucial event of the revolution. In Sidi Bouzid, the causal sequences of events that led to the death of Bouazizi and the riots can hardly be seen as a direct template for the causal mechanisms of the Tunisian Revolution or the Arab uprisings. The particular combination of long- and short-term causes that can best explain the events of Sidi Bouzid are not necessarily helpful in understanding the mechanisms that produced the fall of the Ben Ali regime (even though the two are causally and cognitively connected). The tragedy of Bouazizi did not 'encapsulate' the failings of the Ben Ali regime.[10] Rather, the fall of the regime has been narrated retrospectively in a way that charged this event with all the meanings that actors wanted to give to the Tunisian Revolution and democratic transition. The same point can be made about the narratives of the Libyan uprising and, with a 'reformist' twist, about those of the Algerian and Moroccan protests.

The emergence of unrest in the four North African countries at the beginning of 2011 did not so much reveal some 'objective' failings of these regimes as made muted discontent about some perceived failings publicly expressed and visible—the distinction between the two being politically significant.[11] The visibility and intelligibility of the protest were sufficient for other actors to be enticed to reproduce such public expressions of discontent in their local context. The emergence of new behaviours articulated as protest mobilization forced a reaction from the ruling elites. In turn, a change in state discourses and policies contributed further to shape protest behaviours. Rather than being 'the straw that broke the camel's back', early protest events illustrate how the very idea of 'breaking point' was constructed and empowered by the different actors involved. Interactions between pro- and anti-regime actors in ad hoc protest events produced unintended consequences that reshaped established arenas and practices of contentions, and in so doing generated new, unexpected situations.

Tunisia: redrawing the boundaries of contestation

The emergence of an extraordinary situation in the Tunisian polity is analysed here from the start of the Sidi Bouzid riots on 17 December 2010 to the televised speech of Ben Ali on 28 December 2010, a period that saw only limited changes to the routine practices of authoritarian governance in the country.[12] The self-immolation of Bouazizi on 17 December 2010, although very unusual, was not the first in the country in recent times. That same year, two other men died in similar circumstances. Abdessalem Trimech set himself on fire in the town of Monastir on 3 March 2010, an event that did not receive any significant media attention. Then on 20 November 2010, just a few weeks before Bouazizi, Chemseddine el-Hani went through the same ordeal in the nearby town of Metlaoui.[13] The immediate circumstances of all these events bore some degree of resemblance, particularly the dire socio-economic situation faced by these individuals. In one case, the person was a street vendor who, like Bouazizi, encountered bureaucratic hindrances and police harassment. While these actions undoubtedly pointed to some generic socio-economic and political tensions in the country, it cannot be said that these incidents illustrated a 'typical' predicament or protest strategy. In addition, it is difficult to make a case even after the event for a significant worsening of the socio-economic situation in the country in 2010 that would help explain a sudden increase in such desperate actions. Just a few months before the uprisings, an IMF report on the country even stressed that 'Tunisia weathered the global crisis well'.[14]

Seasoned analysts of the region would remark that the macroeconomic perspectives adopted by the IMF hardly provide the best set of lenses to assess the practical impact on the population of socio-economic changes. As the studies of the 'food riots' induced by the IMF structural adjustment programmes of the 1980s indicate, the way in which citizens experienced and reacted to macroeconomic adjustments was repeatedly misjudged by both national governments and international institutions.[15] Commenting on 'bread riots' in the MENA region at that time, Larbi Sadiki stressed that to understand political pressure from below, greater attention had to be paid to the perspectives of 'the *khubz-istes* (the quietist bread seeker who abandons quietism as soon as his livelihood is threatened by the state) and the *hitiste* (the quietist unemployed who becomes active in bread protests)'.[16] By 2010, in the aftermath of the global financial crisis, even slight variations in the domestic economy had a greater chance of having a negative impact among the poorest in society. This is not to say, as Schraeder and Redissi did post hoc, that 'several socioeconomic and political-military indicators suggested that Tunisia was ripe for change'.[17] Before the uprisings, domestic actors with a more fine-tuned grassroots perspective than the IMF did note how socio-economic tensions persisted and sometime grew in intensity in Tunisian society, but no one suggested that 2010–11 could be a watershed moment.[18]

Conjunctural approaches generally stress that while discrete tensions or breakdowns in different sectors of activities may not in themselves threaten the survival of a regime, a particular combination of challenges could in certain circumstances create a 'perfect storm'. The difficulty remains that prospectively there is no convincing method to separate the 'non-significant' factors, with the potential to become significant, from the 'non-significant' factors that will remain so. Prospectively, had this 'perfect storm' been predicted, events would have unfolded differently due to the forewarnings that the regime would have received. Had the mayor of Sidi Bouzid been well aware of the prospects that a self-immolation could have for social unrest in town, he might have dealt with Bouazizi's threat in a different way.[19] Had the provincial governor been aware of the risk of local riots in the central provinces being a catalyst for a national revolt, he might have dealt with the initial unrest in Sidi Bouzid differently.[20] The inability to understand the transformative potential of such protest events is not simply a failure to predict accurately what might happen. It also reflects a particular mastery of techniques of authoritarian governance which are known to be effective, up to that moment. From a regime's perspective, cognitive failure is therefore not simply a lack of anticipation; it is also the result of having too much experience of a particular kind.

Already in 2010, there had been violent clashes in August between police and protesters in the town of Ben Gardane, near the border with Libya, when the Libyan regime first increased taxes on goods crossing the border, and then temporarily closed the border crossing. Earlier that year, in February, in the coastal town of Skhira, unemployed youth demonstrating so as to obtain jobs from the Tunisian administration went on the rampage and confronted the police.[21] Similarly, but on a larger scale, a couple of years earlier in the Gafsa mining basin there had been several months of disturbances centring around the issue of employment in state-owned mines and poor living conditions. Tunisian specialists often pointed to the Gafsa protests to illustrate the growing difficulties encountered by the Ben Ali regime in coping with social and economic discontent. Yet, the successful if uneasy containment of these protests reinforced the dominant perception that, despite its failings, the regime was still very much in control of the situation.[22] In all these cases, the regime had responded with a rather similar mixture of policies—a carrot and stick approach. On the one hand, it offered financial rewards, with programmes and funds for local development and, on the other hand, it used a securitarian approach, with police and judicial repression targeting those identified as troublemakers. Hence, in a similar fashion after the riots in Sidi Bouzid, on 20 December 2010, while security officials branded the rioters 'thugs' and promised swift retribution, the minister for rural development, Mohamed al-Nouri al-Juwayni, travelled to the town to announce that funds were being made available for a new local employment scheme.[23]

As the population in neighbouring localities became aware of the troubles in Sidi Bouzid, mainly through word of mouth initially, there were similar demonstrations in other towns. On 20 December, protests were organized in the towns of Meknassi, Sidi Ali Ben Aoun and Menzel Bouzaiene, all situated inside the Sidi Bouzid governorate.[24] At this stage, however, it remained unclear how far these protest behaviours represented 'extraordinary' choices and how far they were alternative social tactics located within a still relatively stable system of authoritarian governance. This is not to say that rioting was an informally institutionalized form of political expression in Tunisia, but it could have its place within a stable authoritarian system. The few media reports available at the time described these local episodes of unrest as gestures of solidarity with the people of Sidi Bouzid.[25] There is little doubt that expressions of solidarity were present, particularly in connection to the different clans of the region, such as the Hamama (to which Bouazizi's family belonged).[26] However, these protests were also a more tactical call for attention in order to obtain the same socio-economic rewards that the regime was then offering the population of Sidi Bouzid to appease the situation.

The slogans most commonly heard during these early protests strongly suggested that the protesters' main focus was on socio-economic demands and not on politically construed challenges. Illustrative of these concerns, on 22 December a new fatality occurred during another demonstration in Sidi Bouzid when Houcine Neji, an unemployed young man, threw himself on high-voltage electricity cables after shouting out: 'I don't want any more of this poverty.'[27] As violence erupted after he killed himself, the police fired tear gas at stone-throwing protesters. In their turn, the demonstrators attacked and set fire to police vehicles, to the offices of the National Guard (a branch of the police) and those of the ruling Constitutional Democratic Rally (RCD) party, as well as looting goods from a nearby freight train. In the circumstances, the actions of local security forces in trying to contain these sudden eruptions of violence often constituted an additional cause of popular mobilization. One such case of police over-reaction occurred on 24 December in the town of Menzel Bouzaiene, some 40 miles from Sidi Bouzid. When some members of the police felt threatened by the demonstrators, they fired live ammunition into the crowd, killing a young demonstrator, Mohamed Ammari, and seriously wounding several others (one of them, Chawki Hidri, would die a few days later). The regime then endeavoured to convey the message to the public that the security forces had fired in self-defence, with mixed results.[28]

On 25 and 26 December, the wave of protests reached new provincial towns located in nearby governorates (Bizerte, Sfax, Kairouan, Meknessi, Regueb, Souk Jedid, Ben Gardane, Medenine, Siliana, Sousse). Up to that time, despite the expanding geographical reach of the unrest, the focus of the protesters remained on police brutality and on socio-economic demands. Tellingly, the first small protest to reach the capital at that time was organized by unemployed graduates demanding jobs from the government. Common slogans in this demonstration included 'we need work' and 'stop the corruption', alongside expressions of solidarity with Sidi Bouzid and recriminations about police violence.[29] The socio-economic demands of the protesters in their turn began to generate political tensions, particularly visible in the growing internal disagreements in the Tunisian General Workers Union (UGTT). This new wave of unrest reignited the internecine struggles between the co-opted national leadership of the UGTT and the more independently minded local branches of the union that were more responsive to the demands of the local population.[30] Overall, however, the first ten days of what would become the Tunisian Revolution remained notable for their un-revolutionary character. This is not to say that immolation by fire and violent riots are unremarkable events. Instead, it is to stress that these actions were not accompanied at the time by a visible, self-reflective political discourse that directly challenged the legitimacy of the regime. In the early days of the protest, individually and collectively, people expressed less a desire for regime change than a desire for the regime to change.

The protest behaviours indicated that protesters did not focus on having a different state system, but instead wanted the existing system and institutions to work better. In many ways, this is an unremarkable observation to make. Scholars of revolutions have repeatedly noted that the early stages of a revolution are not characterized by revolutionary thinking and behaviour but by a more tactical approach to the use of violence and public disobedience.[31] Hence, at this stage we did not have in Tunisia a deinstitutionalization of the system which would enable the entrenchment and routinization of extraordinary choices and strategies. What we had instead was an increased likelihood that people would opt for a riskier set of individual and group tactics designed to extract resources and concessions from an authoritarian system that was still seen as the main (if not sole) interlocutor. On 28 December, the first televised speech of President Ben Ali about the unrest illustrated well that this was precisely how the Tunisian regime understood the situation at the time, and why it responded in the way it did.

On national television, Ben Ali declared that these protests were unacceptable in the first instance because such behaviours would 'hamper economic development'. Instrumentalizing the socio-economic rationale of the protest, the president made the demonstrators responsible for the very worsening of the situation that they were complaining about. In this context, he warned that 'the force of law would be used to punish the protesters', and blamed 'foreign interference' for blowing these protests out of proportion. Indicative of the regime's perception of the normality of this level of discontent was Ben Ali's public advice to the state administration to be 'more aware of the psychological impact of unemployment' and to 'deal sensitively with difficult situations'.[32] In the aftermath of Ben Ali's televised intervention, the principal practical initiatives taken by the regime to appease the protesters were the removal of the governors of Sidi Bouzid, Jendouba and Zaghouan (the regions at the heart of the protests). The president also organized a mini-reshuffle of his government by replacing the minister for trade and handicraft, the minister of communications, and the minister of religious affairs. None of them were key figures within the regime and were thus easily expendable from Ben Ali's perspective. In practice, this episode provided an opportunity for jockeying for position among the inner circle of the regime, as indicated by the replacement of the minister of religious affairs by a friend of Sakher el-Materi, Ben Ali's son-in-law (and potential successor). The small scale of the reshuffle indicated that the ruling elite did not consider the situation to be serious enough to warrant a dramatic change of personnel in government.

While these moves constituted a rather unremarkable political response to the situation, the decision of Ben Ali to go on national television to answer the protesters personally was in it itself a new development in the authoritarian routines of the regime. Not only had earlier episodes of unrest not elicited this kind of public intervention by the president, but the regime had maintained up to that point an information blackout about the riots in the Tunisian media. This change of strategy by the regime was reflected from this moment onwards by the increasingly more critical editorial line taken by the privately owned TV station Nessma.[33] Nonetheless, for all the post-uprising talk of an Internet/Twitter/Facebook revolution, the early period of the Tunisian Revolution did not include a significant role for the new media in the organization of anti-regime protests.[34] The practical opportunities provided by new technologies of communication, from cellular phones with video capabilities to Twitter, did not upstage those of more 'traditional' communicative practices.[35]

Reporting on Tunisia, the Al Jazeera journalist Yasmine Ryan argued that 'the key difference in Sidi Bouzid was that locals fought to get news of what was happening out, and succeeded'.[36] She stressed how a video of the first protest after the death of Bouazizi was posted on Facebook and then picked up by Al Jazeera's new media team and aired on Al Jazeera's Mubasher channel on the evening of 17 December. At the same time, she also remarked that 'aside from a solid core of activists, most Tunisians did not dare repost the videos on Facebook or even to "like" them, until President Zine El Abidine Ben Ali's final hours'. In a similar vein, journalists from *France24* noted that a prominent protest-focused Facebook group entitled 'Mr. President, the Tunisians are setting themselves on fire' had about 11,000 endorsements by the end of 2010—not a negligible but neither an overwhelming level of endorsement in the circumstances.[37] What was most conspicuous at the time was the diffusion of information about the Tunisian protests through a combination of old and new media outlets.[38] Already by 20 December, major French newspapers were covering the riots though their associated reporters in Tunisia. Journalists noted that although Facebook was a popular source of information among students and high school pupils, more traditional forms of information remained very relevant for other social groups. The importance of older channels of information was illustrated by the efforts made by the Tunisian regime to maintain a news blackout using tried and tested methods, including beating up journalists (even during a live radio interview, as with Moez el-Bey on 24 December).[39]

In the initial stages of the Tunisian protests, in small towns like Sidi Bouzid in rural governorates, sophisticated communication tools were not necessary for the local population to be aware of what was happening down the road. A distinction can be made between two dimensions of the media's role during these protest episodes: informational and organizational.[40] On both counts, however, not one media format had a visibly crucial impact on the dynamics of the early protests. New media alongside more traditional information channels (foreign press and satellite TV) were part of a network used to bypass the blackout imposed by the state. In the first couple of weeks of unrest, new media technology was not reportedly used directly to organize or coordinate protests against the regime in any significant way. Even the first significant protest to reach the capital on 27 December was organized by a network of independent union activists using fairly traditional means of communication and mobilization.[41]

The evolving communicative strategy of the Tunisian regime, from news blackout to televised interventions by the president, also had an impact on the growing relevance of the media for the articulation of a counter-discourse by the protesters. At the time of the first presidential appearance on national television, the official political narrative of the regime still dominated the media sphere, and it posited the regime as the sole interlocutor for opposition actors. In the aftermath of the presidential speech, a coalition of small left-leaning opposition actors, the Alliance for Citizenship and Equality, declared that the situation was not simply an accumulation of isolated incidents, as Ben Ali had suggested, but the outcome of a profound social crisis that required more radical policy changes. Mustapha Ben Jaafar, the leader of the Democratic Forum for Labour and Liberties (Ettakatol), asked the government to 'reconsider its social, economic and political options'.[42] These mild demands indicated that while locally, in provincial towns, the boundaries of contestation were beginning to shift, the formal political arena had not (yet) accounted for these grassroots transformations.

Algeria: renewed challenges to routine authoritarianism.

Like Tunisia, Algeria did not appear to experience a dramatic change of circumstances in the months preceding the Arab uprisings. The political unease that characterized the beginning of President Bouteflika's third term in office in 2009 had slowly subsided. The socio-economic climate in the country remained harsh, but state subsidies and infrastructural investments kept the situation relatively calm despite the vagaries of the economy.[43] This relative calm has to be set in the context of a tumultuous recent Algerian history. By comparison with its North African neighbours, peace and order remained a rather elusive goal in the country. Although the security situation had improved since the widespread political violence that characterized the civil conflict of the 1990s, the activities of armed Islamist organizations like the GSPC and the AQIM remained a constant nuisance throughout the 2000s.[44] Politically, although state institutions reclaimed a degree of legitimacy after the civil conflict, mainly through the entrenchment of a weak parliamentary system, the regime had also been rocked by powerful social and political protests such as the 'black spring' of 2001 in Kabylia.[45]

Despite a substantial oil and gas rent, periods of popular unrest induced by a deterioration of socio-economic conditions marred the polity throughout the 2000s. In a leaked diplomatic cable from 2008, the US ambassador in Algiers, Robert Ford, indicated to Washington that there were strikes almost weekly in the country and that 'almost daily there are isolated demonstrations with the occasional government office in some distant town attacked'.[46] In 2010, in the *El Watan* newspaper there were 76 riots worthy of news coverage (an average of nearly one and a half per week). According to the *Liberté* newspaper, there was an increase in policing operations designed to restore order, peaking at 112,878 interventions in that year alone.[47] At the end of 2010, if the Algerian regime did not appear to be on the brink of collapse, it was clearly not in a more advantageous position than its neighbours, either. As in neighbouring countries ruled by ageing autocrats, significant changes were not expected in Algeria until at least the end of President Bouteflika's third mandate in 2014.[48]

The first stirrings of a serious uprising in Algeria were the sequence of rioting that brought the country to a halt at the beginning of January 2011. During this period of unrest, protest behaviours briefly came into play on a large scale and disrupted the regime's routine mechanisms of governance. The initial impulse for the riots was economic: sharp increases in the price of staple goods—oil, sugar and flour—at the beginning of the year. Food prices had been increasing gradually throughout the year, reflecting a global upward volatility in prices and new budgetary regulations for subsidies introduced by the Algerian government.[49] The last instalment of deregulatory policies triggered a price hike as well as a shortage of subsidized goods. This increase took place at a time when public awareness of the unrest in neighbouring Tunisia was becoming widespread in Algeria owing to coverage in the Algerian press.[50] In Algeria, protests started in several of the poorer suburbs of Oran and Algiers on 3 January. The next day the riots continued in these suburbs and spread to other areas near the capital. On 5 January, major unrest broke out throughout Algiers and Oran as well as in many other towns all around the country.[51] The demonstrators— mainly young men—protested against a variety of socio-economic ills that had long been a cause of concern and that had given rise to violent protests before—increased living costs, demolition of shantytowns, unemployment, and so on. 'We have no job and no future,' complained one of the protesters in the Algiers suburb of Bab-el-Oued, 'and now we cannot even eat.'[52] To justify their actions, another added that they wanted 'to wake up those who remain deaf to people's misery', and that in order to do so they had to 'bring violence to the table'. As the rioters blocked roads, burned tyres and ransacked local government buildings—again, not unusual forms of protest in Algeria—it became clear that the initial discontent about staple goods had provided people with an opportunity to voice their anger about a much wider range of socio-economic issues.[53]

The Algerian newspapers swiftly covered these events and news of the protests quickly spread around the country. At the same time, videos of the demonstrations and of police repression started to circulate online.[54] Within days, the riots had spread to twenty Algerian regions. The protesters commonly targeted symbols of the state such as town halls and other government buildings, as well as shopping centres, which were regularly looted in the larger towns. The lack of political demands, as well as the lack of visible coordination between the protesters and established political and social movements, was noticeable during the first few days of unrest. At most there was the beginning of an online mobilization among activists.[55] Writing at the time, a journalist from the Algerian newspaper *L'Expression* pondered that it was 'paradoxical for such a sizeable protest movement affecting all the regions of the country to be devoid of political slogans and clear demands'.[56] The memory of the riots of October 1988 also cast a shadow over these events, not least because the press kept making comparisons with this early Algerian 'spring'.[57] While the socio-economic impulse behind the 2011 riots resembled what had happened in 1988, the military and Islamist aspects were clearly quite different. Although the former Islamic Salvation Front leader Ali Belhadj, turned up in the Bab-el-Oued demonstrations of 6 January to say that he would 'defend the demands of the youth at any cost', Islamist activists were hardly driving the protest or even providing large crowds of demonstrators.[58] In addition, the response of the security forces, mainly the police, was nowhere near as brutal and lethal as it had been in 1988, when several hundred demonstrators were killed in less than two weeks by army units firing live ammunition at the crowds.

The security response of the Algerian regime was mainly concerned with ensuring that the rioters did not ransack important government buildings in the centre of towns. Algerian journalists reported how on 7 January the security forces were deployed in key areas of central

Algiers (such as around the parliament, the senate, the governorate, the central post office), and waited for another night of rioting to take place in the suburbs.[59] In Algiers, inhabitants complained that rioters looted shops 'without encountering any opposition from the police'.[60] Local activists suggested that this (lack of) police response illustrated the Algerian regime's worries about making 'martyrs'—by then, only one person had died in these protests. In this context, the security forces dealt with this nation-wide wave of protests in very much the same way as they had done with more localized unrest before, even though this meant abandoning some areas to the demonstrators and rioters for various periods of time. On 8 January, the government announced a complete U-turn on recent price deregulation measures and started to implement emergency policies to reduce quickly the cost of living.[61] In the ensuing few days not only were taxes on food products decreased, but firms importing staple goods were given new subventions to ensure they would lower their retail prices, and the government dipped into its savings to buy additional food supplies on the international markets.[62] Some opposition actors began to argue that this was the beginning of 'a revolution', and that the economic response of the government 'could not buy the silence of the Algerians'.[63] Yet within a couple of days, the protests had subsided in most of the regions and were limited to a few provincial towns. The rapid economic response of the government appeared to have met the demands of the protesters, thereby limiting the scope of the contestation. The relative restraint shown by the security forces was also instrumental in ensuring that state repression itself did not become the cause of further unrest (as had happened in Tunisia at the same time). By 10 January, 'only' three demonstrators had died, there had been over 800 people injured (many from the police), and about 1,000 arrested.[64]

Although there were some reports that online social media platforms like Facebook and Twitter had their access restricted, the role of online mobilization was not particularly significant in this first wave of rioting.[65] In parallel, the more organized efforts by political activists to demonstrate on 11 January in Algiers and to re-energize the protest movement were effectively suppressed by the police in a context where the momentum for mass public disobedience was rapidly decreasing. It was noticeable at the time that most institutionalized social and political actors remained silent about these riots. Few Islamist leaders voiced their solidarity with the protesters—and none from the MSP, the junior partner in the governmental coalition—while at the other end of the political spectrum the very official General Union of Algerian Workers simply blamed 'speculators' for the price increases. In this period of deflation of protest behaviours, even the first act of immolation as a radical form of protest, which occurred on 12 January, did not reignite a wave of demonstrations— there would be a dozen more attempted or successful self-immolations in the following few weeks.[66] As in the initial stages of the Tunisian Revolution, the Algerian protesters during that first week of rioting in January 2011 demanded that the regime change its policies, not that there be a change of regime. In so far as this spontaneous movement of social revolt had articulated demands, they were expressed in socio-economic terms. In response, the government quickly backtracked on its unpopular economic policies to appease the protesters.

In terms of repression, what characterized the response of the regime in January 2011 was not so much the capabilities of the Algerian security apparatus—the police and the gendarmerie together had over 300,000 personnel—as the limited use of these repressive tools. 2011 was not 1988, when the army intervened with live ammunition and killed over 500 demonstrators in less than two weeks.[67] It was not even the 'black spring' of 2001 when the gendarmerie shot dead over 100 protesters in Kabylia during regional protests.[68] In 2011, the deployment of riot police, gendarmerie and plainclothes police was mainly designed to contain the protests by circumscribing them to non-essential areas for the government, while avoiding making 'martyrs'. During the protests, the interior minister, Ould Kablia, declared that 'the security forces are doing all they can, with firmness and intelligence, to avoid things getting out of control and to avoid violent confrontations with the rioters'.[69] In parliament, he indicated that by 10 January over 700 policemen had been injured, but only 53 rioters, and he vaunted the 'smart response and patience, as well as firmness, displayed by the security forces'.[70] This 'patience' of the security forces has to be seen in the context of an institutional and legal background that gave the security apparatus a sizeable freedom of action.[71]

Far more than was the case in Tunisia, episodes of unrest and violence were part of a more routine, longer-term trend in the articulation of socio-economic demands in Algeria. The country had been frequently rocked by such local protests in previous years. At the start of 2011, the national consequences of the food price increases, as well as the example set by Tunisia, facilitated the multiplication of local flashpoints. By quickly addressing the key concerns of protesters and by not unleashing deadly repression, the regime was able to induce a reversion to the situation that prevailed before. After a week of violent nation-wide protests, the contestation subsided to levels that were once again 'manageable' by means of routine security practices.[72] In turn, by acting as if the situation was quite ordinary, the regime contributed to a return to the kind of 'normality' that existed before—unlike Ben Ali, Bouteflika would not appear on national television at that time to call for order. Equally, a return to 'normality' in Algeria in the second half of January still included routinized and ritualized protest performances (clashes with police, ransacking of buildings, strikes, roadblocks, and so on), but in a disparate fashion rather than as part of a nation-wide event. A return to ordinary contentious politics does not imply a 'natural' process of reverting to know repertoires and arenas of contestations—things could of course have happened otherwise. An accidental shooting attributable to the security forces, the fortuitous capture of a symbolic government institution by the protesters, a miscalculation by some members of the ruling elite to seize more power for themselves, could have contributed to the strengthening of the protest dynamic. The reversion to 'normality' was the result not so much of the Algerian regime using the 'correct' combination of repressive and cooptative measures to diffuse unrest, as of behavioural and ideational shifts that unfolded without sufficient speed and directionality. As a result, new arenas of contention and protest dynamics failed to become self-reproducing.

Libya: creating new arenas of contestation

Like all its neighbours before 2011, the Libyan regime had been able to deal with violent uprisings and protest movements at a local level. From the challenges of armed Islamists and of tribal groups in the 1990s to the social protests of Berber activists and of the families of the Abu Salim prison massacre in the 2000s, crises and tensions had never turned into nation-wide events.[73] These past confrontations did lay some foundations for subsequent protest practices and actors. In Benghazi in February 2011, the protests that gave the initial impulse to the uprising can be directly linked to the mobilization of the families of the Abu Salim inmates in front of the town courthouse.[74] Over the years, their network and the sit-ins they organized had become a tolerated expression of discontent that did not cross the lines set in place by the regime for oppositional behaviour in civil society. In this sense, they benefited from the civil society initiatives that Saif al-Islam used to promote his reformist brand of leadership at home and abroad in the 2000s. Other localities that were the scenes of some of the earliest anti-regime protests in February 2011 also indirectly benefited from the changing attitude of the regime towards civil society. The Berber-dominated areas of the Nafusa Mountains had seen a notable increase in Berber cultural activism in the 2000s, as both local and transnational NGO networks began to organize here. In response, the Libyan regime, again under the impulse of Saif al-Islam, sought to co-opt and instrumentalize these Berber associations. In particular, it set up an official 'civil society' organization to control local activism and cut it off from transnational Berber networks.[75] Although they remained constrained in their capacity to organize and mobilize, these Berber associations nonetheless provided a semi-formal structure for communication and coordination of local activists.

To note the pre-existence of limited contention does not in itself provide an explanation for the relevance of these tolerated practices and actors to subsequent protest dynamics. Precisely because these actors expressed grievances through known repertoires of contention, some light needs to be shed on how actors moved beyond routine forms of opposition to support new forms of contestation. It does not follow that, because Berber activists in the Nafusa Mountains opposed the ideology and policies of the Gaddafi regime and sought greater recognition of Amazigh identity and rights, they would necessarily support an armed insurrection or regime change. For such a transformation to take place, the agendas and practices of the different actors would have to co-evolve to sustain new arenas and practices of contentious politics. This process was anything but self-evident, particularly in the face of efforts made by the regime to sow divisions among the protesters in order to remain the final arbiter between competing claims. This predicament was visible in the mid-1990s when the armed insurrection led by the Libyan Islamic Fighting Group (LIFG) in the east of the country did not stir into action other social and political actors opposed to the regime elsewhere in Libya.[76] The strategic use of repression and cooptation by the regime served precisely to construct opportunities and constraints for different constituencies. An illustration of the disruptive tactics of the regime was provided just a few weeks before the beginning of the February uprisings. In late January 2011, after street protests against housing shortages, Gaddafi went on national television to encourage young people in search of housing to take what was rightfully theirs.[77] As a result, in the days that followed, hundreds of Libyan families started occupying new, often unfinished housing projects. In doing so, the protesters turned an initial popular discontent with the regime's economic management of housing issues into actions that appeared to be in line with the will of Libya's 'Supreme Guide'. Before the uprisings, Libyan analysts had presented such situations as an indication that the regime had the ability to buy off social discontent by redistributing the oil rent, and was thus unlikely to be destabilized.[78]

The unrest that flared up in the town of Benghazi on 15 February 2011 is commonly presented as the starting point of the Libyan uprising. On that day, the first protest event was mainly the conjunctural outcome of the coming together of two sets of protesters, those linked to the Abu Salim massacre and those cyber-activists planning a 'day of rage' against the regime (for 17 February).[79] The arrest of Fathi Terbil, a lawyer for the Abu Salim families and one of the activists promoting the 'day of rage', led to the initial gathering of a protesting crowd in front of the courthouse in central Benghazi on the evening of the 15th. A BBC news report aired at that time included a description of the event in a phone interview with a local witness who explained that 'a couple of people in the crowd started chanting anti-government slogans and the crowd took that on'.[80] The harsh response of the security forces late that night strengthened the resolve of the protesters, who kept on demonstrating until the next day. On 16 February, news media reported violent clashes between protesters and security forces in Beyda (just east of Benghazi) and Zintan (in the Nafusa Mountains, in the west of the country).[81] The following day new protests were gaining momentum in the towns of Ajdabiya and Derna, not far from Benghazi. By that time, a revolutionary agenda modelled on the January events in Egypt and Tunisia was already evident in the demonstrations, with footage showing protesters explicitly calling for the fall of the regime.[82] Foreign media were quick to pick up this virulent anti-regime rhetoric and to make direct parallels with regime changes in neighbouring countries. The BBC analyst Frank Gardner turned previous assessments of Libyan stability on their head and stressed that the resources at the disposal of the regime did not make it 'immune from the breeze of revolutionary change that is blowing across the region'.[83]

Locally, at the same time that a virulent anti-Gaddafi rhetoric was being voiced in the public sphere, more conventional repertoires of contention were still in use. In Benghazi, the lawyers' association was still asking the regime for political and economic reform. The Libyan branch of the Muslim Brotherhood for its part called upon the ruling elites to rein in the repression unleashed by the security apparatus.[84] These more routine critiques and demands for concessions addressed to the regime were still effective in the first few days of the protest. On the evening of 16 February, the Libyan regime released about a hundred Islamist prisoners from jail in an attempt to appease the Islamist opposition. What became clearer by the end of 17 February and by 18 February was that in those localities where protesters had mobilized early, the balance between newer, more confrontational anti-regime behaviours and older, more subdued forms of contestation had tilted in favour of the former. This shift was directly linked to the inability of the regime at that time and in those locations to repress or co-opt the protesters sufficiently to make open defiance a non-viable option for local people. In central Benghazi, one eyewitness described how a few hundred protesters were attacked by 'civilians wearing yellow helmets and yielding batons, knives and even hatchets; some of the protestors were killed. The following day, thousands more took to the street, carrying the dead from the previous day; soldiers and mercenaries then opened fire with submachine guns.'[85] Fortunately, the eyewitness added, on the third day members of the armed forces joined the protesters. In part these responses were a longer-term consequence of the organization of the Libyan security forces, and particularly the limited capabilities and motivation of the regular police and armed forces in

Benghazi and the eastern regions more generally. Gaddafi's underlying distrust of the army and of Cyrenaica-based security forces had brought about a purposeful weakening of these security actors in the region.[86] Hence, after a brief initial confrontation with the demonstrators, many security personnel decided individually or collectively to stay at home or in their base, or even to join the protesters. These localized failures of the security apparatus weakened further the capacities of state institutions, as illustrated by the mutiny in the Benghazi jail on 18 February, which led to the escape of about a thousand prisoners. In this increasingly chaotic context, clashes kept occurring not only between the security forces and the demonstrators but also between different groups within the security forces themselves. As police sharpshooters were reported to have shot dead demonstrators in Bayda and Gaddafi's revolutionary committees to have killed protesters in Benghazi, journalists indicated that some members of the police and the army were siding with the demonstrators in these towns and handing them weapons.[87] These perceptions of violence were not necessarily accurate representations of the situation, but they contributed to an overall narrative that shaped the strategies and choices of the participants. Ill-applied repression by the security forces helped to elicit an increasingly violent protest reaction, while failing at the same time to be sufficiently brutal to stop people from mobilizing.

Although the wave of unrest that erupted in mid-February was problematic for a regime that had tolerated little public dissent, such protests could still be seen by the regime as part of a managed process of contestation. Hence, on 20 February Saif al-Islam went on national television to propose a series of vague reforms in an attempt to reclaim the political initiative and placate some of the demands of the protesters. These propositions included the creation of a commission of inquiry into the actions of the security forces to 'investigate the circumstances and events that have caused many victims'. Already, however, this reform proposal was accompanied by more dramatic threats: the alternative to reform was presented as the regime fighting 'to the last bullet'.[88] This attempt at restoring some form of political dialogue took place at a time when in several eastern towns (Benghazi, Bayda, Derna, Tobruk) and in towns of the Nafusa Mountains the protesters found themselves in control as, after several days of confrontation, most state security actors had given up, withdrawn or joined them.[89] Observers present at the time remarked that these local reorganizations of power were not initially seen as the beginning of a process of regime change, but primarily as ad hoc responses to unusual circumstances. Protesters developed local self-help networks in order to cope firstly with repression, and then in order to deal with the withdrawal of the security forces and the progressive shutdown of state institutions and public services.[90] 'We have to re-establish everything ourselves,' said a member of the newly created Benghazi municipal council in the last week of February; 'we have to take care of provisions, of security, of hospitals'.[91]

These local rearticulations of power—outcomes of protests that developed relatively independently of one another—began to create an ideational and material challenge for the regime at the national level. The near simultaneous emergence of violent unrest in different parts of the country put the security apparatus under pressure, as the regime could not send out at once as many reinforcements as required. These difficulties were most visible in Benghazi on 22 February when the military brigade led by General Abdul Fatah Younis, which had been sent to reinforce the security apparatus in town, defected to the opposition under the impulse of its commander. Younis's decision illustrated growing divisions within the Libyan regime at the time.[92] Under pressure, the regime opted in late February for a tactical withdrawal from the locations that it could not control, instead of sending out troops whose loyalty could not be assured. In the process, the security forces had to destroy some of their own equipment to avoid the weapons falling into the hands of the insurgents. In addition, the ruling elites could not as easily portray these simultaneous, multiple protests as self-interested demands by specific groups with personal agendas, as they had done successfully before.[93] The raving speech of Gaddafi on 22 February blaming the unrest among youth on hallucinogenic drugs revealed the limited discursive resources then at the disposal of the regime.[94] The apparent lack of a well thought-through response by the regime, shown by the unscripted TV interventions of Gaddafi and his son, contributed to the reframing of the regime's repression and of the protesters' actions. Locally, in a context of apparent wanton acts of brutality by sections of the state apparatus, the regime's threats to unleash more violence upon the protesters facilitated the diffusion of a counter-discourse of legitimate violent retribution against Gaddafi and his supporters.[95]

Internationally, the ill-calibrated use (and threats of use) of force undermined the reformist image that the regime had been trying to promote under the direction of Saif al-Islam, and brought about a return to previous stereotypes of the Libyan dictator as a 'mad dog'.[96] At this juncture, the redrawing of the arenas of contestation within Libya became increasingly informed by the international positioning of the protests. In the global media and among foreign policy-makers, the regime was increasingly portrayed as on the brink of collapse and disposed to use lethal force in a haphazard manner in a desperate attempt to curb an ever-growing protest movement. Rumours also abounded about the imminent departure of Gaddafi.[97] In late February 2011, the political and discursive adaptations generated by earlier uprisings in Tunisia and Egypt coloured perceptions of the unrest in Libya. Taking a cue here from cognitive psychology, we should note the relevance of factors like availability heuristic (the tendency to be impressed by recent events more than by older ones) and representativeness heuristic (the tendency to take surface similarities as objective evidence) in framing the Libyan uprising at the time.[98] European and US policy-makers were more inclined to see in this wave of protests the beginning of a revolution than previously. In this context, a level of unrest and repression which may not have stirred foreign governments into action in previous years gained a new significance for policy-making. On 25 February 2011, only nine days after the beginning of the Libyan uprising, French President Nicolas Sarkozy declared during an official visit to Turkey: 'Gaddafi must go.'[99] The following day, US President Barack Obama urged Gaddafi to step down from power.[100] Having played the 'War on Terror' card well so as to come in from the cold in the mid-2000s, and having presented the protesters as being manipulated by dangerous Islamists, Gaddafi may have been genuine when he declared himself 'surprised that we have an alliance with the West to fight al-Qaeda, and now that we are fighting terrorists they have abandoned us'.[101]

Reshaping protest actions in Morocco

In the last of the North African uprisings, the wave of protests that started in Morocco on 20 February 2011 was clearly informed by the uprisings that had affected its neighbours. At the same time, the dynamics of unrest in Morocco eschewed some of the more violent revolutionary practices witnessed elsewhere. While many North African countries experienced extraordinary political changes in 2011, Morocco witnessed a more conventional form of social and political contestation that resulted in the implementation of a reform agenda by the ruling elites. Such a reformist path was what regional specialists of democratization had considered for the country in the 2000s under the leadership of the new Moroccan king, Mohammed VI. By 2011, in a more tumultuous regional context, such partial reforms of authoritarian governance suddenly seemed to be rather 'exceptional' in the circumstances.

As had happened in Libya with online mobilization for a 'day of rage', one of the main impulses for what would become the 20 February Movement was a call to demonstrate by online activists. This movement-in-the-making relied at first on social media—notably its Facebook page—to gather momentum for the first demonstrations.[102] Although the 20 February Movement mainly remained an umbrella organization for very different civil society associations (Islamist, leftist, liberal, Berber, etc.) throughout this protest episode, the initial effort at mobilization was more systematically planned than those in neighbouring countries. Successful online mobilization even led some of the leading cyber-activists to organize a press conference for the mainstream media ahead of their planned demonstration on 20 February in order to outline the main themes of the protest. The semi-open authoritarian system in place in Morocco meant that despite low-intensity routine harassment by the security services, these activists were able to voice their demands in the public sphere, online and in local meetings.[103]

The meetings organized before the 20 February demonstrations came about as grassroots associative networks took note of the growing popularity of the online mobilization and began to consider participation in the event. They were also the result of the outreach efforts of some of the cyber-activists who directly engaged with them. Ahmed Benchemsi stresses that this organizational aspect varied from place to place throughout the country depending on the choices of local organizations and activists regarding joint action.[104] In practice, therefore, while the nation-wide protests that started on 20 February 2011 were coordinated by the 20 February Movement, different organizations and networks were in actual fact in charge of mobilizing the demonstrators in different localities.[105] In this diverse associative landscape, several organizations with a national following brought their weight behind the movement and boosted its capabilities. They included, on the Islamist side, al-Adl wal-Ihsane (Justice and Charity); on the leftist side, the Unified Socialist Party; and, from the liberal associative sphere, the Moroccan Human Rights Association and ATTAC.[106]

The demonstrations that took place in most of the main Moroccan cities on 20 February 2011 gathered tens of thousands of protesters in what constituted the largest protest event ever to take place under Mohammed VI's rule. The size of the event took the regime and its security forces by surprise. Their unpreparedness played into the hands of the protesters, who could on the whole demonstrate without too much police hindrance on the day. As soon as these protests started, the cohesiveness of the 20 February Movement's project, as presented in the first press conference by cyber-activists, came quickly under pressure. The different organizations which had associated themselves with the protest began to voice rather different views on change. Divergences within the movement reflected not only the varied interests of its diverse components, but were also an outcome of local articulations of the protest, which conveyed specific local concerns in addition to national themes.[107] These local articulations also generated different security responses and dynamics: repressive measures were far more visible against the smaller protests organized subsequently under the 20 February Movement umbrella.[108] Beside the lack of a clear short- to medium-term protest strategy, the different actors of the movement also struggled to find a common view on the role of the monarchy. Some organizations, like al-Adl wal-Ihsane, had long advocated a political system in which the king would have no executive power. Slogans such as 'down with the Makhzen' also appeared in the first demonstrations, even though they remained relatively uncommon throughout. By far the largest set of demands voiced by the protesters focused on the inefficiency and corruption of the administration, the government and the king's advisers, and gave greater expression to socio-economic concerns. Sélim Smaoui and Mohamed Wazif note how the negotiations between the different groups present during demonstrations and sit-ins generally produced a lowest-common-denominator agreement on using bland generic slogans in order not to upset any of the participating groups.[109] While this wave of protest redefined the boundaries of contention given its broad appeal, it did not entrench a new physical arena of contestation (à la Tahrir Square). Instead, it forced institutionalized political actors, such as the political parties, to position themselves openly in relation to the protest movement and the monarchy.

The cycle of protest initiated by the 20 February Movement started outside the formal political arena and bypassed political parties. By demonstrating the vitality of such a model of contentious politics, this protest movement could have gained the support of the political opposition, most notably the Justice and Development Party (PJD), the largest opposition party, in the early stages of the contestation. After several days of internal debate, however, the PJD leader, Abdelilah Benkirane, decided not to involve the party in a rapprochement with the 20 February Movement but asked party members instead not to participate in the demonstrations as PJD members. This strategy was the outcome of a difficult internal process of assessing the situation. On the one hand, the PJD leadership wanted to strengthen relations with the palace in order to normalize its role as the country's leading political party. On the other hand, many militants and some prominent cadres wanted to become involved in the demonstrations, as the protesters were demanding the kind of reforms that they themselves wanted. A group of well-known PJD cadres publicly said at the time that the party should join the protesters, and put out a list of economic and political demands similar to those voiced by the 20 February Movement.[110] Ultimately, Benkirane and his supporters decided against this strategy of frontal opposition to the monarchy and sought to strengthen the PJD position as the official opposition party. Abdellah Bouanou, leader of the PJD parliamentary group, indicates that at the time one of the principal arguments in favour of keeping their distance from the protest movement was the assessment that 'we cannot control the street'.[111] As the grassroots dynamics of contention could not be expected to follow the party line, there was a fear that the blame for any 'extreme' demand or violence from demonstrators would fall on the PJD. As a result of these internal tensions, three prominent members of the general secretariat of the party—Mustapha Ramid, Lahbib Choubani and Abdelali Hamidine—left the PJD executive body.[112] The youth branch of the party, which had pushed for formal involvement of the PJD, eventually toed the party line and did not participate as the PJD youth organization (even though many members participated in their personal capacity).

Across the board, in the largest political parties there was a noticeable generational divide between the younger party activists and the older cadres regarding the 20 February Movement. This tension is well illustrated by the Socialist Union of Popular Forces party (USFP), in which a group of young militants organized themselves (as 'The Shout') to lobby the leadership for party involvement in the demonstrations. The cadres of the party, caught between this militant base and their desire to have good relations with the palace, eventually decided against a clear line of action. On 24 February, Ahmed Zaki, the head of the USFP parliamentary group, declared that his party 'neither call for a boycott nor for support of the 20 February demonstrations'.[113] In this context, the party leadership timidly called for an acceleration of the political reforms previously proposed by the king. The smaller socialist party, PPS, found a similar compromise between the demands of its more active (young) militants and its desire to maintain good relations with the palace. It too endorsed a mild reformist agenda by stressing that the demands of the 20 February Movement were 'the very same demands that have been featuring on the reform agenda of progressive political parties for years'.[114] A group of dissident cadres led by the former general secretary of the party, Said Sadi, went against the party line and joined the demonstrations. Among the established political parties, the least ambiguous response was that of the Istiqlal party, which headed the government at the time, and which clearly expressed its opposition to the protests. The party called upon its supporters not to take any part whatsoever in the actions of the 20 February Movement. The general reluctance of political parties to take a firm position on the protest movement facilitated the repositioning of the monarchy towards the contestation.

In the days that followed the first wave of demonstrations, two competing dynamics were visible. The protests organized by the 20 February Movement delimited through their actions new arenas of contestation by physically taking control of the public space during sit-ins and by discursively challenging the status quo, forcefully voicing their claims in the public sphere. At the same time, political parties and the Makhzen (the regime) tried to strengthen pre-existing structures and mechanisms of formal contestation, by creating opportunities for specific types of demands which only marginally overstepped traditional boundaries of contestation.[115] This institutionalist approach was well exemplified in the TV interview of Benkirane on 28 February, when he clearly expressed his desire to work within the existing governing structure, according to the existing electoral agenda.[116] The formal embodiment of this reformist dynamic was the televised discourse of King Mohammed on 9 March 2011.[117] By presenting his proposals for reform as part of a larger pre-existing initiative of the Moroccan state for decentralization, and not as a direct answer to the demands of the 20 February Movement, the king sought to reinscribe from the start the response of the regime within the existing political status quo.[118] The gist of the king's intervention was to provide a framework for change that concerned primarily institutional and constitutional reform in order to sidestep the more troublesome issue of socio-economic reform.

The new constitutional and political proposals of the king had some appeal because they were well-targeted responses to the demands of particular opposition actors linked to specific political and social networks. In particular, he focused on the demands of the Berber associations by addressing the recognition of Amazigh identity and language. He also proposed to answer some of the demands of the human rights associations regarding the protection of civil liberties and the reform of the justice system. Finally, his proposals were directed at political parties and their supporters not only to ensure that they would not join the protest movement, but also to encourage them to channel the demands from the street into a more formal process of negotiation. In particular, the king addressed directly some of the parties' main concerns by proposing to strengthen the role of parliament and the prime minister. By proposing to deliver on some of the demands of these social and political groups, the monarchy merely redeployed its practices of divide and rule in a way that forced the actors involved to choose explicitly between an improved institutional path towards change and a riskier extra-constitutional one. At this juncture, the grassroots redrawing of protest practices and arenas had only just begun, and institutionalized opposition actors responded cautiously to the new dynamics of the uprisings.

5

REDRAWING CONTENTION
AND AUTHORITARIAN PRACTICES

While the four North African countries under scrutiny experienced significant periods of unrest, each uprising generated different political dynamics and institutional changes. In two of the polities, Tunisia and Libya, unrest gained momentum as new protest behaviours and discourses diffused widely and became entrenched. In the other two polities, Morocco and Algeria, new protest dynamics were upstaged by the return of older practices of contention and of governance. These interactions between new and old practices underpinned the emergence of new 'revolutionary' actors, as much as the reaffirmation of pre-existing social and political identities. The strategic interactions between the pro- and anti-regimes actors, and their unintended consequences, shaped the trajectories of the uprisings and produced different outcomes. These ranged from the complete destabilization and deinstitutionalization of the regime, to the reform and stabilization of the existing authoritarian order.

Tunisia: from wanting the regime to change to triggering regime change

The emergence of a revolutionary situation in Tunisia during the first two weeks of January 2011 underscored the process of deinstitutionalization unfolding in the country at the time. Although I use the term 'revolution' from the start for the sake of analytical consistency, it must be stressed that this vocabulary only came to the fore in Tunisia towards the end of the revolutionary episode.[1] Initially, the Ben Ali regime applied its usual mixture of socio-economic incentives and police repression to weather the storm of protests, which slightly reduced in intensity around the turn of the year. Then, starting on 3 January, unrest turned more violent in the province of Kasserine, next to the Sidi Bouzid governorate, as the result of an ill-applied use of lethal force by the police. With this renewed violence lasting several days, even the Tunisian General Workers Union (UGTT) began to defy the regime openly, as Abid Brigui, the deputy general secretary, publicly declared on 8 January: 'We support the demands of the population of Sidi Bouzid and of the central regions.'[2] Adding that it was 'not normal to respond with bullets', he demanded the release of all the protesters jailed during these protests. The regime decided to step up police repression to contain this new wave of rioting and, as a result, the death toll kept increasing among protesters. By 10 January, the official death toll for the provinces of Kasserine and Sidi Bouzid reached 21, with the towns of Kasserine, Thala and Regueb being the main flash-points.[3] During that week, while the unrest still retained a clear socio-economic agenda, the protests also became more political as protesters focused on the illegitimate violence unleashed by the regime's security forces. In Thala, an eyewitness described how a peaceful demonstration was moving toward the town centre when 'policemen started to throw tear gas and it all went awry; the protesters set fire to tires and threw them in courtyard of the police station, and they also set fire to the RCD [Constitutional Democratic Rally] local office.'[4]

It is a common observation that an ill-applied use of force by the state can act as a rallying crying for opposition forces. David Hess and Brian Martin note that 'for a repressive event to generate backfire, two factors must be present. First, an audience must perceive the event to be unjust. Violent repression of a social movement with claims that are widely perceived to be legitimate is one example of a situation that some people will perceive as unjust ... Second, information about the event or situation needs to be communicated effectively to receptive audiences that are substantial enough that authorities must take their outrage into consideration.'[5] While parts of the Tunisian public may have been irked by some of the demonstrators' outbursts of violence, the sharp increase in the number of protesters shot dead by the police at the start of January swung the pendulum of perceived injustice firmly against the regime.[6] Earlier explanations given by the government that the police were acting in self-defence were increasingly no longer credible as the death toll grew. In this sequence of events, the increasingly negative public response to the actions of the security forces was underpinned by the effective media coverage of the protests.

The impact of the new media during this sequence of events became more noticeable, as it facilitated the emergence of a new discourse about 'revolution' that formalized and advertised the transformative nature of these protests. In informational terms, the media helped raise the profile of the revolt and articulate a perspective that countered the official version given by the regime at home and abroad. As before, a combination of new and old media outlets proved most effective at conveying counter-discourses. In particular, during the most violent episodes of confrontation in Kasserine, Thala and Regueb, the evidence gathered via mobile phones with video capabilities, and then relayed via social media sites like Nawaat or Facebook to satellite television channels like Al Jazeera, enabled local activists to broadcast their message beyond their own context.[7] The informational and mobilizational dynamics at the time were characterized not so much by the relevance of specific media as by the synergy between different types of media and technologies—Ben Wagner talks about 'co-evolution' in this context.[8] Mehdi Mabrouk argues that the increasingly effective use of these media dynamics enabled the Tunisian protesters to move from a defensive depiction of their action in the face of state propaganda to a more offensive media campaign criticizing the actions of the regime. He remarks that, by the second week of January, 'information-providers gained unprecedented access to public opinion by providing video clips showing the legal violations, security abuses and financial corruption linked to the ruling family. Such detailed documentation of their abuses created a vivid impression amongst the wider public, inciting it to ever greater mobilization in order to reach its revolutionary goals.'[9]

At the beginning of January the increased level of material and discursive confrontation between the protesters and the regime led to a qualitative shift in the articulation of the protest. Explicitly 'revolutionary' anti-regime behaviours became more entrenched, and previously common authoritarian practices and discourses began to be deinstitutionalized in everyday life. Slogans like 'no to corruption' become intermixed with new ones like 'Ben Ali go away'.[10] As part of this process, the death of Bouazizi and the events of Sidi Bouzid were recast as the founding events of a revolutionary movement that no longer interacted with the regime on the basis of the preceding authoritarian bargain. Realizing the danger, on 10 January 2011 the regime made another effort at reinstitutionalizing the authoritarian contract that had prevailed before. Ben Ali went on national television for the second time since the beginning of the revolt and announced new terms of engagement by the regime with the protesters. The president began by addressing the increase in deadly violence in the country and blamed it on 'gangs of thugs' perpetrating 'acts of terrorism'.[11] Turning to the issue of the emerging revolutionary discourse of the demonstrators, Ben Ali cautioned the population against listening to such misguided views and 'falsehoods'. Forced to acknowledge the importance of the events of Sidi Bouzid in view of their growing symbolic value for the protesters, he expressed 'his regrets' for the victims and 'his compassion' for the local population. At the same time, Ben Ali tried to reimpose a socio-economic explanation of the unrest and invoked in his defence 'the advances' made by Tunisia under his rule, as well as the 'international recognition' of the Tunisian model of development. He stressed how much his government had been doing to maintain good socio-economic conditions in the country, including subsidizing the price of staple goods. He also promised to do much more by announcing the creation of 300,000 new jobs before the end of 2012. This initiative included a guarantee of 'full employment of all the graduates who have been unemployed for over two years'. Concluding more tentatively on the issue of political liberalization, the president proposed the organization of a national conference involving 'representatives of civil society' and a relaxation of media censorship, while promising that state institutions and political parties would be 'more responsive to the demands of the citizens'.[12]

This formal attempt to relegitimize routine authoritarian governance through a combination of stick (against 'thugs') and carrot (for the unemployed) was accompanied mainly by a stiffening of repressive

policies, since the new economic programmes would only be introduced over many months. A UGTT member from Kasserine declared
that it was 'chaos here in Kasserine after a night of violence, of snipers'
fire, of looting and stealing from shops and homes by plainclothes
police units'.[13] In the aftermath of Ben Ali's speech, the first reports
emerged of a systematic attempt by the Tunisian authorities to block
social networking sites such as Facebook in order to halt counter-discourses. In addition, the ministry of education announced that high
schools and universities would be closed until further notice. These
two measures were designed to reduce the opportunities for the vir-
tual and physical gathering of regime opponents, particularly students.
In Tunis, the day after Ben Ali's speech, journalists recorded the presence of anti-riot police at all the main intersections of the town centre,
and witnessed the systematic dispersal of gatherings of more than a few
persons by plainclothes policemen.[14] For the protesters, the discourses
and policies of the regime hardly appeared to have changed since the
first televised appearance of Ben Ali some two weeks earlier, even
though the pace, reach and intensity of the revolt had increased. In the
circumstances, the regime's ability to redirect protest behaviours
towards the narrow forms of routinized dissent that had prevailed previously remained limited. On 11 and 12 January, rioting continued in
many Tunisian towns, and increasingly the unrest reached the capital,
Tunis, where protesters were met by heavy police repression. On 12
January in particular, police and demonstrators clashed in the centre of
the capital. Rioters threw stones at government buildings, bringing
unrest right to the doorstep of the ruling elite. In response, that evening the same night-time curfew previously imposed in several provincial towns was extended to Tunis.[15]

In an increasingly dysfunctional institutional order, established opposition actors found it as difficult as the regime not to be hostages to
fortune. The leaders of the centre-left movement Ettajdid, one of the
few parties that Ben Ali had authorized in his ultra-dominant party system, declared at the time that they too were 'frightened by the turn of
events'.[16] When the UGTT and the Progressive Democratic Party called
for a general strike on 12 January, it was clear that they were responding
to events on the ground rather than directing the protest.[17] These institutionalized actors walked a fine line between adopting a confronta-

tional stance against the regime, as a means of strengthening their hand to extract concessions, and fully opposing the regime in order to contribute to its downfall. Until the very last moment, the discourses and actions of most of these established actors indicated that the first option still headed their agenda. Mahmoud Ben Romdhane declared to journalists on 11 January that Ettajdid was 'not saying today that Ben Ali has to go, but that the situation is serious and that there is a need for dialogue'.[18] Taking stock of its rather ineffective (if not counterproductive) strategy of increased repression, and slowly realizing that it might need the support of previously sidelined opposition actors, the regime began to re-evaluate some of its options. On the evening of 12 January, Prime Minister Mohamed Ghannouchi, announced that the president had replaced his much despised interior minister and had decided to free all those arrested in recent protests that were not involved in looting.[19] He also declared that Ben Ali had given instructions to set up a committee of inquiry into the abuses by security forces that had occurred during the protests, and a second committee to look into the issue of corruption and misbehaviour by state officials. For the students demonstrating in Tunis at the time, these concessions were a sign of failure of the regime's earlier policies. Talking to journalists, one of them argued that it was 'a declaration of failure from the regime' and an indication that the regime was afraid of the demonstrators, 'so afraid that it preferred to shut down all the universities'.[20]

On 13 January, Ben Ali went on national television for the third time in an increasingly desperate attempt to help restore some order in the country. This media outing, which would be the last for Ben Ali as Tunisian president, highlighted the increasing disruption and deinstitutionalization of authoritarian governance in the face of continuing mass unrest. In this third televised address, Ben Ali's language was clearly different—literally and symbolically. The president delivered his speech mainly in colloquial Tunisian dialect (rather than in the standard literary Arabic that was habitually used in official discourse) in an effort to convince ordinary Tunisians that he was close to them. Substantively, Ben Ali no longer focused on socio-economic issues (which were only occasionally mentioned this time), but addressed directly the political nature of the unrest. The president told his audience that he 'had understood them' and that 'the situation requires a serious change to be made', 'a profound and systematic one'. In a rather desperate bid to cast his words as authoritative, he twice loudly exclaimed, 'Enough violence! Enough violence!' Ben Ali declared that he 'had instructed the interior ministry, and repeated his instructions ... to stop the use of live ammunition'. He stressed that he 'expected all Tunisians, whether they supported him or not, to endorse such an effort to appease the situation and to banish any recourse to violence'. Then he outlined some of the more important political changes on offer, including press freedom, an end to censorship, the freedom to express political views and organize (peaceful) political demonstrations, and a reform of the electoral and associative codes. Indicating that he would not seek another presidential mandate at the end of his term, he attempted to shift the blame for past political repression, saying that 'many things did not turn out the way I wanted them to, particularly in the domain of democracy and of liberties. Some people have misled me at times by hiding the facts from me.'[21]

At that juncture in the process of popular uprising, even such groundbreaking concessions from an otherwise unyielding authoritarian regime did not alter the dynamics of mass opposition to the regime, not least because the actions of the security forces did not always validate the president's call for calm and appeasement. As several political movements voiced their willingness to engage with the regime on the basis of these proposals for political reform—including Ahmed Nejib Chebbi of the Progressive Democratic Party, Mustapha Ben Jaafar of the Democratic Forum for Labour and Liberties, and Ahmed Brahim of Ettajdid—popular unrest continued unabated.[22] Mehdi Mabrouk comments that at the time 'the overall political movement was characterized by the inability of civil society, particularly its formal institutions, to formalize the protests of youth into specific demands and it was this lack of formalization that created the revolutionary situation'. Taking the example of a leaked telephone conversation between Ben Ali and the dean of the Lawyers National Association, in which the dean told Ben Ali that the lawyers refused to follow his instructions to end their protest, Mabrouk remarks that when the regime's usual tactics did not work, 'it had no access to any alternative mediatory mechanisms'.[23] As political instability reached a peak in the second week of 2011, the very cautious strategies favoured by institutionalized opposition actors, still reacting to years of repression and cooptation, directly contributed to their inability to control or direct the dynamics of protest.

The continuing violence on 14 January, particularly in Tunis, brought home the message to the regime that neither the changing discourse of Ben Ali, nor the modicum of support for reform voiced by the opposition was sufficient to alter significantly the revolutionary fervour that was increasingly on display among protesters. That day, demonstrators in Tunis even managed to get access to the roof of the Interior Ministry. These apparently unpredictable and uncontrollable outbursts of violence so close to the seat of power led Ben Ali to reconsider his options in a worst-case scenario in which security forces would not be able to guarantee his safety. Earlier in the week his wife and his two daughters left the Tunisian capital for various foreign destinations as a precautionary measure. Subsequent declarations by Ben Ali's chief of security, Ali Sariati, would also suggest that the president was worried about his own security in the palace, especially after he replaced his chief of staff, General Ammar, for refusing to order the army to use lethal force against the demonstrators on 13 January.[24] In a letter written from exile to explain his actions, Ben Ali himself stressed that he had received information from his security chief concerning a possible attempt on his life in the palace.[25] Later statements by Sariati and the defence minister, Ridha Grira, indicated that at that time various officials responsible for security in the regime were increasingly concerned with looking after their own interests or started jockeying for position to retain control of the institutions after the possible departure of Ben Ali.[26] Such doubts about the reliability of the chain of command and the loyalty of the security forces in a situation where the president felt that he was potentially directly under threat helped to concretize Ben Ali's plan to leave the country, at least until the protests had weakened.

The actual flight of the president appears to have been an ad hoc decision taken by Ben Ali on the day in view of continuing violence near the presidential palace and the reluctance of soldiers to use lethal force to quell dissent. Unlike in earlier revolutionary episodes in the region (such as Iran in 1979) or in those that would follow in 2011 (Egypt, Libya, Yemen, Syria), in the Tunisian case the issue of the removal from office of the president did not explicitly drive the protests until the very last moments of the revolt-turned-revolution. The protesters, as well as established political actors inside or outside the regime, did not raise this issue until the last few days or hours of the regime.[27] At that time, the ad hoc aspect of Ben Ali's change of strategy was highlighted by the position of foreign governments, which until the very last day still held firmly to their belief in the resilience of the regime. On 12 January, the French foreign minister, Michèle Alliot-Marie, even proposed to provide police assistance to the Tunisian government to help it contain the demonstrations 'with less bloodshed'.[28] Later that day, the US State Department merely indicated that it was concerned by reports of the use of excessive force by the regime, a position echoed the following day by the French prime minister, François Fillon, who condemned the 'disproportionate use of force by the authorities'.[29] The formal deinstitutionalization of the Ben Ali regime on the international stage only came about on 14 January, when Ben Ali's ad hoc decision to leave Tunisia was matched by the equally ad hoc decision of the French government not to allow him to enter France, and by the unlikely exile to Saudi Arabia of this once trusted ally of the 'West' and forceful advocate of secularism.[30] The flight from Tunisia of the president forced a redrawing of the institutional arenas of contention and opened the door for a reconstruction and repositioning of political identities and actors.

Libya: from local areas of revolutionary protest to international conflict zone

The redrawing of new arenas of contestation in Libya in February–March 2011 was a direct outcome of the deinstitutionalization of authoritarian governance in different areas of the country. As extraordinary protests became routine, they entrenched a revolutionary discourse that drove social and political practices further away from the authoritarian status quo, at home and abroad. At the local level, by the end of February organized resistance to the Gaddafi regime became less of an extraordinary behaviour and more of a routine affair in those locations where unrest had started early. Protesters in the areas where the state security forces had withdrawn no longer protested but turned their attention to local governance and to supporting protest movements elsewhere in the country. For many would-be revolutionaries, the experience of the uprisings changed from confronting the regime to managing everyday social, economic, political and security problems without support from the central government. For many others, the routinization of the revolutionary moment came in the form of a quasi-military lifestyle through incorporation into self-defence groups and revolutionary brigades.[31]

By the beginning of March 2013, as the demarcation lines between pro- and anti-Gaddafi areas began to stabilize, the process of uprising and the uncertainties that had facilitated the shaping of protest identities and practices began to solidify into a more conventional armed conflict, with military activities at the front line and routine forms of insurgent governance at the rear. Detailing the situation in the town of Misrata, Brian McQuinn notes that different networks of insurgents collaborated with each other and coordinated their efforts without having a unified authority or command structure.[32] The local civilian committees that formed the basis of the Misrata City Council and ran the city's affairs on a daily basis collaborated with the Misrata Military Council, which was headed by armed brigades, but had no political authority over it. In a similar way, the many Misratan revolutionary brigades formed at the time collaborated with each other under the umbrella of the Military Council but retained their autonomy of action. In practice, the Military Council served mainly as an intelligence-gathering and military supply office, not as a command centre. The brigades also collaborated with the City Council, but each had its own logistical and financial supply chain organized by local businessmen and notables.

Domestically, the routinization and institutionalization of the pro-test-turned-armed insurrection became formalized on 27 February 2011 with the establishment of the National Transitional Council (NTC). After a few tentative meetings between local leaders from the eastern towns controlled by the protesters, national actors who had defected from the regime and opposition actors from other parts of Libya, the NTC was established to coordinate anti-regime resistance. Its first official meeting on 5 March was preceded by the dissemination of its founding statement.[33] The four main points highlighted in this communiqué indicated the orientation of this putative leadership of the Libyan insurrection. First, the NTC recognized the prominence of 'the youth' in driving the protest movement and in being 'the foundation of the revolution'. By the time of the communiqué, however, the tide had already begun to turn against the revolutionary youth and in favour of the more structured armed brigades. Unlike in the Tunisian context, where ill-applied lethal repression by the regime helped to mobilize protesters, in Libya the use of lethal force by the regime and by the opposition was by March 2011 beginning to be seen as standard practice between two fighting forces. Secondly, the NTC presented itself as the sole representative of the Libyan population and listed the towns that had dispatched members to the Council (while recognizing that it was still waiting to hear from several regions of the country). Thirdly, the Council stressed the importance of the military aspect of the revolution by specifically naming its head of military affairs, Omer el-Hariri, in its communiqué. As the NTC sought to position itself as a political and institutional alternative to the Gaddafi regime, its own process of institutionalization underscored the fact that one of the main challenges it faced was the emergence of multiple centres of political and military authority. Amazigh groups from the Nafusa Mountains in particular recognized the leadership of the NTC for tactical purposes—mainly to negotiate external military support for the insurgency—but de facto organized their activities at arm's length from the Council.[34] While the NTC had formally established a National Liberation Army, this military institution was in practice a loose coalition of independent brigades and not a unified command structure. Lastly, the NTC declaration emphasized the importance of the international community by stating that its foreign affairs representatives, Mohamed Jebril and Ali el-Esawi, were to 'negotiate and communicate with all members of international communities to accomplish international recognition of the Council'.[35] The foreign policies of the insurgents, and the role of foreign policies in the insurgency, were confirmed as one crucial set of interactions shaping the arenas and practices of contention of the Libyan conflict.

At the international level, French President Nicolas Sarkozy, had voiced the possibility of a no-fly zone to hinder the Libyan regime's capacity for violent repression and, on 28 February, this idea was taken up by the British prime minister, David Cameron. Cameron announced in the British parliament that he had 'asked the Ministry of Defence and the Chief of the Defence Staff to work with our allies on plans for a military no-fly zone'.[36] While earlier declarations by the French president may have amounted to posturing and over-compensation for the lack of reaction by Western powers to the Tunisian and Egyptian revolutions, the planning of a no-fly zone pointed to a more direct involvement of international actors in the Libyan uprisings. At the time, however, the relevance of a no-fly zone for this uprising remained questionable. The Libyan air force was particularly weak—and it got even weaker as several pilots joined the rebels' camp, sabotaged the planes at their base, bailed out and crashed their planes in the desert, or fled abroad with their fighter jets.[37] Overall, the air force did not play, and was unlikely to play, a significant part in stopping the uprising or in inflicting large casualties on the insurgents. Although it was presented by the British prime minister as a means of preventing the bombing of civilian populations, only a handful of attacks by helicopters had taken place against rebel-held areas in February. As for the subsequent argument that the no-fly zone would prevent the airlifting of mercenaries, this was also of limited pertinence considering the continuing influx of mercenaries by land throughout the conflict. Regardless of the considerations of foreign governments, the outcome was that military intervention set apart the Libyan revolution from the other uprisings in the region, which mostly took place without external military involvement.[38]

The international military intervention in Libya, initiated by the French, British and American air forces, began in earnest on 19 March with the bombing of armoured vehicles of the Libyan army on their way to retake Benghazi. This air campaign helped to entrench a process of militarization of the Libyan conflict and to delimit new arenas of contention. By working to stabilize the front line between pro-Gaddafi and anti-Gaddafi areas, the bombing campaign that started on 19 March entrenched a situation of multiple sovereignties in Libya. This process further structured the resistance to the regime by supporting specific ideational and behavioural dynamics. Protest dynamics ceased to be grounded primarily on mass mobilization during (more or less violent) street demonstrations and became a more regulated use of force by armed groups. 'Revolutionary' violence lost its extraordinary quality by becoming more programmatic and strategic. The contrast is striking between the first unplanned offensives of youthful revolutionaries in early March in the Gulf of Sirte and the subsequent planned military efforts to conquer or retain the same territory. The initial violent upsurge, inspired by earlier street battles against the police, showed little coordination and method, as most of the rebel fighters had no training and no inclination to follow a military strategy. 'There is no comparison between our weapons and theirs,' said one disappointed rebel fighter; 'they're trained, they're organized … We're not an army, we're the people, and even if we had weapons, we wouldn't even know how to use them.'[39] As journalists and analysts noted at the time, front-line 'soldiers' often simply disregarded 'orders' from field commanders and fought or withdrew from the battlefield on their own initiative.[40]

The issuing of an NTC directive at the end of March declaring that fighters could not join front-line troops without having completed their military training illustrated the formal downplaying of the initial 'revolutionary spirit' in favour of military efficiency.[41] Armed groups initially created to resist early repression by the state security forces became over the weeks more professional military units with an offensive capability. The militarization of the Libyan conflict led to a professionalization of the revolutionaries—a domestic process linked to the internationalization of the conflict, as foreign powers provided weapons and training to the insurgents. This build-up of a military structure and capability was also a bottom-up process, with logistics chains being created throughout the country and transnationally.[42] Revolutionary behaviour began to be reinstitutionalized through these interactions, which strengthened both the ideational and material capacity of local power centres. This situation was explicitly recognized by the NTC on its official Facebook page in May 2011 when it stated, 'The Council derives its legitimacy from the decisions of local councils set up by the revolutionary people of Libya on the 17th of February. These local councils facilitated a mechanism to manage daily life in the liberated cities and villages.'[43] The routinization of military confrontation entrenched a system of multiple sovereignties in which different actors and practices became institutionalized in different parts of the country.

Algeria: from social unrest to political protest

In early January 2011, the tension between routine authoritarian governance and the new protest behaviours did not produce a 'revolutionary' dynamic of mobilization beyond the first few days of rioting. These protest dynamics were, however, tentatively formalized and reintroduced in the aftermath of the riots by opposition actors who organized a second, and ultimately far less spectacular, wave of political protest in late January and February 2011. On 20 January several opposition parties (including the Socialist Front (FFS), the Rally for Culture and Democracy (RCD), and several small leftist parties), unofficial labour unions and civil society organizations (notably the Algerian League for the Defence of Human Rights (LADDH)) joined forces to give voice to what they presented as the (implicit) demands of the rioting crowds. Inspired by the example of the Tunisian 'January 14 Front' created a week earlier in Tunis, they formally announced on the 21st the formation of the National Coordination for Change and Democracy (Coordination Nationale pour le Changement et la Démocratie, CNCD).[44] The CNCD called, in particular, for greater democracy and social justice, for an end to the state of emergency in place since 1992, for a relaxation of the media laws, for the release of all previously arrested protesters, and for new employment opportunities. As the CNCD declared its intention to organize a protest march against the government, its call was swiftly echoed by the Islamist activist network, Rachad.[45] The Rachad website (repeatedly blocked by the Algerian regime) even proposed at the time 'documentation on non-violent activism that can produce a radical change in Algeria'. By then, however, the FFS had decided not to join the protest movement, thereby illustrating some of the difficulties of alliance building among opposition actors that would keep hindering the action of the CNCD.[46] At the same time, without coordination with other CNCD members, the RCD leader, Said Sadi, announced that he was organizing a 'march for democracy' in Algiers the next day. The governorate of Algiers promptly issued a communiqué read out during the evening news which stated that such gatherings were considered a breach of public order and were not authorized.[47]

On 22 January, the demonstration of a few hundred RCD supporters in central Algiers was quickly broken up by an extremely large police contingent that was estimated at around 20,000, specially mobilized throughout the city. Busloads of RCD supporters coming for the day from Kabylia, the RCD heartland, were stopped on the outskirts of Algiers by police units deployed there to prevent them from reaching the city centre.[48] Although this initial protest march ended up being a non-event—and the RCD was promptly criticized by the FFS for its strategy[49]—the CNCD indicated that it intended to organize its own demonstration on 12 February. Following this announcement, the Algerian regime made good use of the lull in the protest cycle to refine the policy options that could best ease the socio-economic and political tensions in the country. After a meeting between the president and his cabinet on 3 February 2011, government spokespersons leaked to the press that the 19-year-old state of emergency would soon be lifted. They also indicated that opposition parties would be allowed greater airtime on state-controlled television and radio stations. The government then announced that new job-creation schemes were about to be implemented.[50] In so acting, the regime effectively met some of the key demands of the opposition, while not giving the impression of caving in under pressure, as none of these announcements was yet official policy.[51]

On 12 February 2011—which, coincidentally, was the day after the resignation of President Mubarak in Egypt—protesters responding to the call of the CNCD converged on May First Square in central Algiers. In an event which some viewed as a miniature reproduction of Egypt's Tahrir Square, about 3,000 protesters managed to occupy the square for a while after breaking through police lines.[52] In Algiers, unlike Tahrir Square, the security forces outnumbered the protesters by ten to one, for about 30,000 security personnel had been mobilized by the regime on that occasion. Journalists reported that for most of the afternoon the demonstrators stayed on the square chanting anti-government and pro-democracy slogans—'free and democratic Algeria', 'the regime out' and 'yesterday Egypt, today Algeria'.[53] The riot police blocked attempts by would-be protesters from neighbouring suburbs and from other towns to reach the centre of Algiers. In one incident, Ali Belhadj, former leader of the Islamic Salvation Front (FIS), and several dozens of his supporters who were trying to join the demonstrators on May First Square were pushed back from the scene. In what proved damaging for the attempt of the CNCD to unify the opposition—and indicative of the deep mistrust between the left and the Islamists—the expulsion of Belhadj was not the work of the police but of the CNCD demonstrators themselves.[54] Fearing that the Islamists might hijack their protest, CNCD activists decided to do without their support—or hindrance, as they might have seen it. By the end of the day, as protesters began to go home or were dispersed by the police, it was clear that May First Square had failed to be an Algerian Tahrir Square.[55] Said Sadi might well have been right when he pointed out that 'when you mobilize 30,000 police in the capital, that's a sign of weakness, not strength'.[56] This protest event did confirm the common reliance of the Algerian regime on security measures to cope with political pressure.[57] But the 12 February protest also illustrated the limited capabilities of the CNCD to mobilize and unite different opposition forces in the country and, more importantly, to connect with the tens of thousands of youths from the suburbs who had rioted a month earlier.[58] 'When Bab-el-Oued rose in January, opposition parties did not join the youths in the streets,' noted a sceptical inhabitant of Algeria; 'today they join the revolt bandwagon by pure opportunism. This demonstration is not the revolt of the youths of 5th January.'[59]

Undaunted by the regime's show of force and by their limited success, the CNCD called for demonstrations to continue every Saturday on May First Square in an effort to remobilize protesters.[60] The following week, on 19 February, a similar demonstration was duly organized by the CNCD, with rather similar results. A few thousand protesters managed to gain access to May First Square only to face a deployment of police as impressive as that of the week before. The government also ensured that its security forces were positioned at strategic points throughout Algiers to prevent would-be demonstrators from making it to the town centre.[61] Just as had happened the week before, the CNCD call for protest failed to mobilize enough opposition actors and depoliticized youths to generate an overpowering movement of contestation. By then it was apparent that the choice of a weekly demonstration on Saturday had also entrenched the divide between Islamic activists— the Rachad movement had called earlier for demonstrations on Fridays—and leftist and liberal activists. Further divisions over strategy within the CNCD undermined the appeal of the movement, especially when on 22 February the organization split into two opposing factions after a tense general meeting.[62] The formal lifting of the nineteen-year-old state of emergency on 24 February did not assist the protest strategy of the CNCD, as newly introduced security measures applying to Algiers still banned demonstrations and sit-ins in the capital.[63] The Algerian interior minister, Dahou Ould Kablia, justified these measures by invoking the terrorism threat in the country and the targeting of state institutions in Algiers by terrorist organizations.[64]

Over the weeks political protests slowly subsided as discontent became channelled once more through routine mechanisms of authoritarian governance. The weakness of this protest mobilization was on display on 5 March when a small CNCD demonstration came under attack by pro-regime supporters trying to assault the RCD leader, Said Sadi, who was leading the march in the Al-Madania neighbourhood of Algiers.[65] In the aftermath of this event, other opposition movements openly criticized the tactics of the RCD. Karim Tabbou, the FFS first secretary, addressing a crowd of supporters a few thousand strong in Algiers, declared that his own organization would not 'get caught in confrontation and violence'.[66] The symbolic end-point of the CNCD-inspired 'new' contestation was the demonstration by tens of thousands of communal guards in Algiers on 7 March, demanding better recognition and pay. This protest, not addressing in any way the political demands of the opposition, was able to draw protesters in far larger numbers than the CNCD had ever managed to, and, in doing so, was able to upset temporarily the police control of central Algiers. This one-off demonstration illustrated that even the well-oiled security apparatus of the Algerian regime could be outplayed, as long as protesters turned up unexpectedly in sufficient numbers.[67]

According to Jack Brown, it was counterintuitive that, compared with Tunisia, the Algerian riots of January 2011 were not better relayed by civil society actors, as Algeria under Bouteflika had a freer and livelier civil and political society than Tunisia under Ben Ali.[68] What the political protests of February 2011 revealed was that a lively and diverse civil and political society could constitute a hindrance to large-scale mobilization when opposition actors were powerful enough to mobilize their core constituencies but too weak to attract support beyond them. Political unrest in Algeria in February was far less significant in scope than social unrest in January because the articulation of a political agenda helped to fragment the mass of potential protesters into different constituencies. Unlike in the January riots and unlike in Tunisia, where a motley crew of demonstrators could join any protest for any reason, in the February demonstrations protesters had to subscribe to a particular agenda to join the movement—as witness the turning away of Islamists by CNCD activists. In this context, the political framing of common grievances did not so much empower the crowds than divide them into competing factions. As had happened before in situations of intense contestation, such as the 'black spring' of 2001 in Kabylia, the tension between the articulation of specific demands by specific actors and the generic reasons of discontent hindered the diffusion of the unrest.[69] Rather than reshaping arenas of contestation where new discourses and practices could gain momentum, organized political protests entrenched existing divisions and established behaviours—'Go back to your village, you dirty Kabyle,' shouted counter-demonstrators at Said Sadi during the CNCD demonstrations.[70]

In this stabilized context, the actions of the security forces assisted this return to routine protest practices by preventing the protest movement from accidentally reaching a critical mass. Unlike in January during the wave of rioting, when the regime had asked the police to limit their involvement, in February security forces intervened more systematically to ensure that better-planned protests would not instigate further unrest. The role of the security apparatus cannot be reduced to its actual repressive capabilities, as the issue of willingness to use force remained a key factor in this security dilemma.[71] In Algeria, the military had shown repeatedly over the years that it was both willing and able to use lethal force on a massive scale to support the regime it thought was best for the country (and for its own interests).[72] Although this neo-praetorian influence might well wane over time, in 2011 it still set very tangible constraints upon the kind of political changes that protest actors thought they could initiate successfully.[73] In January–February 2011, the Algerian ruling elites were confident that the military would not suddenly choose to let a popular protest topple the existing institutional order—unless, that is, the counter-elites leading the protest reached an agreement with the military leadership. The creation of a vicious circle between low mobilization and the low costs of repression was an important self-reinforcing mechanism of routine authoritarian governance in this context. Common social interpretations of the determination of the security forces reinforced the tendency to avoid an all-out confrontation with the military-backed regime. In Algeria particularly, the perception that latent violence in society could resurface if the regime was to be swept away by an uprising strengthened these risk-averse attitudes. For those citizens who had experienced the civil conflict of the 1990s, the spectre of widespread violence was 'in everybody's mind'—even though this observation increasingly no longer applied to the youth.[74]

Morocco: a transition to pre-existing practices of contention

The reform agenda proposed by the Moroccan king on 9 March 2011 targeted three different constituencies. Firstly, it was aimed at the general public and any would-be protester enticed by the call of the 20 February Movement. Secondly, it was directed at the established political parties, which were still in the process of formalizing their strategy towards the protest movement. Thirdly, it addressed more broadly the international community and the foreign governments that had been most involved in the regional uprisings.

Internationally, by proposing a reform platform, the monarchy tried to convince foreign policy-makers that the Moroccan regime was not only different from the repressive systems of Tunisia or Egypt, but that it provided an alternative, negotiated solution to the havoc created at the time by the Libyan conflict. On 10 March 2011, the day following the king's speech, the palace-controlled Maghreb Arab Press (MAP) service duly provided for public consumption a lengthy selection of all the positive endorsements of the king's proposals by foreign governments. MAP stressed that the Spanish prime minister, José Luis Zapatero, responded 'very positively to the large-scale reform of the constitution announced by the king'. Similarly, from Washington, MAP reported comments by a spokesperson for the State Department, also welcoming the king's speech and indicating that Mohammed VI was 'a reformer', 'listening to his people' and 'taking appropriate action'. From London, after a meeting with the Moroccan foreign minister, his British counterpart, William Hague, also expressed his approval of this discourse, which constituted 'a strong indication that the king is listening to the demands of his people'. MAP similarly reported that the French president, Nicolas Sarkozy, had told the king that 'through the measures granted, His Majesty demonstrates his ever-present readiness to listen to his people, and his willingness to lead a peaceful but resolute evolution of his kingdom that enables it to keep adapting harmoniously to the transformation of our world.'[75] And Sarkozy added: 'In the troublesome period now encountered by the Arab world, the wisdom and foresight of His Majesty are a major factor for the stability of the entire region.' The following day, the French Foreign Ministry issued a statement indicating that the foreign minister, Alain Juppé, had phoned his Moroccan counterpart, Taieb Fassi Fihri, to tell him that such reforms heralded 'a historic change in Morocco'. Juppé stated that 'the lucid, courageous and visionary discourse of King Mohammed VI … creates the prospect of a serene and peaceful democratization process for Morocco and its model of governance, which can constitute an inspiration for the region.'[76]

The position of the French government revealed some of the difficulties that France and other international players had in rearticulating their Middle Eastern and North African policy. A few days earlier, during an official visit to post-Mubarak Egypt, Juppé had been keen to make amends for the tendency of Western policy makers to be 'intoxicated these past few years by arguments that said that the authoritarian regimes in place were the only bulwark against extremism'.[77] Emphasizing this tension, at the extraordinary European Council meeting of 11 March 2011 dedicated to the Libyan conflict, European leaders issued a joint communiqué supportive of the announcement of elections in post-Ben Ali Tunisia, of constitutional changes in post-Mubarak Egypt, and of the formation of a consultative committee to revise the constitution in Morocco.[78] Equally, at the United Nations, in his speech of 17 March 2011 calling for the adoption of a no-fly zone in Libya, the French foreign minister welcomed, alongside the democratic transitions in Tunisia and Egypt, the news that 'in Morocco, King Mohammed VI announced in a courageous and visionary speech the establishment of a constitutional monarchy'.[79] In an international context dominated by the prospects of military intervention in Libya, many foreign governments were so eager to believe in the possibility of a reformist pathway in the region that they equated the stated intentions of the Moroccan regime with actual political and institutional changes in the other countries of the Arab uprisings.

The form and timing of the Moroccan monarchy's response to the challenge of the 20 February Movement enabled the regime to convey a message to the international community. It signalled that there was a reformist approach to political change in the region that could strengthen democracy without a violent upheaval. This positioning helped foreign policy-makers to frame the strategy of the monarchy in a positive light, and in so doing they ended up discounting the actual demands of the protesters and minimizing the reluctance of the regime to address them. The emerging transnational connections made at the time between the 20 February Movement and European associative networks were in this context insufficient to force European governments to take into account popular resistance to the limited reforms offered by the Moroccan regime.[80] For foreign policy actors at the time, the new contestation created by the 20 February Movement was not seen as an effective counter-discourse or protest practice in the face of the reformist approach of the monarchy. As the endorsements of the actions of the king by foreign actors were reprised in the Moroccan press, this positive framing of the Moroccan regime constrained even further the options available domestically to the main political parties.

The Moroccan political parties had not anticipated the initial success of the 20 February Movement. Their ambiguous reaction to the protest and lack of clear strategy between the start of the protest and the announcement by the monarchy of a reform programme revealed their difficulties in dealing with a new practice of contestation disconnected from party politics. The formal positioning of the king in favour of a limited reform agenda conformed with their cautious response to the 20 February Movement. From a strategic perspective, for most established parties the street protests provided an opportunity to speed up political reforms that would strengthen their institutional role. In this perspective, it was important for the parties that the unrest should not purposely or inadvertently endanger the very institutional infrastructure that they inhabited. In mid-March, many dissident party cadres and members who had asked their party to support the 20 February Movement were placed in a difficult position by the opening of formal negotiations on constitutional reforms between the palace and the political parties. In a situation where many leading activists of the 20 February Movement chose to boycott the negotiations initiated by the palace, most of the parties' dissidents eventually decided to return to the fold of their political organizations. In early April, the dissidents of the Justice and Development Party (PJD), Ramid, Choubani and Hamidine, returned to the secretariat and became involved in the negotiations about constitutional reform. Similarly, the youth wing of the Socialist Union of Popular Forces (USFP), Shabiba, which had taken a stance in favour of the 20 February Movement early on, progressively changed its position in May in order to toe the party line. Smaoui and Wazif note that this evolution is to be understood not solely in relation to internal competition within the USFP, but also as an outcome of the dynamics of the 20 February Movement. The failure of the USFP dissidents to induce a policy shift within the party had meant that their influence also declined among the leadership of the 20 February Movement. This situation would eventually force the USFP activists back to the party, where they ended up supporting the constitutional referendum proposed by the monarchy.[81]

The decision of the main political parties to remain within established arenas and practices of contention and not push for a more ambitious reform programme was reflected in the proposals that they sent to the reform commission. In the main, they stayed within the framework already outlined by the king on 9 March and did not seek directly to challenge the dominance of the palace over parliament.[82] Only some of the smaller parties with ties to the 20 February Movement opposed openly the constitutional model proposed by the palace. In a communiqué dated 27 March, the Unified Socialist Party (PSU) spelled out its opposition to such limited reforms and demanded 'a true parliamentary monarchy on the model recognized around the world'.[83] Regarding the role of the king, the PSU added that 'one cannot invoke some religious quality to elevate oneself above the constitution'. At that time, the unequal competition between the main Moroccan parties and the smaller ones was not compensated for by a level of street mobilization that delegitimized the minimalist reform agenda of the monarchy. While the protests remained substantial throughout March and April, and the regime had to use police repression carefully to contain the unrest, the demonstrations did not generate an upward spiral of mobilization. Instead, the process of cooptation of parties by the regime and the disagreements on strategy within the 20 February coalition reduced the level of protest mobilization over time.[84]

After the king's speech, some of the leaders of the 20 February Movement had welcomed some of the proposals made. However, most of the leading activists of the movement wanted the regime to make further concessions.[85] The king had appointed Abdellatif Menouni at the head of the newly created Consultative Commission for the Revision of the Constitution (CCRC) on 10 March. Menouni invited several of the main social and political associations forming the 20 February Movement to participate in the debate over the reforms, and in doing so he exacerbated the internal tensions within the movement. Reflecting the views of many activists who did not trust the commission appointed by the palace, founding members of the 20 February Movement, including Oussama Khlifi, Abdallah Aballagh and Nizar Bennamate, refused Menouni's invitation. Several organizations, including the PSU and the Moroccan Human Rights Association, also declined to participate.[86] The Islamists of al-Adl wal-Ihsane for their part had not been invited. The daughter of Sheik Yassine, Nadia Yassine, had already declared that the promises made by the king were insufficient and that al-Adl wal-Ihsane would keep demonstrating alongside the 20 February Movement.[87]

Besides this effort at drawing protest actors into a formal, institutionalized process of negotiation, the regime used its patronage networks to undermine the dynamics of street mobilization. Smaoui and Wazif illustrated in the case of poor suburbs of Casablanca that local 'bigmen' used as relays between the local elites and the population positioned themselves differently in order to mobilize people for or against the regime at various points during the protests.[88] While some of these local actors supported the 20 February Movement at the beginning of the unrest, over time regime patronage provided enough rewards to these 'bigmen' that by the time of the referendum they mobilized their clients to vote yes to constitutional reforms. This process was evidently more than a mere cost-benefit analysis on their part—that is, raising the stakes in order to sell their services at a higher price. It was a complex and at times ambiguous evolution of their social strategy and worldview in changing circumstances. Smaoui and Wazif stress that at some stages these 'bigmen' did genuinely protest against the lack of involvement of the state in their community, even in the face of police repression. As with the case of the party dissidents, whatever cost-benefit analysis these actors made, their calculations were predicated on an evolving protest situation in which patronage was conditional on the ability of particular ruling elites to use the political system for profit. The successful (re-)cooptation of local actors into the networks of the regime made it clear that the unrest started by the 20 February Movement was no longer gaining momentum, and that repression by the regime had not produced a backlash.

The limited role played by repression in the spring of 2011 during the main period of activism of the 20 February Movement helped contain the situation mainly within pre-existing arenas of contention. The reign of Mohammed VI had been a period of renegotiation of the prerogatives of the security apparatus and of reassertion of civil liberties and political rights.[89] The actions of the 20 February Movement tested further some of the routine authoritarian practices of the Moroccan regime. While demonstrations and sit-ins had been commonly tolerated under Mohammed VI, once the weekly demonstrations of the 20 February Movement started, the police repeatedly, though not systemically, intervened to disperse these gatherings, especially in the main urban areas. This approach often left the protesters unsure of what to expect: 'We were disappointed and surprised by the intervention of the repressive forces,' said one participant about a brutally repressed demonstration in Casablanca a few days after the king's speech.[90] A leading member of the PSU present at the time saw it as 'a political fault and an action directed [by the prefect of Casablanca] against His Majesty, who had promised a strengthening of individual liberties'.[91]

This flexible repressive strategy of the security forces was informed by the trajectories of the other uprisings in the region, notably the Tahrir Square scenario. In this perspective, it was important for the regime that the protesters did not permanently occupy a significant public space in which more opposition to the regime could rally and which could become a focal point for the international media.[92] Repression was thus tailored to the location of the demonstrations and sit-ins, with the areas close to the centre of power in Rabat being more controlled than peripheral areas. In addition, gatherings in front of disputed symbols of the regime, such as the buildings of the security apparatus, were particularly targeted by repression. The headquarters of the National Surveillance Directorate (DST) in Temara, near the capital, an organization accused by human rights organizations of routinely using torture, was the location for a sit-in in mid-May that was put down particularly brutally.[93] This event marked the start of several weeks of increased police repression aimed in particular at demonstrations and sit-ins in the capital, Rabat, especially near official buildings.[94]

The boundaries of the arenas of contestation were also tested by the protesters themselves as they sought to mobilize ever larger numbers of participants. After a month and a half of regular protests, when weekly sit-ins became in some ways banal occurrences, some of the organizers of the 20 February Movement opted for marches through the city centre. These tactics, which recalled the marches of the workers' unions against the regime in the 1970s and 1980s, were less acceptable than sit-ins for the regime as a protest practice, and repression was usually harsher. In this case, too, the location of the marches was significant for the level of repression applied. Security forces targeted in particular those marches through the very centre of towns, as well as those starting from the most disadvantaged areas towards the centre. On the Egyptian Tahrir Square model, the Moroccan regime seemed to be particularly worried by the possibility of a mass mobilization of the people in the poorer suburbs which would overwhelm police units and occupy the town centre. Targeted repression also operated effectively in the new and old media. Instead of virulent denunciation of the 'traitors' à la Gaddafi, or technical control of the Internet traffic à la Ben Ali, the Moroccan regime let the more mainstream activists express themselves relatively unhindered online and in the press, while undermining their credentials behind the scene. Most of the critical cyber-activists had their websites, blogs, Facebook pages and emails hacked at one point or another by pro-regime hackers. Journalists too were targeted by the judicial system on trumped-up charges in order to dent their credibility and reduce their capacity for action. One of the most notable illustrations of this trend took place at the end of April 2011, with the jailing of Rachid Nini, the editor of the *Al-Massae* newspaper, one of the most read print media in the country. While he was officially found guilty and jailed for one year for having 'challenged institutional bodies and state officials' and 'endangered state security and national integrity', the underlying cause of his arrest was his denunciation of the DST torture at the time of the protests.[95]

Soon afterwards, to display his credentials as a reformer, the king showed his goodwill towards the opposition by freeing scores of political prisoners, notably Islamists.[96] He then announced more instrumentally a salary increase for civil servants and a rise in the basic pension rate. During this conciliatory phase, the security forces also reduced the level of repression against street demonstrators. While the protesters pushed the boundaries of the permissible in the Moroccan public sphere, the regime and the security forces in their turn adopted a gradual set of repressive responses that made some types of mobilization easier than others. Instead of trying to prevent protests as much as possible, the security forces targeted those protest actions that the regime found most subversive of the authoritarian status quo. The mobilization of the 20 February Movement had initiated a tentative reorganization of discourses and practices in social and political arenas. Over the weeks and months, however, the ability of the institutionalized actors to implement risk-averse strategies helped moderate the protest dynamics to the degree that it could once more be channelled into pre-existing routines of contentious politics.

6

DEMOBILIZATION AND RECONSTRUCTION OF THE ACTORS OF THE UPRISINGS

In the extraordinary situations of the 2011 uprisings, new practices and arenas of contestation shaped 'new' social and political actors. Any assessment of the actors leading or symbolizing change in the countries of the Arab uprisings has been and remains an arduous task for both practical and conceptual reasons. Empirically, the evaluation of the successes and failures of the pro- and anti-regime actors in this historical episode has lacked determinacy due to the fluidity of the situation after the uprisings. Conceptually, a major challenge has been to frame those actors that became prominent through the uprisings, without defining them mainly according to pre-existing social and political trends or identities. In some cases, it has been relatively easier to analyse the political trajectories of the uprisings, as they followed pre-existing patterns of regime change (as in Tunisia) or resilience (as in Algeria). The Tunisian Revolution can be said to have followed what Donatella Della Porta calls a process of 'eventful democratization'.[1] The emergence of liberal-democratic institutions in the post-uprising period enables us to track those 'new' actors who were not effectively politicized before or who significantly changed their behaviours and discourses to position themselves inside this normative and institutional framework. These actors then entrenched a model of governance that was sufficiently different from the old regime and sufficiently attuned to protesters' demands for the protesters to reduce their disruptive action to a level where routine, institutionalized state governance was again possible.

At the other end of the spectrum of change, Algeria illustrated the continuing relevance of established authoritarian processes and identities. In 'reformist' contexts, new practices and arenas of contestation only marginally transformed the behaviours and discourses of established actors, as emerging protest identities were unable to position themselves as credible alternatives to the prevailing authoritarian system. As new forms of mobilization failed to provide tangible outcomes, extraordinary protests reverted to standard expressions of discontent which authoritarian institutions had learnt to manage reasonably well. Whether in situations of change or stability, the establishment of post-uprising routines enabled the affirmation of new and old actors whose identity and practice were shaped by the trajectories of the uprisings. The strengthening of the patron–client networks of the regime and of the FLN in Algeria, the normalization of the PJD as party of government in Morocco's 'constitutional' monarchy, the institutionalization of Ennahda as the main political party in a functioning Tunisian electoral democracy, and the entrenchment of armed brigades as the main components of political order in a divided Libya were all actors affirmed or reaffirmed by the Arab uprisings in North Africa.

Entrenching the democratic actors of the Tunisian transition

The Tunisian Revolution did not end with the departure of Ben Ali. This event marked the high-water mark of revolutionary violence in the country and paved the way for a return to routine politics. Hence, social and political actors framed it retrospectively as the transformative event that marked the beginning of the institutional reconstruction of a democratic political system in the country. Many accounts of political change in Tunisia naturalized a posteriori this process of democratic transition, especially after the successful founding elections of 23 October 2011. In this way, the beginning of the revolt, the fall of Ben Ali, and the setting up of a functioning electoral democracy could be seamlessly woven into a democratic narrative about the 'Arab Spring', for which Tunisia was 'a beacon of hope'.[2] In practice, however, the transition from revolutionary behaviour and authoritarian deinstitutionalization to formal democracy in 2011 was an ambiguous process with multiple rationales and potentialities.[3] This ambiguity derived from the hazardous transformation of processes of mobilization against the regime into routine behaviours facilitating the institutionalization of democratic politics.

Causally, the mere vacation of power at the head of the state cannot explain why and how the anti-regime mobilization that had gained momentum up to that time would end. In Tunisia, the departure of Ben Ali was only one of many demands of the protesters. In effect, when the president left Tunisia on the evening of 14 January 2011, the deinstitutionalization of authoritarian governance that had prevailed in the country reached its highest point. There was de facto a power vacuum at the highest institutional level, a situation formalized by the imposition of a state of emergency. Retrospectively, the departure of Ben Ali would be portrayed as a transformative event that mobilized actors away from anti-regime protests and towards more participatory forms of political engagement. Yet, like earlier transformative events of the uprisings, such a framing of Ben Ali's departure is only meaningful as part of a new narrative about democratic revolution. It is a common observation that participants find it difficult to reach consensus about what a revolution is meant to achieve and, therefore, when mobilization has achieved its objectives.[4] Beyond the revolutionary dynamics, what needs to be understood is the re-emergence of routine institutionalized governance legitimized by the discourse and practice of electoral democracy.[5] In Tunisia, that the departure of President Ben Ali did not simply result in a palace coup, military takeover or descent into civil conflict shaped all subsequent framings of this event, as the end of the Tunisian Revolution. The successful organization of foundational elections in October 2011 signalled formally that a particular protest episode had ended in in the country. However, even this specific political outcome could not have been announced with much confidence in January 2011 when Ben Ali left, given the heightened uncertainty and deinstitutionalization that prevailed at the time.[6]

In January 2011, after the flight of Ben Ali, political instability and violence were in part the result of the continuing bottom-up mobilization of demonstrators who reoriented their anger and their calls for change at the newly created transitional government.[7] The most spectacular and effective grassroots mobilizations at this juncture were the sit-ins in the Kasbah of Tunis, starting on 23 January (Kasbah I) and 25 February (Kasbah II). 'We want to make a tabula rasa of twenty-three years of Ben Ali's rule,' said one angry demonstrator in the first Kasbah protest.[8] In part instability was also the top-down consequence of sudden and repeated changes of personnel at the head of state institutions, and the decreased ability of both newly appointed personnel and remaining old-regime figures to control their subordinates, especially in the security sector.[9] Besides the uncertainty generated by widespread unrest, the possibility of a democratic transition also depended on the decision of the military to stay out of politics and on the old-regime elites' role in facilitating the emergence of multipartyism. 'We are protecting the constitution,' said the chief of staff, General Ammar, at the time of the Kasbah protest; 'we will not act outside of its framework'.[10] During that period of deinstitutionalization, these three sets of interactions proved to be particularly important for producing a specific electoral and democratic end to the process of revolutionary mobilization.

Among the elites, many actors from the old regime started to reinvent their political identities and that of the state as soon as the president left the country. On the evening of 14 January, Prime Minister Mohamed Ghannouchi went on state television to announce that he was assuming power as interim president. As soon as Ghannouchi stepped in, his authority was questioned not only by the demonstrators, but by parts of the old elite and the opposition.[11] On 15 January, the Constitutional Council indicated that, according to their reading of the constitution, in cases where the president was unable to govern, his authority ought to be transferred to the president of parliament, Fouad Mebazaa. The main institutionalized opposition actors (from the UGTT to the political parties), who had initially agreed to the prime minister taking over, changed tack and endorsed the more legalistic transfer of power to Mebazaa. In a context of deinstitutionalization, these elites were concerned to maintain the formal legitimacy of state institutions and avoid giving further signs of political arbitrariness.[12] Indicative of the frailty of the new provisional authority was the call by state officials and UGTT representatives on state television that same evening for citizens to form vigilante committees to protect their neighborhoods against attacks from RCD activists and supporters of the old regime.[13]

More generally, the need for the state administration to perform once again its routine functions was particularly felt in Tunis, where food and petrol shortages were beginning to be noticeable.[14]

The process of formally reconstructing the identity of the regime through a democratic opening designed to strengthen institutional stability continued apace with the appointment of a 'government of national unity' to oversee political reforms on 17 January. Reflecting the frailty and malleability of these new political identities, on the following day four members of the national unity government representing 'civil society' resigned under pressure from the UGTT—itself under the pressure from the street—which was not satisfied with the significant number of apparatchiks from the old regime that had remained in government (notably Ahmed Friaa, the interior minister).[15] That evening, as several hundred demonstrators in front of the government buildings in central Tunis shouted 'The revolution goes on' and 'RCD out', Ghannouchi, the prime minister, and Mebazaa, the interim president, resigned from the RCD in an attempt to distance themselves and the provisional government from the former ruling party. In addition, the government appointed a High Commission for Political Reform, headed by the opposition lawyer Yadh Ben Achour, to oversee a process of constitutional and electoral reform designed to produce a more democratic institutional system. Publicly emphasizing the regime's change of identity, on 19 January Mebazaa declared on national television that he was ready 'to satisfy the legitimate aspirations of the revolt in order to bring to fruition this revolution for liberty and dignity'. He announced a general amnesty, complete freedom of expression, an independent judiciary and 'the separation of the state and the [RCD] party'.[16] To appease the protesters and distance themselves from the old regime, the new Tunisian authorities also had 33 members of Ben Ali's extended family and ruling circle arrested the following day. In addition, in response to demands from the opposition, the assets of the RCD were seized and the RCD members of the provisional government resigned from the party.[17] Despite this very public reorientation of the ruling elites, daily demonstrations continued throughout the week in the Kasbah to demand the resignation of the provisional government and the appointment of a new government without members of the previous administration. If we are opposed to the new government, said one of the protesters, 'it is because we fear that the ministers from the old regime will try to hide the truth regarding what took place before'.[18] On 27 January, Prime Minister Ghannouchi finally relented and organized a governmental reshuffle that removed former Ben Ali apparatchiks. While opposition politicians made some positive pronouncements about this step, popular discontent continued to focus on the person of Ghannouchi, the main figure of the old regime still in power. The following week, in another attempt to distance the new government from the old regime, the interior ministry banned all activities of the RCD and requested the courts to dissolve it.[19]

Throughout January 2011, the positioning of the military leadership was an important factor shaping both the end of the old regime and the direction of the political transition. After the fall of Ben Ali, many accounts of the role of the Tunisian army during the revolution and transition stressed that, unlike in the rest of the region, the Tunisian military had not been closely integrated in the regime.[20] The army was small and not particularly well equipped compared with the other security forces, and the officer corps was fairly professionalized, not least through the training it received in the United States. Robert Springborg and Clement Henry argue that 'the Tunisian military had few economic interests under its control. It was largely cut off from the patronage networks that enmeshed President Ben Ali, his family and a few other sycophantic hangers-on.'[21] There may also have been distrust between the top brass and Ben Ali, as there were lingering doubts over the role of the president in the 2002 plane crash that killed the previous chief of staff, General Abdelaziz Skik, and 13 of his senior officers.[22] However, while such overall considerations might have been accurate, they do not amount to an explanation of the actions of the military during and after the revolution.[23]

Looking back in time, many of the reasons advanced in 2011 to account for the refusal of the military to participate directly in Ben Ali's repressive strategy were not sufficient to generate opposition to Bourguiba's repressive strategy during the 1984 unrest. When in January 1984 rioting erupted throughout Tunisia and a state of emergency was declared, army units used live ammunition against the crowds in the streets of Tunis, as the police proved incapable of controlling the situation. Eventually, order was restored after several days of violence, when Bourguiba withdrew his unpopular economic policies.[24] In that particular context, the professionalization of the military and their non-involvement in politics meant that the army obeyed the orders given to them and repressed the demonstrators. Ware noted at the time that 'the military has resented having to assume a police function which belongs to other organs of security under civilian control'. He also remarked that 'a certain distrust between armed forces and Interior is beginning to make its appearance in the context of an uneasy feeling that the civilians cannot cope with the problems of social disorder'.[25] While these observations could appear potent in the context of the 2011 uprising, throughout the 1990s and the 2000s the issues of army morale, tensions between the branches of the security apparatus, and military corporate interests were hardly considered as serious problems for the regime.[26] At the same time, it is equally difficult to assert that because the military did not play a political role previously, it would remain politically neutral in a new political context.

The military top brass might not have had a personal agenda before the 2011 uprising, but neither did they have a record of opposition to the regime.[27] Journalistic reports in January and February 2011 indicated that there was a degree of suspicion among many social and political actors regarding the real intentions of the military leadership.[28] The multiple breakdowns of institutionalized politics after the fall of Ben Ali, which occasionally led to confrontation between different branches of the state security apparatus, gave the military new opportunities to (re-)define its role in the country. As Ben Ali left the country, the military leadership recognized the legitimacy of Prime Minister Ghannouchi and General Ammar resumed his role as chief of staff at the request of the prime minister. As multiple transfers of power took place at the top of the security apparatus—e.g. Ben Ali's security chief was arrested, the interior minister was dismissed—security actors competed with each other to establish their authority. Within a few days, the military chain of command began to supplant that of other security agencies set up by Ben Ali, and army units began to take charge of law and order. For some time, the army had to deal with both anti-regime demonstrators and security personnel still supporting the old regime. On 16 January, notably, army units had to launch an assault on the presidential palace where the presidential guard, faithful to Ben Ali, refused to stand down. Meanwhile, for several days numerous clashes between army units and National Guard and police units occurred in Tunis and in several other towns.[29] For the transitional government, the involvement of the army in routine policing was a pragmatic policy choice to deal with tasks that the police units, having spearheaded the repression, could not easily perform in the early post-Ben Ali period.[30] "The police had exited town,' commented a doctor from Bizerte, 'leaving the town on its own.'[31]

On 24 January, in a rare public intervention, General Ammar made a speech in front of a crowd of protesters in the centre of Tunis. Telling demonstrators who were calling for the resignation of the provisional government that 'our revolution is your revolution', he encouraged them to listen to the new authorities and not create chaos that would play into the hands of the 'enemies of the state'.[32] At the time, this public appearance of the chief of staff appeared as an expression of support for the democratic political transition, and not as a declaration of military intent to take charge of politics.[33] In Tunisia, the military chose not to take advantage of the state of emergency and of repeated challenges from below against the provisional government. They did not visibly push for greater inclusion of their corporate interests through closer association with the political decision-making process, nor did they visibly back specific political actors. Material constraints (such as manpower, equipment, training) as well as the relative success of the process of reinstitutionalization certainly facilitated this choice, but it remained nonetheless a contingent outcome that is only partially explained by the reasons given by these actors subsequently.

In the 'revolutionary' camp, on 11 February the formation of the National Council for the Protection of the Revolution brought together 28 political parties, many from the left, as well as the Islamists of Ennahda, the UGTT, the Bar Association and several human rights organizations, in an attempt to structure the demands of the opposition and put pressure on the provisional government. These opposition actors also used this National Council to solidify their claims to lead the process of political transition and to speak in the name of the protesters. Despite the risk of implosion, this coalition remained reasonably united throughout February and became de facto the main institutionalized body of the protest movement. It was, however, only partially able to control the protest dynamics, as the Kasbah I and II demonstrations against the provisional government showed. This unrest culminated in a mass demonstration on 25 February in the Kasbah of Tunis when over 100,000 people demanded Ghannouchi's resignation.[34] This constituted the largest protest event in the country since the fall of Ben Ali. To diffuse popular defiance against the transitional government, Ghannouchi finally decided to resign in favor of Beji Caid Essebsi on 27 February.[35] As Essebsi took the reins of the transitional process, a swift process of legalization of political parties—including Ennahda on 1 March—gave momentum to the democratic transition among the elites and (at least part of) the population. In turn, the working agreement between the former state elites and the main opposition actors helped to channel popular discontent towards more formal bargaining processes (including strikes) and weakened the appeal of protests to bring down the system. To buttress the legitimacy of his new provisional government, Essebsi facilitated the inclusion and institutionalization of the opposition-led National Council for the Protection of the Revolution. In early March, the government nominated a High Commission for the Realization of the Objectives of the Revolution, Political Reform and Democratic Transition, charged with overseeing the process of transition to democracy.[36] The High Commission was effectively a merger between the National Council and the Ben Achour Commission. It stamped a 'revolutionary' identity on the actions of the new government, which assisted the progressive realignment of popular demands and state governance.

On 3 March, the High Commission announced a 'road map' for the democratic transition, which included the election of a national constituent assembly to draft a new constitution. This was formalized by a presidential decree the following month. Parliament (on 7 March), followed by the senate (on 9 March), voted for a law allowing the interim president, Fouad Mebazaa, to issue law-like decrees without consulting parliament and senate (which thereby surrendered their constitutional legitimacy) until the election of a new constituent assembly later in the year. On 9 March the RCD was also dissolved, and the High Commission proposed a (presidential) decree that excluded any RCD leader and any Ben Ali minister from all political activities for ten years. By making the legislature and the lawmakers of the old regime redundant, the provisional government cleared the way for a democratically elected constituent assembly with revolutionary credentials—the combination of these two aspects being particularly important at the time. Finally, on 23 March, the High Commission also suspended the Ben Ali-era constitution and replaced it with Decree 14, outlining the provisional organization of state authorities and empowering the provisional government with executive and legislative authority. That these executive and legislative changes did not entrench another form of autocratic governance in the country was facilitated by the 'pre-institutionalization' of the role of the opposition in this political system, most significantly through the involvement of the National Council for the Protection of the Revolution within the High Commission. Composed of 71 members at the beginning of March, the High Commission grew to 120 members by the end of the month and it finally reached 155 members in April as it sought to increase representativeness. [37] The High Commission became in this respect the principal tool to ensure the operationalization of the process of democratic transition, not least through the revision of the electoral code and the scheduling of parliamentary elections. [38]

If the departure of Ben Ali had marked the highest point of revolutionary deinstitutionalization, the 25 February Kasbah II demonstrations marked the beginning of revolutionary demobilization, as no protest would reach this size and intensity again in the transitional period. The departure of Prime Minister Ghannouchi had removed an important symbol of the old regime that protesters could easily frame as the embodiment of their discontent with the state. The new provisional government nominated by Essebsi on 7 March continued to face popular resistance and more or less violent mass demonstrations, but never again on the same scale. Tellingly, this winding down of the protest dynamics, as the failed Kasbah III mobilization showed, occurred even though some members of the new Essebsi government had obvious connections with the old regime (notably Habib Essid, the interior minister). [39] In the weeks that followed, the discourse of the protesters also became noticeably different, turning away from demands for a change of government and reverting to demands for policy changes. As the Kasbah III protest ended, thousands of people came together in another suburb of Tunis at a meeting organized on the theme 'Let us build our country, let us study and work'.[40] In March and April, the discourses about revolution that had become ubiquitous at the beginning of the year and that remained effective in mobilizational terms slowly gave way to another set of mobilizational symbols and mechanisms focusing on producing a working electoral democracy.[41] The growing success of these new discourses and behavioural routines could be witnessed over the ensuing weeks and months, notably in the lack of mobilization induced by various difficulties or failures of the new 'democratic' institutions and processes.[42] The publication of regulations for the new electoral system and constituent assembly, initially scheduled for the end of March, was postponed to mid-April without generating disquiet. The date of the foundational elections, first announced for the end of July, was moved to the end of October, again without generating much overt concern for the democratic transition.[43] Even the withdrawal from the High Commission of the increasingly influential Ennahda party on 27 June, following a spat over the rules for the organization of the elections, only minimally disrupted the start of the electoral campaign. In practice, even without the formal involvement of the Islamist party, the High Commission was able to generate a wide political consensus, which informally included Ennahda, about the role of the electoral commission, the electoral code, party financing and freedom of association.[44]

As the time of the elections drew nearer, social and political mobilization was increasingly channelled through party activism.[45] Finally, the democratic transition was marked by the formal deinstitutionalization of those institutions that were the direct products of the revolution. On 13 October, ten days before the elections, Mebazaa, the interim president, brought to a close the activities of the High Commission. The fairly straightforward election of representatives for the Tunisian National Constituent Assembly on 23 October 2011 formally marked the end of the period of deinstitutionalization in the polity and the beginning of new routine governance legitimized by electoral democracy. Ennahda came first in the elections with 37 per cent of the votes, followed by the Congress for the Republic (CPR) (9 per cent) and Ettakatol (7 per cent). The three parties constituted a ruling coalition (troika), with Moncef Marzouki (CPR) becoming president of the Republic, Mustapha Ben Jafar (Ettakatol) becoming president of the

Constituent Assembly and Hamadi Jebali (Ennahda) prime minister. This last transformative event marked the end of the period of democratic transition and the beginning of a new narrative less grounded on the revolution or on democratic transition than on democratic consolidation. The emergence of this new narrative consolidated post hoc explanations of the 'revolution' that were concerned less with actual depictions of these events from an actor's perspective than with building a consensus around a democratic revolution narrative.[46] This new narrative and its institutional embodiments would then increasingly define a posteriori the identities and behaviours of the actors of the Tunisian uprisings, revolution and democratic transition.

Democratic and military transition in Libya

The international military intervention in Libya led by French, British and American armed forces set apart the process of (re)construction of the actors in the Libyan revolution from the rest of the North African uprisings. From March to October 2011 Libya was characterized by a situation of multiple sovereignties.[47] Rather than a sudden wave of protests followed by regime change or 'reform', Libya witnessed a more protracted episode of civil war during which political authority was directly linked to military occupation of territories. For many months, violent retribution by the regime became the de facto answer to the demands for justice and respect for rights and liberties that were voiced at the start of the protests. A war economy was the de facto answer to the demands for socio-economic reforms, in both regime-controlled and rebel-held territories. Unlike in neighbouring countries, where new or reformed political processes diverted social and political actors away from violent revolutionary behaviour, in Libya the behaviours of protest actors were shaped by the militarization of the uprising for a significant period of time. This form of socialization created political opportunities that were not readily available in the other countries of the Arab uprisings (with Syria becoming the next country to illustrate this trend from 2012 onwards).

The militarization of the Libyan civil conflict helped to professionalize the revolutionary actors. Armed groups initially created to resist the repression of the security forces became over time more professional military units with offensive capabilities. This militarization and professionalization of the regime's opponents were also tied to external military support, which helped structure the armed resistance and provided military training.[48] The routinization of military confrontation and the development of a war economy contributed in their turn to the entrenchment of local power centres and to the legitimization of their rule.[49] Even in the tumultuous settings of a civil conflict, insurgents were able to re-establish a quasi-institutional system of governance at the local level—the besieged town of Misrata provides a vivid illustration of this process.[50] During the civil war (and, indeed, for most of the period of political transition that followed), anti-regime behaviours were expressed in and mediated by local patterns of interactions, not least revenge actions. 'It is difficult to control a revolution,' said a rebel commander, 'it is a difficult situation and we wouldn't know how to stop it.'[51] This situation strengthened the ideational and material capacity of local power centres at the expense of a central authority.[52] The de facto legitimacy of local authorities was already visible during the conflict in multiple high-profile disputes between them and the National Transitional Council (NTC) which were not resolved in favour of the latter.[53] From a security perspective in particular, the National Liberation Army, which the NTC had formally established, failed to become a unified military structure that could control large revolutionary brigades, both during the conflict and after the fall of Gaddafi.

For the NTC, the strategic necessity of maintaining internal divisions to a minimum during the conflict meant that discussions and agreements about the structure of the post-Gaddafi regime were not particularly developed, even as the regime began to fall apart in the summer of 2011. The preamble of the Libyan interim constitutional declaration issued by the NTC on 3 August 2011 stated that the new political system being set up in the country came 'in response to the desire of the Libyan people and their hopes to achieve democracy'.[54] The production of the document itself was a top-down formulation of a political framework that formalized the Council's leadership and set out broad guidelines for the establishment of new political institutions. While this document was well received by those foreign governments supporting the NTC, it was mainly ignored by the revolutionary brigades, as it said little about the security apparatus.[55] In effect, the centrifugal trends within the insurgents' camp were strengthened as brigades began to score significant victories against Gaddafi's troops. After the capture of Tripoli in August 2011, brigade commanders became even more reluctant to follow a central command and even more wary of competitors on their side.[56] Days after planning a joint military operation against Gaddafi's forces in the capital, the revolutionary brigades from different Libyan regions that had participated to the fight tried to boost their position within the insurgents' camp by carving out for themselves areas of exclusive control in the capital. This set the scene for an uneasy coexistence between the units of the Tripoli Revolutionary Council (headed by Abdullah Naker) and the Tripoli Military Council (led by the former LIFG commander Abdelhakim Belhadj), alongside powerful brigades from Misrata and Zintan. To maintain the peace and retain the brigades' support, the NTC sought to formalize this situation by appointing the commanders of the most important factions to key ministerial positions. Misrata's brigade leader, Fawzi Abdul A'al, and Zintan's brigade leader, Osama al-Juwaili, were thus nominated to head the interior and defence ministries respectively.

The situation prevailing in the capital after the fall of the old regime signalled the resilience of the militarized behaviours and identities generated by the conflict. 'The people in the West say, "We paid a huge price, and we want to be in charge", and Misrata the same,' summarized an NTC member at the time.[57] Both before and after the official end of the 2011 Libyan conflict, the Misrata and Zintan brigades ignored calls from the NTC to disarm and vacate their positions in the capital. Instead, they boosted their operational capabilities by taking control of the military bases of the former regime and looting their arsenals.[58] Fully aware that their strong bargaining positions vis-à-vis the NTC and the new government depended on their retaining a distinct military chain of command, the brigade leaders kept alive the discourse of military professionalization and revolutionary legitimacy in the post-Gaddafi period. The formal cooptation of brigade commanders into the state security apparatus without an accompanying centralization of the command structure of the different brigades was an important feature of the Libyan security system during the period of democratic transition. After the official end of the conflict on 23 October 2011, the efforts of the NTC to redirect revolutionary actors away from their previous practices and towards more routine electoral behaviours occurred in parallel with the consolidation of militarized identities and practices. 'We have sacrificed for this revolution and you haven't, and now we will take what we want,' a young fighter told a Tripoli businessman after seizing his property.[59] Commonly in periods of political transitions, actors who remain primarily defined by their revolutionary discourses and behaviours find it difficult to organize in the face of the legal and repressive apparatus of a relegitimized state system. In the Libyan case, the transitional period was also, and in some cases above all, a post-conflict situation in which many of the former revolutionaries could back their claims with military force and thus better compete with the new state institutions. The post-revolutionary construction of a democratic political system in Libya was characterized by the recurrence of military actions draped in revolutionary rhetoric designed to challenge the new regime.[60] One of the earliest illustrations of this tension was the refusal by the Zintan brigade to hand over Gaddafi's son, Saif al-Islam, to the NTC authorities after his capture on 19 November 2011.[61] It was one of the many interactions between the central government and local power centres that underscored the continuation of a de facto system of multiple sovereignties in the country.

The situation in the town of Misrata at the beginning of 2012 provided a new illustration of these centre–periphery dynamics, ahead of Libya's foundational elections scheduled for that summer. On 20 February 2012, Misrata was the first major city to hold local elections in post-Gaddafi Libya. Over 100,000 voters were able to choose between 28 independent candidates for their new local council. In the process, they elected a new town major, Yousef Ben Yousef, to replace Khalifa al-Zwawy, who had headed the council during the civil conflict. The persistence of a pattern of dual sovereignty was visible on election day, as the military brigades that provided security for this event did not consider that the elected council had authority over them. A brigade member securing a polling booth declared at the time: 'We'll give them a bit of time, because we are starting from zero. If they do something good for the country, then fine. But otherwise we'll remove them just as we removed Gaddafi. It will be another revolution.'[62] Like the Misrata City Council and the Misrata Military Council during the conflict, civilian and military organizations collaborated but maintained distinct authority structures. Even the successful mobilization of voters, with a respectable 57 per cent turnout in Misrata, did not imply the demobilization of the brigades or the abandonment of 'revolutionary' strategies (that is, extra-constitutional political change) in favour of electoral politics. In practice, after these local elections, elected Misratan politicians were no more in a position to control the actions of the Misratan revolutionary brigades than they were before, and their repeated calls for the brigades to disarm or leave Tripoli went unheeded.[63] In these situations, democratic legitimacy did not straightforwardly trump revolutionary legitimacy.

At the national level, the NTC faced a predicament similar to that of the local councillors during the transitional period when they sought to create new, centralized military and police institutions. Frederic Wehrey stresses that the NTC not only had to confront brigade commanders and fighters who did not place electoral legitimacy above revolutionary legitimacy, but it also had to deal with the deep suspicion of former rebels towards those members of the army and police that had served under Gaddafi before defecting.[64] This tension translated into an unwillingness on the part of the brigades to follow the leadership of politicians associated with the old regime and to serve under the command of officers linked to the old regime. In February 2012 scores of small brigades from the Tripoli region agreed to join forces to form the Military Council of West Libya. Representatives of the new coalition stressed that this show of unity was a means to pressure more effectively the transitional government to reform itself and particularly to revise its policy of integrating security personnel within a new military and police structure. The leader of the newly created Military Council, Colonel Mokhtar Fernana, declared that the NTC committee in charge of integrating revolutionary fighters was attempting to 'hijack the revolution' by taking in men who had fought for Gaddafi.[65] One of his fellow commanders on the Council concurred and added that in this context his fighters 'would not give up their arms to a corrupt government'.

Such tensions and resistance throughout the country meant in practice the continuation of multiple, parallel security structures with overlapping responsibilities and often conflicting relations. Throughout the transitional period, the NTC had sought to defuse post-conflict tensions gradually and indirectly by offering mainly financial incentives to former fighters to integrate within its new security structures. Paul Salem and Amanda Kadlec note that, while by March 2012 almost 80,000 ex-fighters had registered for an integration programme that gave them a salary in exchange for leaving their brigade or militia, there were few measures in place to monitor their actual behaviour. They point out that, in practice, 'among those that registered, only a minority have actually been integrated into the army and police, while many others continue serving in militia brigades, arguing that their compensation is for the security service they are providing in their area'.[66] If the transition period marked the beginning of the formal implementation of a system of electoral democracy and the mobilization of citizens as voters, it did not empower political mechanisms that entirely superseded those of the mobilization of citizens as fighters.

In parallel, while the entrenchment of local power centres meant that regional divisions were routinely expressed as opposition to central rule, this process did not give rise to a regionalist reorganization of political authority. Rather, it added another layer of complexity to the multiple sovereignties already created by the armed brigades. In the Nafusa Mountains, for instance, there were palpable tensions between the Berber brigades and the Arab units of the Zintan brigade. While both sets of actors put pressure on the central government to advance their agenda, they repeatedly clashed with each other in the region.[67] In the eastern region of Cyrenaica, revolutionary brigades reorganized themselves in larger coalitions, with the Barqa Military Council and the Union of Revolutionary Brigades emerging in the spring of 2012 as two of the most powerful groups.[68] In March 2012, at a meeting of 3,000 tribal and local leaders in Benghazi, the newly created (civilian) Council of Barqa called for a federal solution for the region of Barqa (Benghazi and historic Cyrenaica) and appointed as their representative Ahmed al-Senussi, a descendant of King Idris. The high visibility of the Barqa Council, due notably to their support of the blockade of the main coastal road and, later, of the oil terminals, did not signify the emergence of a cohesive political and military Cyrenaican entity.[69] In effect, other brigades in the eastern region not supporting the federalist agenda or Barqa leadership worked to undermine their actions, politically and militarily.[70]

At the time of Libya's foundational elections on 7 July 2012, the identity and behaviours of many important armed actors had not significantly changed from the time of the fall of Gaddafi. Although in the aftermath of the civil conflict, the 'revolutionary' brigades were starved of 'revolutionary' action, friction over the distribution of resources, security interventions on behalf of the new state authorities, and the brigades' own efforts to influence elected politicians created sufficient room for alternative political rationales to remain alive. Although the NTC had some success in promoting the democratic electoral process as a political avenue for members and leaders of armed groups, fighters retained in parallel an allegiance to their 'revolutionary' military leadership. The results of the 2012 parliamentary elections themselves illustrated that the civil conflict, despite its unifying anti-Gaddafi rhetoric, reinforced many of the tribal, ethnic and regional divides that had been played upon by Gaddafi.[71] Although Libya's foundational elections were reasonably free and fair in the circumstances, the fragmented parliament that resulted ensured the continuing weakness of the national political elites. In this context, the revolutionary brigades, when they were not primarily concerned with translating their military capital into economic advantages, accompanied their support for electoral democracy with a particular agenda regarding how to deal with the remnants of the old regime. Their reluctance to disarm, demobilize or be formally placed under the control of the central government in part reflected the importance of this 'revolutionary mission'.

The direct and forceful intervention of the brigades into politics, and their temporary confiscation of the state authority when they deemed it necessary, continued after the 2012 elections. The blockade of parliament by gunmen protesting again ministerial nominations on 1 November 2012 was one of the first blatant illustrations of how failure to deconstruct war identities and behaviours undermined democratic consolidation.[72] The primacy of force over dialogue and of revolutionary rhetoric over political compromise was reaffirmed early in 2013 when armed brigades coerced the elected parliament into voting for a law on 'political isolation' that applied to anyone having held an official position at any time in the Gaddafi regime.[73] This policy in turn intensified the dynamics of socio-economic and political exclusion in the country and undermined the ability of the new regime to act as a fair arbiter. The identities and behaviours of the actors of the Libyan uprisings, revolution, civil war and democratic transitions thus continued to be shaped after the elections by this dual dynamic of political centralization through electoral democracy and social fragmentation through the continuation of armed militancy.

Reasserting authoritarian routines and normalizing discontent in Algeria

By March 2011 it was clear that the Arab uprisings would not impact on Algeria in the way it had done on its eastern neighbours. While Tunisia increasingly institutionalized a dynamic of democratic transition and Libya witnessed a routinization of militarized interactions, Algeria reverted to known mechanisms of authoritarian governance. Neither the leaderless riots of January nor the political protests of February had created enough momentum for new dynamics of mass mobilization to become entrenched. No event had been recognized as sufficiently 'transformative' by large swathes of the Algerian population to enable the transformation of protest behaviours into a system-challenging mass phenomenon. In addition, the regime's own response to the partial disruption of established authoritarian routines in January and February did not itself lead to a greater destabilization of the dominant practices of governance. Rather, the regime's strategy encouraged the consolidation of the contentious practices, arenas and actors that predated the uprisings. By March 2011 it was quite conspicuous that such 'routine' instances of unrest were again becoming widespread. In Algiers, these included, for instance, a crowd of 100–200 youths throwing Molotov cocktails at the police on 16 March, and a slightly larger crowd of protesters attacking in a similar way the police and contractors coming to bulldoze a shantytown on 23 March.[74] A few weeks later, during a similarly violent confrontation in another shantytown, an inhabitant insisted that these people were not 'rioters' but 'people who made demands' and who 'asked for nothing more than their right [to live there]'.[75] A return to 'normality' in Algeria in the spring of 2011 did not mean the end of violent social unrest. Instead, it translated into the routinization of discontent within mobilizational pathways that were non-threatening for the ruling elite. This evolution resulted in part at least from a strategic effort by the regime to address the material demands of three categories of actors: unionized workers, security personnel, and social and political entrepreneurs.

In March 2011, socio-economic protests led to at least 70 instances of strike action in the country by professional associations and unions, from teachers to railway workers and from doctors to court clerks.[76] The dynamics of these strikes provided a good illustration of the social contract which the regime entrenched to legitimize its rule in the face of structured contestation. On each occasion, the state administration agreed to provide better social and economic incentives in exchange for the (grudging) quiescence of the strikers and an end to the strikes. In practice, in response to the challenges of January and February, the government opened up its coffers to entice protesters to revert to pre-existing negotiated protest tactics by giving these a higher probability of success. In this particular context, the Algerian government was simply inclined to settle financially any claim that was being voiced forcefully enough. As Ali Chibani remarked at the time, 'this position of weakness is well understood by Algerians who understand that now is the time to obtain promotions, improve their working condition and their social circumstances'.[77] As the administration kept responding positively to the demands of the strikers, it incited other groups to organize similar actions, which were addressed in a similar way.[78] The demands of the protesters as much as the response of the administration illustrated that these routine forms of opposition, despite their recurrence and number, had entrenched a consensus about asking the regime to change its policies rather than encouraging thinking about regime change. Even the surprisingly strong students' demonstration of April 2013 was less about 'regime out!' than 'Harraoubia [the education minister] out!' and better job opportunities after graduating.[79] That month, nonetheless, the security forces would fence off Martyrs' Square in central Algiers to avoid any accidental duplication of a Tahrir Square situation.

The ability of the Algerian regime to reorient system-challenging unrest into more mundane benefit-seeking protests has long been a function of the instrumentalization of the oil rent by the ruling elites. Luis Martinez argues that the utilization of the oil and gas rent by successive Algerian governments illustrates less a concern with developing a viable national economy than with creating patronage structures to ensure the dependence of social and political actors (and the population at large) on the ruling elites.[80] Authoritarian resilience had long been bolstered by a form of economic 'mismanagement' that strengthened the importance of the regime's patron–client connections. In the spring of 2011, the Algerian regime relied heavily on this particular mechanism of governance to generate an economically unsustainable but politically advantageous use of the oil rent. In addition to specific concessions on salaries made to various striking sectors, public spending increased by a massive 25 per cent (from 64 to 80 billion euros) in the amended 2011 budget.[81] To improve the cost of living more generally, the Algerian government had scrapped its 5 per cent tax on imports, its 17 per cent VAT tax on food products, and an array of taxes on private businesses. These generous pay-outs were possible because of the utilization of the country's (oil and gas) 'stabilization fund', which contained $155 billion in foreign currency reserves at the time.[82] The Algerian finance minister himself recognized at the time that this spending policy could only constitute a short-term option for the government.[83] With an ever-larger public sector and ever-increasing public sector wage bill, the health of Algerian finances depended on a continuous rise in oil and gas prices.[84] Although the fire-fighting tactics adopted by the regime during the uprisings had worsened the medium-term economic prospects for the country, this was a price that the ruling elites were more than willing to pay in the circumstances.

The regime's drive towards consolidating rent-seeking behaviours was also a strategic effort to ensure the continuing support of the security forces for the ruling elites. While the cohesiveness of the officers' corps derived in part from their socialization of patterns, not least during the war of independence and the civil conflict of the 1990s, it also rested on more materialistic considerations. These included not only an ever-increasing military budget for the leadership to redistribute to their clientele, but also a more direct involvement in public and private sector ventures. Looking back at the process of economic liberalization of the late 1980s to early 1990s, Steven Cook proposes a mafia imagery to describe the role of generals acting as 'godfathers' for entrepreneurs seeking business licences and distribution contracts, and taking a share of the profits in return.[85] The socio-economic rewards associated with the military had come under threat during the civil conflict but were reasserted during the Bouteflika presidency. Unsurprisingly, as internal competition for these new opportunities increased in the 2000s, key military figures were involved in various corruption scandals, most spectacularly in relation to the national oil company, Sonatrach, in 2010.[86]

During the decade of the 2000s, the military and security budget of Algeria had kept increasing year on year.[87] Significantly, just before the eruption of social and political unrest in 2011, the government announced in December 2010 that the wages in the police (totalling 170,000 personnel) were to increase by a massive 50 per cent and to include a three-year back-pay deal. In the same way, in December 2011 the salaries of military personnel were similarly increased by a sizeable 40 per cent, also with a three-year back-pay package.[88] In doing so, the ruling elites ensured that the social contract proposed to the Algerian population, involving immediate socio-economic gratification in exchange for quiescence, was also applied to the rank-and-file members of the security apparatus to ensure their loyalty. In the security sector, these benefits were provided in exchange for more active support of the regime, demonstrated by a willingness to suppress protests when commanded to do so by their hierarchy.

The final component of the regime's strategy of normalizing unrest concerned social and political entrepreneurs. In April 2011, the Algerian president unveiled on national television a programme of political reforms designed to 'deepen the democratic process and to enable the citizens to better contribute to the choices that shape their future'.[89] This limited initiative focused mainly on a modification of the electoral code to facilitate the creation of new political parties within the pre-existing pseudo-democratic political system. The first consequence of this initiative was to reaffirm the divisions between pro-governmental organizations, which supported it, and the main opposition parties and civil society organizations, which decided to boycott the consultative reform process. A more medium-term impact of this reform was the expansion of the regime's patronage network through business politics after the formation of new political parties. This process was facilitated by the multiplication of micro-parties—the number of parties nearly doubled in 2011, from twenty-two to forty. The great majority of these new parties were either splinter groups from pre-existing organizations—especially the former state party, the FLN; the pro-regime RND, as well as the co-opted Islamist party, the MSP—or vehicles for self-promotion by personalities and businessmen close to the regime.[90] 'They are killing the last remaining shreds of interest that we had for politics,' commented a Kabyle youngster during the electoral campaign; 'we see on posters candidates without any morality who never had any political engagement in their life.'[91]

In this context, mobilization for the parliamentary elections of May 2012, as well as the elections themselves, did not bring many surprises. The multiplication of opposition parties in a winner-takes-all system boosted, by default, the electoral performance of the established parties, especially the FLN, which fell just short of an absolute majority in parliament—it obtained 221 seats out of 462, even though it only received about 17 per cent of the votes.[92] The micro-parties that the regime had encouraged in order to make the political field appear more pluralistic ended up strengthening an ultra-dominant party system. This more pluralistic pseudo-democratic system received the approval of the main international supporters of the regime, including France and the United States.[93] Domestically, however, these electoral results generated a usual level of suspicion and incredulity among the Algerian public and political society, and strengthened the already well-established drive towards both formal depoliticization and clientelism. In Algeria, more than anywhere else in the region at that time, the reforms proposed by the regime and the post-uprising political divisions favoured the status quo.

Reforming authoritarian cooptation in Morocco

The principal strategy of the Moroccan regime in the aftermath of the unrest initiated by the 20 February Movement was to consolidate the identities and practices of those political actors that had agreed upon a negotiated approach to political change. On 17 June 2011 the king of Morocco formally announced the constitutional reforms devised by the reform commission and set 1 July as the date for a referendum on the new constitution. In so doing, the palace sought to move public debates further away from the protest practices of the 20 February Movement and towards routine voting behaviour. In the weeks preceding this announcement, the regime had bet on a loss of momentum of the 20 February Movement demonstrations and sought to speed up the process of demobilization by increasing the level of repression.[94] Although in May–June 2011 the protests were less powerful than they had been in February–March, they still constituted a visible and recurring challenge to the state authorities, and a source of new behaviours and identities. Starting in mid-May, the security apparatus stepped up its use of repression against the protesters to limit the scope of demonstrations.[95] The bombing of a tourist area in Marrakesh on 28 April, orchestrated by Islamists linked to al-Qaeda, provided a useful context for the hardening of security measures.[96] The government stressed that the police only responded to provocations from protesters, and blamed the ongoing wave of protests for the increasing socio-economic difficulties experienced by ordinary Moroccans.

By organizing the referendum on the constitution, the monarchy sought to formalize its elite-driven political consensus as a working alternative to the demands of the 20 February Movement.[97] The constitutional reforms devised by the (palace-appointed) drafting committee followed closely what the king had proposed on 9 March, and they received an implicit go-ahead from the main political parties participating in the consultation process.[98] As soon as the campaign for the referendum started, all the main Moroccan parties campaigned in favour of a yes vote for the new constitution. The monarchy also mobilized its own patronage networks to generate additional support among other actors in civil society, such as the Sufi orders. On 25 June, the Boutchichia Sufi brotherhood gathered several thousands of its supporters in Casablanca for one of the largest pro-constitution demonstrations.[99] 'We didn't have to pay for the bus fare,' pointed out one of the *imams* of the brotherhood; 'the Islamic Affairs Ministry asked us to come to Casablanca and we did so happily.'[100] In this case, the cooptation of the brotherhood was facilitated by the role played by of one of its prominent members, Ahmed Toufiq, who also headed the ministry of Islamic affairs. Pro-regime mobilization in the Islamic public sphere also involved pressuring imams (as civil servants) to call for a yes vote for the new constitution in their Friday sermons.[101]

Effective mobilization by the regime of co-opted social and political actors during the very short campaign for the referendum helped drown out the critical voices from the 20 February Movement who had called for a boycott. This dynamic was facilitated by the use of intimidation and repression to control the flow of information, including pressures on the domestic media not to broadcast messages in favour of a boycott.[102] By running a short campaign and hindering open discussion, the regime sought to avoid the reopening of a public debate on the monarchy's role in the political system. Opponents had long argued that the reforms did not go far enough, and they had criticized in particular the political prerogatives of the king (such as the power to nominate governors and judges). Directly or indirectly, these criticisms targeted the very identity of the monarchy as near absolute and the role of the king as commander of the faithful.[103] However, neither before nor during the referendum campaign was this opposition sufficiently effectively relayed by powerful street protests and the media to challenge the discourse of the institutionalized elites. In this context, it came as little surprise that the results of the referendum formally validated the traditional political role of the monarchy and revealed that the king was in charge of the reform agenda. The official results announced a participation rate of 73.5 per cent, with the share of the yes vote totalling 98.5 per cent of the votes cast. Although opposition actors expressed concern about flaws in the electoral system, voters did not perceive that vote rigging had reached such new heights that it required them to take action.[104] For all its failings, the referendum process facilitated the beginning of the transition from street protest to formal politics. This transition was speeded up later that month when the king called early parliamentary elections. On 30 July, in his annual speech from the throne, Mohammed VI announced the holding of new parliamentary elections in the fall of 2011 as a means to entrench the new political agreement embedded in the constitution.

For the leadership and the militants of the main political parties, this announcement completed the move away from contentious politics and marked the beginning of electoral campaigning. Political mobilization centred on the parliamentary elections weakened the mobilization of the 20 February Movement, as public debates refocused on the competing agendas of the parties engaged in these elections.[105] During the summer months and in the autumn, supporters of the 20 February Movement still punctually mobilized to demonstrate their opposition to the regime, but the movement had clearly lost momentum. Although the routinization of their protests reduced the relevance of the movement as a challenge for the monarchy, the regime remained wary that these protest dynamics could impact on participation in the elections. Throughout the 2000s, electoral participation in Morocco had been declining as voters increasingly reckoned that parliament was a largely ineffective institution and the most important decision-making processes remained firmly in the hands of the monarchy.[106] In the fall of 2011, therefore, an important aspect of the demobilization of the actors of the 20 February Movement was linked to showing the relevance of electoral democracy in the kingdom.[107] The protesters sought to keep alive popular scepticism about the role of parliament, especially as the constitutional reforms did not significantly alter the balance of power between elected politicians and the palace. 'The elections are a charade, you will not fool us this time,' shouted participants in a sizeable demonstration in central Rabat in October.[108] The boycott campaign of the 20 February Movement sought to amplify the phenomenon of formal depoliticization induced by perceptions of the ineffectiveness (if not corruption) of parliament in a political system controlled by the monarchy.[109] The postponement of elections from October to November to allow more time for voter registration reflected the anxiety of the regime about the level of electoral participation.

The parliamentary elections of 25 November 2011 appeared to reverse the downward trend in voters' participation. The participation rate was officially announced at just over 45 per cent—a notable improvement over the rate in the 2007 elections of 37 per cent. This increased mobilization of voters, or, more precisely, the perception that there had been a larger electoral turnout despite the boycott of the 20 February Movement, publicly validated the reformist agenda of the monarchy and the political parties. Tellingly, after the elections, al-Adl wal-Ihsane, which had been one of the main sources of participants in the movement, declared that it would formally end its association with the 20 February Movement.[110] Citing divergences within the movement, Fathallah Arsalane, one of the leaders of the Islamist organization, concluded that in view of 'the evolving situation in the country this form of activism is no longer effective'.[111] The withdrawal of al-Adl wal-Ihsane underscored the strategic success of its main Islamist competitor, the Justice and Development Party (PJD), which had embraced conventional forms of political contestation through participation in electoral processes as a means to increase its influence in the institutional system. The election results illustrated that voters' mobilization had been quite effective among Islamic-leaning constituencies, as the PJD headed the poll for the first time in parliamentary elections, with 23 per cent of the votes (and 27 per cent of the seats).

The electoral victory of the PJD was also significant because the 2011 constitutional reforms established that the party which came first in elections would be given the responsibility to form a government. In December 2011, the PJD thus had to opportunity to redefine its identity from opposition party to governing party. This evolution underscored both the continuing normalization of this Islamist party in the political sphere and the pragmatism of the monarchy in co-opting new actors in the ruling circles.[112] When Mohammed VI nominated as prime minister the PJD leader, Abdelilah Benkirane, the monarchy effectively ruled out the desirability of an anti-PJD coalition that would artificially patch together a parliamentary majority against the Islamists.[113] In return, the PJD indicated its willingness to collaborate with other political parties to form a large coalition in which governing responsibilities would be shared across partisan divides. The ruling coalition formed on 12 December 2011 included, in addition to the PJD, the Independence Party (Istiqlal), the Popular Movement, and the Progress and Socialism Party (PPS). The negotiations between the different parties eventually forming the Benkirane government on 3 January 2012 indicated that these actors (and at least some of their supporters) had for the time being moved away from the idea of renegotiating the formal boundaries of politics with the monarchy.

The formation of a new Moroccan government symbolized the closure of the episode of contentious politics initiated a few months earlier by the 20 February Movement. The monarchy had successfully diffused the challenge to its authority by reaffirming, and having other social and political actors reaffirm, its 'reformist' approach to political change. In effect, at the start of 2012, the responsibility for handling the country's socio-economic difficulties, corruption and other social ills was foisted upon the PJD-led government. The PJD's non-challenging stance towards the monarchy was illustrated by its acceptance of key ministerial nominations from the palace.[114] The 20 February Movement's mobilization continued under a PJD government, but it was in continuous decline; and the impact of the repressive apparatus increased as mobilization slackened. Illustrative of the resilience of authoritarian enclaves in the Moroccan regime was the inability of Rachid Nini's lawyers to obtain a revision of the journalist's jail sentence, even though one of his lawyers, Mustapha Ramid, had become justice minister in the new PJD-led government.[115] More traditional forms of mobilization against specific policies of the new government returned in 2012. Even the self-immolation of an unemployed youth during a protest in January 2012 did not attract much media attention or rekindle popular mobilization.[116] The discontent initially directed at the regime and the old ruling elites widened to include the ruling Islamist party, the PJD, thereby turning one of the main political challengers of the regime into a component of a stable, reforming authoritarian system.[117]

This situation ensured that the monarchy and the PJD had a growing common interest in working together, even as each tried to shift the blame towards the other when facing popular discontent. The new ruling elites were aware of the ever-present possibility of a 20 February–like movement resurfacing. As the leader of the PJD parliamentary group, Abdellah Bouanou, noted at the time of the toppling of President Morsi of Egypt in July 2013, 'The 20 February Movement is an idea; it will return if the government fails.'[118] In the medium term, however, most of the actors of the 2011 Moroccan uprisings were pushed back towards formal depoliticization and ordinary forms of disobedience. Even the new activists of the 20 February Movement became just another opposition group with known arenas and practices of opposition to the regime.[119] 'We prefer to be 200 with clear and precise demands,' said the organizer of a small protest marking the anniversary of the movement in Casablanca, 'than thousands with ambiguous messages.'[120] The identities and behaviours of the actors of the uprisings had co-evolved with those of the regime to produce a situation in which they could coexist and conflict with each other within the symbolic and institutional order imposed by a 'reformed' monarchy.

7

CONCLUSION

MOBILIZATION AND DEMOBILIZATION
IN THE NORTH AFRICAN UPRISINGS

Whatever happened during the Arab uprisings—the lived uprisings, that is—commonly does not matter much in academic and policy debates about the evolution of the region. Certainly, for the participants themselves, the uprisings could have been the stage for personal achievement or, at worst, personal tragedy. There are, however, political insights to be drawn from this protest episode that go well beyond the now common-sense arguments about the common causes of success and failures in the region. Looking back at the case of the 1979 Islamic revolution in Iran, Charles Kurzman noted that social sciences have a general tendency to produce retroactive predictions whenever unexpected changes occur.[1] Since political science is principally concerned with explaining institutional regularities, in extraordinary circumstances analysts are inclined to recast earlier arguments in a new light to explain why some causal factors were underestimated rather than question the relevance of the overall framework of analysis. In the aftermath of the Arab uprisings, as authoritarian routines came back to the fore and new models of governance were institutionalized, the longer-term causal mechanisms and factors previously emphasized in analyses of the region reclaimed centre stage. The narrative proposed by Jason Brownlee, Tarek Masoud and Andrew Reynolds regarding the pathways of reform and repression in the region highlights well these longer-term dynamics, but at the expense of what happened during the uprisings themselves.[2] Their approach illustrates a trend towards prioritizing the structural, 'objective' opportunities for change (or stasis) that social scientists can qualify (or quantify), over the interactions between the different actors who craft revolution, democracy or authoritarianism.

Brownlee, Masoud and Reynolds stress that 'many who took to the streets may have perceived a structural opportunity where one did not exist ... Demonstrations "diffused" partly because of a misperception that regimes were vulnerable.'[3] This is not quite the kind of 'moment of madness' that Sidney Tarrow took from Aristide Zolberg to emphasize that the specifics of revolutionary situations are too elusive to be analysed meaningfully.[4] Yet, the view that sidelines the dynamics within uprisings remains common. What is prioritized is explanations of state and society that best capture causality before and after an unexpected event, but that largely fail to reflect on causality during the episode of contention itself. Once a particular political event has been reduced to a mere historical curiosity, the drive to explain its unexpectedness loses its primacy. Once more, for scholars and policy-makers alike, the ability to explain routine politics becomes the main objective of the analysis. The political causality of extraordinary episodes is discounted, and so are the interactions at work at the time.

Regarding crucial protest episodes, Kurzman noted in the context of the Iranian Revolution that 'the greater the degree of deinstitutionalization, the harder it is to argue that people are falling back on an established pattern of behavior without being aware of doing so ... the greater the break from routine, the more likely that people will be aware of the break. The more aware they are, the greater the role played by conscious decision.'[5] During the Arab uprisings, the processes of partial or complete deinstitutionalization of authoritarian regimes (understood as sets of routine practices of governance) brought to light the dynamics of these interdependent constructions of political causality. In the four North African polities considered, consciously extraordinary political choices were made and translated into actions that further eroded the dominant representations of social normality. The unrest that started for a number of usually unconnected reasons created the conditions for a transformation of attitudes towards the dominant political order by establishing and (sometimes) entrenching new arenas of contention. In those arenas, new logics of situation and of action meant that 'extraordinary' choices became less tied to pre-existing interpretations of the authoritarian social and political order.[6] Instead, these choices and logics became primarily the product of the protest event itself, gaining momentum whenever the new arenas of contention acquired political depth and public recognition.

The evolution of the various regimes' strategies of repression and cooptation, which simultaneously constrained and enabled protest dynamics and arenas of contention, was causally connected to these cognitive and behavioural changes. In each of the four North African polities, the organization of routine authoritarian governance had produced distinct costs and benefits for the ruling elites. The choices of these elites and the responses of the state apparatus during the uprisings were directly informed by these known strengths and weaknesses of authoritarian governance. The ability of each regime to adapt those previously dependable policies and discourses that constituted 'normality' in each polity to address specific protest actions, arenas and actors helped shape the trajectory of each wave of unrest. The processes that produced such acts, arenas and actors of contention (in that particular order) were similar in all country cases. Nonetheless, the specific interactions between these elements of contention, and between them and the actions of the regime, produced different outcomes. In each case, however, the first phase of the uprisings was dominated by acts of contention that triggered further contentious events, regardless of the intention of the actors involved. The second period was a situation of heightened crisis characterized by the (possibility of) entrenchment of arenas of contention, which constituted an alternative discursive and material space to that of the established authoritarian order. The third and final moment of the uprisings corresponded to the reinstitutionalization of actors of contention and of governance, whose identity shaped new or reformed routine practices of governance marking the end of the protest episode or regime crisis.

Acts of contention: events creating events

Event-making as contingent mobilization

In the four North African polities, the early process of mobilization in protest events best illustrates the contingent dynamics of events-generated action. What marked these sequences of mobilization was not their planned or unplanned character, as both could be found, and hybrid situations were common. In the first wave of unrest in Tunisia and Algeria, friends, families and neighbourhood solidarities commonly structured the protests. By contrast, in the Moroccan case, cyber-activists and civil society organizations prepared themselves and negotiated for several weeks before organizing the first demonstrations. Finally, in Libya these two types of dynamics of mobilization coincidentally met. In all these cases, beyond the strategies and tactics of the protesters, the unintended consequences of these first acts of protest amounted to a strengthening of the dynamics of mobilization. An unusually potent uptake in protest mobilization was at the same time the main cause and the main outcome of these first noticeable instances of public dissent.

Events-generated mobilization repeatedly bypassed conventional tools of social and political control because the rapidly shifting loci of contestation and the (intended and unintended) actions of the protesters generated unpredictability regarding the content and scope of the unrest. This does not mean that new actors, practices, strategies or arenas of contestation were suddenly created out of nothing at the start of each period of unrest. Mobilization emerged out of a combination of rather ordinary elements of social contention and authoritarian control, which were temporarily out of kilter. The themes of each early episode of unrest, the early protest discourses and practices, not to mention the declared identities and objectives of the protesters, were all fairly commonplace. It was noticeable at the time that many of the actors involved in these events mainly focused on immediate local grievances, and instrumentally challenged the state authorities in order to gain a stronger bargaining position. Emotions may have been heightened, tempers may have flared, and behaviours may have been risk-prone, but the objectives of the early protests were initially rather down-to-earth.[7] While localized instances of unrest were not necessarily problematic for the state authorities, the multiplication of protest events and the recurrence of protest mobilization began to create the perception, among both pro- and anti-regime actors, that these contentious actions could generate generalized unrest. And in the wake of the Tunisian uprising, the framing of unrest was not only local and national, but also regional and transnational.[8] The snowballing effect of these early protest events helped to keep the dynamic of unrest out of kilter with standard state responses in each country in the first few days or weeks of the uprisings.

Event-induced cognitive and policy shifts

As protest events generated more protest events, policy disruption induced by the unrest and resulting cognitive dissonance were soon noticeable (and noticed) at different levels of governance, from the local to the national and the international (with multiple feedback loops). The transformation of localized episodes of unrest into nation-wide movements of unrest was not only the product of the protesters' strategic and coincidental actions but also, and crucially, of the responses of the authoritarian system in place. Just as the protesters did not (and could not) fully assess the consequences of their actions, pro-regime actors, whether members of the administration, the security services, or co-opted social and political forces, inadvertently contributed to the snowballing of the protests and to the disruption of pre-existing authoritarian routines. In practice, authoritarian mismanagement of the early unrest occurred according to two main scenarios.

Firstly, by dealing with out-of-kilter protests with well-known techniques of repression and cooptation, state actors were only marginally able to address the coincidentally stronger mobilization of protests, which kept gaining momentum. State control was relatively ineffective precisely because of the gap between the initial objectives and practices of the protesters and the dynamics of mobilization during actual protest events—that is, the gap between what people set out to do and what occurred. The most vivid example of these causal dynamics was the episode of repression and counter-repression that took place in the very first days of the Libyan uprising. The initial attempt by the regime to intimidate protesters and would-be protesters did not have the intended effect in the face of a slightly larger and better organized opposition than expected. The recourse to police brutality to force the issue only served to galvanize protesters, who were then able to gain the upper hand over the security forces in parts of the city of Benghazi. This first element of state mismanagement of the unrest—the failure to adapt to changing circumstances so as to remain effective—facilitated the emergence of an internal protest dynamic that kept mobilizing more and more protesters.

The other side of the mishandling of nascent unrest by the regime involved ad hoc tactical changes to deal with the non-standard aspects of the protest. In this case, state actors themselves helped to deinstitutionalize routine practices of authoritarian governance. Once Libyan and Tunisian security forces started to use live ammunition locally (for whichever reason) to cope with the protests, they turned the unrest into an even more extraordinary protest event. Discursively too, the televised speeches of President Ben Ali in Tunisia served directly to discredit the regime's 'business as usual' narrative, which it had offered to its supporters and to the population at large. Similarly, the bellicose televised pronouncements of Gaddafi and his son did serious damage on the international scene to the reformist image that the Libyan regime had been building over the preceding few years. These ad hoc tactical changes were conducive to strengthening the disruptions already experienced in the polity and the unpredictability of the dynamics of mobilization. Unpredictability, however, did not always translate into (and ought not to be equated with) increasing mobilization, as the first wave of unrest in Algeria shows, protests died out as the regime opted for an unusually lenient response to the event.

Interactions between protest events and institutionalized actors

Even during events-driven episodes of contestation, the dynamics of mobilization signposted early pathways of institutionalization of dissent. Just as protest events were beginning to gain momentum, exit pathways were shaped by the actions (and non-actions) of both pro- and anti-regime actors. The positioning of institutionalized opposition actors like the political parties or the unions signalled some possible mechanisms for managing the conflict. This positioning remained, nonetheless, ambiguous in the first stage of the uprisings, as unfolding events shaped both new arenas of contention and new identity markers for these established actors. In Tunisia, these ambiguities were noticeable in the tense relations between the local branches of the UGTT union, which repeatedly chose to help organize local protests, and the national secretariat, which was initially reluctant to challenge the regime openly.[9] In Morocco, similar tensions were palpable between the militant base of the opposition parties, particularly their youth wings, which were keen to join forces with the 20 February Movement, and the leadership, worried about losing the political gains they had made in the pseudo-democratic Moroccan system. Finally, this time through non-action, the lack of positioning on the part of the Algerian political opposition towards the early wave of social unrest also pointed to a limited set of options for mobilization facilitated by party politics.

The varying ability of organized opposition forces to link up with the protesters during the early period of mobilization helped to shape in different ways the trajectories of unrest in each country. In particular, hegemonic systems characterized by a lack of pluralism in the interactions between state and citizens (such as Libya and, to a lesser extent, Tunisia) could not swiftly generate a credible reformist option for the regime. Once the initial threshold of open defiance was reached in the face of repression, the ruling elites did not have at their disposal reliable and effective instruments of dialogue with the protesters. Even when institutionalized opposition actors could mediate between the regime and the protesters, their role generally made them hostages to fortune. As acts of contestation intersected with each other and with the actions of the regime and the opposition, new arenas of contention began to be delimited. Within these new spaces of contestation, as well as in relation to them, institutionalized opposition actors would play their part in raising or lowering the scope and intensity of the uprisings.

Arenas of contention: areas of change and routine governance

Creating sites of extraordinary contention

The snowballing protests and the disruption in the routine practices of authoritarian governance coincided with a growing self-awareness among protesters and ruling elites that new arenas and practices of contestations had been created. Newly formed arenas of contestation provided a space for the articulation of protest discourses and practices that infused events and actions with further political meaning. The dynamics of mobilization were shaped by different imbrications between arenas of contention and the social and political actors articulating these discourses and practices. Illustrative of the ineffective configuration of the two were the belated efforts by Algerian opposition parties to use the wave of riots of early January 2011 to challenge the regime's control of the political sphere. This explicit attempt at organizing a more potent arena of contentious politics was undermined by the parties' slow reaction to the initial wave of grassroots discontent. In turn, their inability to occupy the public space with their own supporters led to a spiral of demobilization instead of a strengthening of this public arena of contestation. In a more nuanced fashion, the attempt by the 20 February Movement to change the terms of the political and socio-economic status quo by occupying the street and the public sphere was at first successful in pushing back the boundaries of the permissible in Morocco.[10] However, the movement's inability to convince established opposition political parties to join them in this new arena of contention, and the decision of the parties to remain within the pre-existing arena of formal political contention, were instrumental in the failure to entrench this newly created model and space of contentious politics.

On the other hand, illustrative of an effective configuration of arenas and practices was the unplanned and more violent process of mobilization in Tunisia, which eventually produced a bandwagon effect as unions and parties progressively turned against the regime when Ben Ali reluctantly opened the door to political reforms.[11] This more forceful physical delimitation of new political arenas, which turned into a revolutionary political space during the process of mobilization, triggered the president's decision to flee the country. The flight of Ben Ali further undermined the institutionalized arena of political contention and drew the state institutions themselves to the centre of the arena of contention redefined by the uprising. In the Libyan case, the progressive armed takeover of territories previously controlled by the regime was a more direct form of redrawing the boundaries of the arenas of contention. Although state institutions and authoritarian routines were not challenged everywhere at once, there was a gradual shrinkage of the Gaddafi regime's institutional control over time. Simultaneously, as the regime's opponents strengthened their hold on these territories, the 'liberated' areas became not only arenas of contestation but also sites where political, social and economic relations were reconfigured around new material and ideational resources.

Crafting spaces of contention and governance

As all the uprisings shaped with greater or lesser success some arenas of contestation, a situation of divided sovereignty emerged out of these interactions. In the most dramatic case, that of Libya, owing to repeated failures of the state security forces to contain the challenge of the pro- testing crowds, the protesters found themselves in charge of significant parts of urban areas for a significant amount of time. In this context, in addition to meaning-making, what became important for these actors was governance-making in the face of faltering state institutions. This 'liberated' space publicly embodying anti-regime views and practices strengthened the political dynamics of the uprisings and, in the Libyan case, quickly produced a formal declaration of divided sovereignty by an insurgent government. The formal recognition of this situation by sev- eral foreign governments in turn strengthened the viability and auton- omy of these arenas of insurgent control vis-à-vis the Libyan regime. The military engagement of these international actors in support of the rebels helped to transform areas controlled by insurgents into the basis of a new regime, thereby delegitimizing old-regime institutions and formalizing the emerging democratic government. The domestic strengthening of these arenas of contestation which had become quasi- sovereign entities also induced external actors to revise their own nar- ratives about sovereignty in the region. As foreign involvement in favour of the Libyan rebels increased at the beginning of March 2011, the French foreign minister, Alain Juppé, timeously declared during his visit to post-Mubarak Egypt: 'In truth we may have let ourselves be intoxi- cated these past few years by arguments that said that the authoritarian regimes in place were the only bulwark against extremism.'[12]

The involvement of international actors in shaping arenas of conten- tion as the uprisings gained momentum proved crucial for the viability of those arenas in Libya. However, this factor remained an infrequent and unusual mechanism for carving out new arenas of contention during the Arab uprisings—Libya being the only case of such direct external involvement in North Africa. Elsewhere, foreign governments were generally as taken aback by the uprisings as domestic elites were. In Tunisia, the French government was so surprised by the swiftness with which unrest destabilized the regime that it was still seeking to boost Ben Ali's security forces at a time when Ben Ali was already looking for a safe exit from the country. The Tunisian uprising started a trend in the formation of arenas of contention, which were carved mainly as a result of domestic and even local processes of contestation. The rapid expansion of contested spaces near the centre of power in the capital, Tunis, gave rise to the perception that 'people's power' (in the form of grassroots mobilization) could challenge the omnipotence of the regime. In turn, the decision of the president to flee the country without formally handing over power served to strengthen the protest-induced dynamics of deinstitutionalization of the regime.

By contrast, in Morocco and even more so in Algeria, after the initial wave of disruption the protesters were far less able to entrench new arenas of contention constituting alternative sites of popular sovereignty. In these two cases, the non-violent trajectories of the uprisings also ensured that protesters did not create the perception of an imminent (physical) danger for the ruling elites. In Algeria, the disconnect between the contestation created by social riots in early January and that created by the political protests in early February enabled the regime to deal with these challenges sequentially. In Morocco, the inability of the 20 February Movement to convince the institutionalized opposition parties to join forces with them in order to entrench the contention initiated by the mass protest proved to be highly damaging for the protesters. The decision of the main opposition parties, as well as that of the regime's foreign backers, to support the reform proposals set forth by the monarchy served to reinforce the formal structures of political contestation at the expense of the new arenas of contestation won by the 20 February Movement.

Barriers against contentious politics: the regime in action

The period of heightened unrest was significant in redrawing the boundaries or reaffirming the routine structures and practices of authoritarian governance. This process involved more than the ad hoc revision of policies and tactics by regimes reacting to unexpected events. It was also a case of putting in place mechanisms which were, from the regimes' perspective, effective in shaping practices of contestation in the short to medium term (over weeks and months). When Gaddafi started to deploy his most loyal and best-equipped military units at the beginning of March 2011 in a campaign of military reconquest of the towns that had fallen into the hands of the protesters, he helped to set up the parameters of the ensuing civil conflict. Illustrative of a different method, when the king of Morocco started negotiating with opposition political parties about giving more political and institutional prerogatives to parliament in exchange for their support for his reforms, a medium-term process of formal political mobilization was set in motion in opposition to street mobilization.

The need to control the politically relevant public space was a key policy move of the regimes to stop protests from gaining momentum.[13] In Algeria and in Morocco, crucially, it was implemented through the use of (mostly) non-lethal force. The Algerian regime had learnt from previous episodes of unrest (1988, 2001) in which the use of lethal force by the army and police had energized the protest movement, and revised its tactics. The issue of authoritarian learning in the context of the 2011 Arab uprisings applies beyond this particular episode of contestation, as authoritarian elites learnt from past episodes of unrest.[14] Authoritarian learning remains, however, a double-edged sword, as applying tactics informed by the dynamics of past protests may prove inadequate and even counterproductive in new situations. In Tunisia, the very attempt at handling the unrest through pre-existing techniques of governance served to create an extraordinary situation. The ruling elites' misperception of what constituted effective responses at that time produced policy choices that worsened the situation of unrest. When protest dynamics did not neatly articulate pre-existing opposition to the regime, the actions and discourses of the ruling elites appeared inadequate. The televised speeches of Ben Ali in Tunisia (and of Gaddafi in Libya), as the uprisings were gaining momentum, illustrated these performative difficulties. Before the Arab uprisings, policy-makers in Tunisia and abroad believed that this resilient authoritarian system was unlikely to be destabilized by popular unrest, a perception that guided and informed policy-making until the very last hours of the regime. Similarly, after a swift events-induced paradigm shift, the perception of the Libyan uprising as a powerful grassroots movement that would quickly sweep away a crumbling Gaddafi regime informed policy-making in respect of international military intervention. Eventually this military option had to be forcefully implemented to ensure that new foreign policy orientations were aligned with actual political outcomes.

At the time of the Algerian riots, many observers remarked that in Tunisia, too, the protests could have turned out quite differently had the Ben Ali regime adopted the strategy of the Algerian regime, namely an immediate financial subvention and non-lethal, limited police intervention. This may be accurate retrospectively, but prospectively it made sense for the Tunisian regime to use its usual mechanisms of repression and cooptation to deal with these events. It is also noteworthy that the actions of the Algerian security forces themselves were not a typical response to a situation of nation-wide unrest. Time and again, the Algerian army and gendarmerie used lethal force in situations of widespread rioting to bring unrest under control. The response of the security forces in January 2011 was thus also slightly out of kilter. But in the context of the 2011 Algerian riots, this strategy facilitated a winding down of the initial protest and did not provide the impetus for a politicization of the unrest. In this case, an adaptive evolution of the regime's repressive strategy was instrumental in counterbalancing an out-of-kilter protest event. Importantly, however, the relative success of the 2011 Algerian strategy remained largely dependent on two elements that were outside the control of the regime at that particular time—even though the regime had a hand in the longer-term construction of these dynamics. The first external factor was that opposition actors were unable to produce a united front against the regime because of long-standing divisions. The second aspect was that, partly as a result of this disunity, the institutionalized opposition was unable to reach out to a larger public.

In Algeria and in Morocco, the early winding down of the unrest ensured that the cohesiveness of the security forces was not tested in the same way that it was in Tunisia and in Libya. Historically, the repeated involvement of the Algerian military in politics had laid the foundation for some behavioural and institutional patterns that were unpropitious for a revolutionary trajectory in which the army would simply stand by.

Yet, even in Algeria, the 2011 uprisings do not provide direct insights into the role that the security forces could play when confronted by a system-challenging protest. The same remark can also be made about the role of the Moroccan security forces in a different institutional context, where the military was located further away from political power. The successful cooptation of the opposition political parties by the monarchy and the continuing non-violent nature of the 20 February Movement's protests ensured that the regime did not face a security challenge during which the loyalty of the security forces could be tested.

Actors of contention and governance: institutionalizing identities and practices

Negotiating and institutionalizing new and old identities

The period of political reinstitutionalization following the climax of the uprisings, when deinstitutionalization reached its highest level, corresponded to the entrenchment of the political identities of the actors participating in routine governance. This process could be more or less violent, and more or less articulated through formal political mechanisms depending on the involvement of already institutionalized actors. Among those cases where the uprisings led to the fall of the authoritarian system, the Tunisian transition showcased the mechanisms producing a relatively smooth, negotiated transfer of power from old to new elites. In this process, the 'revolutionary' credentials of the latter were merged with the state credentials of the former. While the institutionalized opposition had not led the protest movement from the start, they were able to position themselves within the revolutionary narrative so as to appear as a legitimate alternative to the old ruling elite once the reigning autocrat had departed. Similarly, some of the actors once associated with the regime, not least the military, were willing and able to revise their role and identity to join the new democratic governance project. The dialogue between members of the old regime and the opposition was instrumental in enabling each actor to reinvent its identity. In the early stages of the transition, the willingness of opposition actors to collaborate with the cadres of the old regime was repeatedly challenged by the street. As well-known authoritarian figures and structures were progressively removed and as street protests began to lose momentum, opposition actors were able to validate a working agreement on those political and institutional reforms constituting the formal outcome of the Tunisian Revolution.

This working consensus between new and old elites continued to operate after the foundational elections of October 2011, as Ennahda sought to build a large ruling coalition with a wide support base in order to avoid new unrest or authoritarian reversal. In April 2013, the leader of Ennahda, Rachid Ghannouchi, declared:

> Al-Nahda cannot and does not desire to lead alone. Our alliance with Marzouki's Congress for the Republic (CPR) and Mustafa bin Jaafar's Al-Takatol [Ettakatol] … is not tactical. It is natural and should continue until the elections and beyond. We have reflected upon the Algerian experience of 1991 and the legislative elections that were suspended by the army. The Islamic Salvation Front (FIS) obtained 80 per cent of the votes, but the remaining 20 per cent carried significant weight (representative of the army, professional cadres, journalists and individuals who influence foreign relations). That minority also carries significant weight here [in Tunisia]. So even if we obtained 51 per cent of the votes, we could not govern.[15]

Among Tunisian parties, repeated efforts at building consensus at the institutional level meant that the interactions between new political actors (and between new and old) were conducive to maintaining the authority of state institutions as power was transferred between successive governments.

In the Libyan uprising, by contrast, the failure to sustain a dialogue between old and new state elites disrupted the process of constructing a new democratic regime. Sharp divisions between old-regime identities and revolutionary and civil war identities were kept alive by the unwillingness of many of the 'new' actors to accommodate the former elites and, repeatedly, each other. Subsequent to the military collaboration established to bring down the Gaddafi regime, the political and military leaders of the revolution and the civil war failed to entrench a dependable framework for collaboration. As a result of continuing clashes between different political and armed factions, the framework and road map for national reconstruction and reconciliation set by the central government remained a fairly weak set of institutional guidelines and mechanisms. In addition, while in Tunisia the discontent of the revolutionary youth against politicians commonly

CONCLUSION

accused of 'stealing the revolution' was relatively inconsequential, in Libya the military capabilities of the former revolutionaries ensured that similar expressions of discontent were far more consequential for the state elites and for governance. The civil conflict had not allowed a straightforward transition from revolutionaries to voters, as had happened in Tunisia, but produced instead an initial transition from revolutionaries to armed revolutionaries. The routinization of wartime behaviours ensured that one of the main identities for actors emerging from the revolution and civil conflict was that of 'fighters'. Such identities, which had to be accommodated and eventually dissolved in the new democratic order, kept challenging the identities and practices of newly institutionalized state actors, and weakened the process of state reinstitutionalization.

Elsewhere in the region, among those countries where the uprisings did not fundamentally reshape the identity of the regime, the interactions between social and political actors changed only superficially. In Morocco, the mutual accommodation of the regime and the opposition parties helped entrench stable 'reformed' identities. Both the monarchy and the opposition parties who had accepted the reformist deal of the palace were keen to present themselves as responding to the demands that people had voiced during the protests. As the 20 February Movement became just another opposition movement, both the king and the PJD portrayed themselves as the leading democratizing actors in the country. Once in government, the PJD behaved like a pragmatic governing party and did not seek to challenge directly the monarchy, while the king did not seek directly to undermine the Islamist-led ruling coalition. With some limited discursive and institutional changes, this situation replicated fairly well the pre-uprising mechanisms of governance in the country. In Algeria, a similar outcome was generated, with even more limited discursive and constitutional changes due to the multiplication of micro-parties unable to challenge the political hold of the regime and the FLN.

Eliminating undesirable actors and practices

As new or reformed practices of routine governance became entrenched in the post-uprising period, actors produced ideational frameworks designed to eliminate undesirable identities from the past. This framing effort could be accompanied by a rather brutal process of physical elimination of those actors representing old political identities, such as members of the old regime during and after the Libyan civil war. In addition, pressure from the revolutionary brigades on the newly elected parliament led to the passing of a 'political isolation law' in May 2013 that barred from public office all those officials who had held position under Gaddafi at any time.[16] In post-uprising Libya, the lacklustre performance of the new ruling elites facilitated the entrenchment of a zero-sum game. In this situation, the military winners of the civil conflict sought to maximize their gains by evicting former state actors altogether rather than by seeking a working compromise to improve the efficiency and capabilities of the new regime. The shifting alliances within the ruling coalition and within the opposition favoured a blaming game for the political and economic failures of the new regime. Before as well as after the elections, elected politicians and brigade commanders retained as a salient aspect of their discourse the need to protect the country against all those elements that threatened the gains of the revolution—be they supporters of the old regime, federalists, Berberists, Islamists, and so on.[17] By contrast, the purchasing power of a unifying narrative about a new Libyan state and society remained far more elusive, as illustrated by the lack of headway made in writing a new constitution for the country between 2011 and 2014.[18]

Identity validation could also be obtained through more consensual and legalistic processes designed, as in Tunisia, to block out the most compromised actors of the old regime, as well as some of the troublesome identities and actors that had made headway since the uprisings, such as the Salafists of Ansar al-Sharia.[19] In the Tunisian case, there was a progressive re-emergence of 'authorized discourses' about what the revolution was about, and what 'the people' wanted, among both government and opposition. Beyond the secular–Islamist divide, a consensus emerged among elites that posited dissonant voices as a danger for the achievements of the revolution. This applied equally well to those actors who were once close to the old regime, to those leftist voices questioning the Tunisian neo-liberal economic model, and to Islamist actors wanting to go further than Ennahda in terms of social and religious reforms.[20] Most visibly, by 2013 the discourse on terrorism and security inherited from the Ben Ali era was once again deployed by both government and opposition to placate the narratives and actions of Ansar al-Sharia, which was officially named a terrorist organization in August 2013 by the Ennahda interior minister.

In situations of 'reform' after the uprisings, as in Algeria and in Morocco, there was a more ambiguous process of adaptation of narratives and identities. The evolution of contestation in Algeria after the social unrest of January and the political protests of February illustrated continuity in protest identities, though expressed now through routinized, non-system-challenging practices. The wave of strikes that followed the initial uprisings retained socially and politically contentious identities but only within their sector of activity and during finite protest sequences. These recurrent but self-limiting challenges were slowly diffused by the regime through repeated (mainly financial) interventions designed to address the demands of particular categories of social and political actors. Similarly, the new Algerian parties that were created after the uprisings formally voiced their opposition to the status quo to mobilize discontented voters for electoral gains. However, their identity as opposition actors quickly melted away as self-interest and self-promotional strategies pushed them towards well-established pork-barrel politics. In Morocco, the structure of the pseudo-democratic system ensured that the PJD was in a stronger bargaining position vis-à-vis the regime, as well as being less driven by immediate or personal gain. Nonetheless, the bargaining process with the monarchy that constituted the basis of the post-uprising consensus ensured that the identities and practices of institutionalized political actors did not stray very far from what they had been in the pre-uprising period. At the same time, the actors of the 20 February Movement had to recast themselves as ordinary social and political opponents to take advantage of the routine opportunities provided by the system and to cope with routine judicial and police repression.[21]

Stabilizing status quo identities

Political mobilization in electoral campaigns has been a common element of institutional stabilization in the post-uprising period. The effectiveness of this formal mobilization in support of the new institutional order, as opposed to tumultuous anti-regime mobilization, depended on both the dynamics of the protests and the capacity of the parties. The greater insertion of political parties in the institutional system facilitated their role as shapers of public opinion. In Tunisia, before the foundational elections, the parties' semi-institutionalized role within the High Commission enabled them to present themselves as the natural gateway for making demands on the provisional government. Their efforts at working together within an agreed framework for the democratic transition, before and after the elections, ensured that their role was seen as important by the population, who turned out in numbers in political rallies (and at election time).[22] In 2013, the emergence of Nidaa Tounes as the main opposition party, bringing together secularists and former supporters of the old regime, confirmed the entrenchment of party politics as the main identity marker for challenging democratically elected ruling elites. It is notable too that 2013 also marked the fall of the Salafi movement of Ansar al-Sharia, which had kept alive 'revolutionary' mobilization with an Islamist stance up to that time.[23]

Mobilization through party politics was also one of the main mechanisms that provided a 'reformist' exit for the Moroccan uprising. In Morocco, this redirection of mobilization was less dramatic and more structured than in Tunisia because of the limited scope of institutional change. Political parties had already been involved in the mobilization process led by the 20 February Movement when some of their members and supporters joined the protest. This applied not only to the small political organizations which were formally part of the movement but also to the larger opposition parties, which were indirectly involved through the participation of their youth wings and independent-minded cadres. The leaders of the larger opposition parties were then able to convince party cadres and many members and supporters that incremental gains made by means of negotiated reforms were the best way forward in the face of resistance from the regime, and in view of the strategies of their political competitors. This positioning as well as the cohesiveness of the parties facilitated the shift from extraordinary street demonstrations to more mundane political rallies, first in support of the reforms and, after the constitutional referendum, during the campaign for the parliamentary elections. These party-centric strategies and dynamics continued to dictate the tempo of political reform after the nomination of the PJD-led government.[24] In their turn, the political opponents of the PJD used parliamentary blocking tactics as well as participation in street demonstrations to contest the more contentious or unpopular policies of the new government—a situation which left the monarchy mostly unscathed.

The limited and limiting role of political parties in Algeria and Libya ensured that they continued to remain marginal to the process of identity production and institutional stabilization after the uprisings. This inability to shape decisively political orientations was an outcome of different processes of party insertion into political society and the state system. In the crude Algerian pseudo-democratic system, ruling elites exerted both constitutional and extra-constitutional pressures on opposition parties to ensure that these actors were not able to mount effective challenges against pro-regime parties during or outside election time. As a result, these parties were not generally judged by the population to be credible vectors of mass mobilization. Even though opposition actors could mobilize their own supporters relatively effectively, partisanship constituted a weakness for mounting a collective challenge against the regime rather than a strength. The multiplication of small parties encouraged by the Algerian regime after the uprisings reinforced this trend and even made party politics more redundant than before. The failure of the Libyan parties, by contrast, derived from their own internal weakness and lack of cohesion, which underpinned their inability to mobilize people effectively around a political programme. Weak party identity, even in the case of the Justice and Development Party (offshoot of the Libyan Muslim Brotherhood), meant that party politics could not easily overcome other forms of partisanship, particularly affiliations with revolutionary brigades. Even after the foundational elections, elected parliamentarians failed to produce a stable ruling coalition that could have strengthened the role and identity of a national political society. Instead, divisions between nascent party elites weakened the authority of parliament vis-à-vis armed actors and, ultimately, vis-à-vis the population.

After the 2011 Arab uprisings

The 2011 protest episodes are not indicative of a brand-new trend in Middle East politics. They are no more a template for change in the region than the 1979 Islamic revolution in Iran ever was. The trajectories of the uprisings in North Africa cannot be used directly to model future patterns of unrest in the rest of the Arab world. The surface similarities between the protest events and the political transformations that they have induced in different countries have been identified already. However, noting family resemblances in order to build a typology of regime change is to reduce the relevance of the uprisings themselves. Conceptually and analytically, it is more useful to understand the sequencing and dynamics of the actions, arenas and actors of contention that produced such political transformations. Regardless of the outcomes, the similarities in the process of mobilization and demobilization provide insights into the varied mechanisms underpinning such events. By understanding the internal dynamics of the uprisings and the interactions that were causally potent, we can acquire new lenses with which to consider attempts at political change in the region.

In democratization and revolution studies, the outcomes of the Arab uprisings can be placed in already well-established categories. We have successful transition processes leading to democratic consolidation, as in Tunisia. We have the entrenchment of liberalized autocracies, as in Morocco. We have situations of authoritarian status quo, as in Algeria. And we have situations of state failure and conflict, as in Libya. None of these outcomes are particularly novel in terms of long-term institutional equilibria, nor are they particularly surprising as historical occurrences for these polities. The Arab uprisings point to a set of processes that led from one known institutional model—in this case, more or less open authoritarian regimes—to other institutional equilibria. Each North African country case provides a different articulation of these processes that helps us understand the logic of particular political trajectories. The dynamics of these rearticulations of power are a key to understanding future changes in the region. Tracking events and analysing arenas of contestation generated by protest events help explain the emergence or success of social and political identities and actors, and the institutional systems that are created by their interactions.

In the few years since the Arab uprisings, it has become common for analyses of the region to downplay the 'extraordinariness' of the events that took place at that time and to note instead the continuities of governance before and after the uprisings. However, to highlight the role played by those actors and factors that are deemed important retrospectively in a new political order is to over-rationalize the trajectories of change. Since any system of institutionalized rule (be it authoritarian, democratic or hybrid) can come out of any preceding institutional order, one is bound to identify continuities in practices and actors if one looks for them. With a limited sample of real-life political transformations at hand to study, it cannot be confidently shown that those factors and actors who were important before and after the changes were crucial for such political transformations. In particular, those factors and actors who had a significant impact during a revolutionary or transitional episode but who waned and faded away subsequently are usually the firsts to drop out of the explanatory narrative. As a result, structural explanations overstate the importance of those elements that remain. Analytically and conceptually, recognition of continuities of governance has to be accompanied by recognition of the contingency of these continuities—things could indeed have happened otherwise, and other continuities could have been showcased.

The different trajectories of change in the four North African countries can be used analytically as counterfactuals to map various scenarios of interaction between different players, and to draw inferences from this.[25] They illustrate the variations in the sequencing of events, formation of arenas of contestation, and construction of actors and practices that shaped the outcomes of the uprisings in each state. Rather than stressing that these transformations were likely outcomes of pre-existing structural trends and tensions, an event-oriented account of these episodes illustrates instead how contingent these institutional rearticulations were. Like a counterfactual narrative, such an account is thus not intended to replace structural accounts of political change in the region. It is meant to unpack the causal dynamics of critical episodes of unrest which are otherwise assumed to be largely irrelevant (if no significant changes occur) or largely predictable in view of longer-term trends (if changes do occur). People do make history in circumstances not chosen by themselves; and revolutionary situations are an important set of accidental circumstances in which people make their histories and that of others.

NOTES

1. INTRODUCTION: UNDERSTANDING AND EXPLANING THE ARAB UPRISINGS

1. Suganami argued that 'narratives are essential to explanations either because explanations are given in a narrative form or because they invariably contain narrative accounts within them. What differentiates explanations of social and natural phenomena is not the absence or presence of narratives, but the ingredients used in the narrative accounts.' Hidemi Suganami, 'Narrative Explanation and International Relations: Back to Basics', *Millennium: Journal of International Studies* 37 (2) 2008, pp. 327–356, at p. 355.
2. Doug McAdam, Sidney Tarrow and Charles Tilly, *Dynamics of Contention*. Cambridge: Cambridge University Press, 2001.
3. Oliver suggested that their quest was doomed to failure because 'a generalizing strategy focused on one process can never explain a historical episode, and should not try to. But conversely, a research program focused on explaining particular historical events cannot yield a general understanding of any process.' Pamela E. Oliver, 'Mechanisms of Contention', *Mobilization* 8 (1) 2003, pp. 119–122, at p. 121.
4. Mounia Bennani-Chraïbi and Olivier Fillieule, 'Pour une sociologie des situations révolutionnaires: Retour sur les révoltes arabes', *Revue Française de Science Politique* 62 (5) 2012, pp. 767–796.
5. Sidney Tarrow, 'Cycles of Collective Action: Between Moments of Madness and the Repertoire of Contention', *Social Science History* 17 (2) 1993, pp. 281–307, at pp. 281–282.
6. For a critique, see Jeff Goodwin, James M. Jasper, and Francesca Polletta, eds., *Passionate Politics: Emotions and Social Movements*. Chicago: University of Chicago Press, 2001.

7. Guillermo O'Donnell and Philippe C. Schmitter, *Transitions from Authoritarian Rule: Tentative Conclusions about Uncertain Transitions*. Baltimore: Johns Hopkins University Press, 1986, p. 5.

8. Capoccia and Ziblatt have developed this perspective by emphasizing the situational perspective of the actors at the moment of change. See Giovanni Capoccia and Daniel Ziblatt, 'The Historical Turn in Democratization Studies: A New Research Agenda for Europe and Beyond', *Comparative Political Studies* 43 (8/9) 2010, pp. 931–968.

9. Charles Kurzman, *The Unthinkable Revolution in Iran*. Cambridge: Harvard University Press, 2004.

10. Dan Slater, 'Revolutions, Crackdowns, and Quiescence: Communal Elites and Democratic Mobilization in Southeast Asia', *American Journal of Sociology* 115 (1) 2009, pp. 203–254, at p. 206.

11. Kurzman suggests instead that one ought to consider meaning-making as constitutive of all variables and mechanisms. Charles Kurzman, 'Meaning-Making in Social Movements', *Anthropological Quarterly* 81 (1) 2008, pp. 5–15, at p. 10.

12. See Jason Brownlee, Tarek Masoud and Andrew Reynolds, *The Arab Spring: Pathways of Repression and Reform*. Oxford: Oxford University Press, 2015.

13. Compare Jason Brownlee, *Authoritarianism in an Age of Democratization*. Cambridge: Cambridge University Press, 2007, with Asef Bayat, *Life as Politics: How Ordinary People Change the Middle East*. Stanford: Stanford University Press, 2010.

14. Charles Kurzman, 'Can Understanding Undermine Explanation? The Confused Experience of Revolution', *Philosophy of the Social Sciences* 34 (3) 2004, pp. 328–351, at p. 347.

15. This is an adaptation of Cox's argument that theory is always for someone and for some purpose. Robert Cox, 'Social Forces, States, and World Orders: Beyond International Relations Theory', *Millennium: Journal of International Studies* 10 (2) 1981, pp. 126–155. I made this argument specifically in relation to political Islam in Frédéric Volpi, *Political Islam Observed: Disciplinary Perspective*. New York: Oxford University Press, 2010.

2. ACTS, ARENAS AND ACTORS: FRAMING THE UPRISINGS

1. Asef Bayat, *Life as Politics: How Ordinary People Change the Middle East*. Stanford: Stanford University Press, 2010, p. 1.

2. Lisa Anderson, 'Searching Where the Light Shines: Studying Democratization in the Middle East', *Annual Review of Political Science* 9, June 2006, pp. 189–214; Thomas Carothers, 'The End of the Transition Paradigm', *Journal of Democracy* 13 (1) 2002, pp. 5–21.

3. Jason Brownlee, *Authoritarianism in an Age of Democratization*. Cambridge: Cambridge University Press, 2007; Ellen Lust, *Structuring Conflict in the Arab World: Incumbents, Opponents and Institutions*. Cambridge: Cambridge University Press, 2005.

4. Oliver Schlumberger, ed., *Debating Arab Authoritarianism: Dynamics and Durability in Nondemocratic Regimes*. Stanford: Stanford University Press, 2008.

5. Zachary Lockman. *Contending Visions of the Middle East: The History and Politics of Orientalism*. New York: Cambridge University Press, 2004; Frédéric Volpi, *Political Islam Observed: Disciplinary Perspectives*. New York: Oxford University Press, 2010

6. In these narratives, the economic dimensions were commonly stressed, as well as the securitarian characteristics of these regimes. See for the former, Michael L. Ross, 'Does Oil Hinder Democracy?', *World Politics* 53 (3) 2001, pp. 325–361; Michael Herb, 'No Taxation Without Representation? Rents, Development, and Democracy', *Comparative Politics* 37 (3) 2005, pp. 297–317; and, for the latter, Eva Bellin, 'The Robustness of Authoritarianism in the Middle East: Exceptionalism in Comparative Perspective', *Comparative Politics* 36 (2) 2004, pp. 139–157.

7. Marsha Pripstein Posusney, 'Enduring Authoritarianism: Middle East Lessons for Comparative Theory', *Comparative Politics* 36 (2) 2004, pp. 127–138; Ibrahim Elbadawi and Samir Makdisi, eds., *Democracy in the Arab World: Explaining the Deficit*. New York: Routledge, 2011.

8. Steven Heydemann, 'Upgrading Authoritarianism in the Arab World', Brookings Institution Analysis Paper, No. 13, October 2007.

9. Bayat, *Life as Politics*, p. 14. Bayat did consider the possibility that non-movements would become conventional social movements and engage in contentious politics when opportunities for such collective actions were introduced by a crisis of the regimes. However, this situation would negate the specificities of nonmovements and of their micro-transformation of the social and political order.

10. For a very pertinent critique, see Mounia Bennani-Chraïbi and Olivier Fillieule, '*Exit, voice, loyalty*, et bien d'autres choses encore …', pp. 43–126, in Mounia Bennani-Chraïbi and Olivier Fillieule, eds., *Résistances et protestations dans les sociétés musulmanes*. Paris, Presses de Sciences Po, 2003.

11. Gregory F. Gause, 'The Middle East Academic Community and the "Winter of Arab Discontent"', in Ellen Laipson, ed., *Seismic Shift: Understanding Change in the Middle East*. Washington, DC: The Henry L. Stimson Center, 2011, pp. 11–27.

12. Nassim Nicholas Taleb, *The Black Swan: The Impact of the Highly Improbable*. New York: Random House, 2007. In the context of the

Arab uprisings, see Nassim Nicholas Taleb and Mark Blyth, 'The Black Swan of Cairo: How Suppressing Volatility Makes the World Less Predictable and More Dangerous', *Foreign Affairs* 90 (3) 2011, pp. 33–39.

13. See for example in the social sciences, Molly Patterson and Kristen Renwick Monroe, 'Narrative in Political Science', *Annual Review of Political Science* 1, 1998, pp. 315–331.

14. James Jasper, 'Introduction: From Political Opportunity Structures to Strategic Inaction', pp. 1–34, in James Jasper and Jeff Goodwin, eds., *Contention in Context: Political Opportunities and the Emergence of Protest.* Stanford: Stanford University Press, 2012.

15. William H. Sewell, Jr., 'Historical Events as Transformations of Structures: Inventing Revolution at the Bastille', *Theory and Society* 25, 1996, pp. 841–881. More broadly, see William H. Sewell, *Logics of History: Social Theory and Social Transformation.* Chicago: University of Chicago Press, 2005.

16. Charles Kurzman, 'Can Understanding Undermine Explanation? The Confused Experience of Revolution', *Philosophy of the Social Sciences* 34 (3) 2004, pp. 328–351.

17. Jasper, 'Introduction: From Political Opportunity Structures to Strategic Inaction'.

18. In the context of the Arab uprising, probably the most vivid illustration of such an arena was Egypt's Tahrir Square. See Jeroen Gunning and Ilan Zvi Baron, *Why Occupy a Square?: People, Protests and Movements in the Egyptian Revolution.* New York: Oxford University Press, 2014.

19. For Bourdieu, habitus are 'systems of durable, transposable dispositions, structured structures predisposed to function as structuring structures, that is, as principles which generate and organize practices and representations.' Pierre Bourdieu, *The Logic of Practice.* Trans. R. Nice. Stanford: Stanford University Press, 1990, at p. 53.

20. Describing the events of the Tunisian Revolution, Hmed also suggests that 'ce ne sont pas les révolutionnaires qui font la révolution, mais bien l'inverse' [It is not revolutionaries that make revolutions, but the opposite]. Choukri Hmed, '"Si le peuple un jour aspire à vivre, le destin se doit de répondre"', *Les Temps Modernes* 664, 2011, pp. 4–20, at p. 17.

21. Like Orientalist accounts of the Middle East, which are good at explaining the present in terms of the past but bad at accounting for anything new in the 'Orient', structural accounts of the Arab uprisings have commonly been far better at explaining how revolutionary uprisings are the conclusion of long-term regional trends than at recognising what the uprisings themselves have changed in the politics of the region.

22. The trajectories of mundane social and political actors becoming 'revolutionaries' in exceptional circumstances have been well documented in diverse revolutionary settings. See Timothy Tackett, *Becoming a Revolutionary: The Deputies of the French National Assembly and the Emergence of a Revolutionary Culture (1789–1790)*. Princeton: Princeton University Press, 1996.

23. See Donald Davidson, 'Actions, Reasons, and Causes', *Journal of Philosophy* 60 (23) 1963.

24. James M. Jasper, 'Introduction: Playing the Game', pp. 9–33, in James M. Jasper and Jan Willem Duyvendak, eds., *Players and Arenas: The Interactive Dynamics of Protest*. Amsterdam: Amsterdam University Press, 2015.

25. James M. Jasper, 'Introduction: Players and Arenas Formerly Known as the State', pp. 9–26, in Jan Willem Duyvendak and James M. Jasper, eds., *Breaking Down the State: Protestors Engaged*. Amsterdam: Amsterdam University Press, 2015.

26. John Foran, *Taking Power: On the Origins of Third World Revolutions*. Cambridge: Cambridge University Press, 2005; Jack Goldstone, 'Comparative Historical Analysis and Knowledge Accumulation in the Study of Revolutions', pp. 41–90, in James Mahoney and Dietrich Rueschemeyer, eds., *Comparative Historical Analysis in the Social Sciences*. Cambridge: Cambridge University Press, 2003.

27. Richard Sakwa, 'The age of paradox: The anti-revolutionary revolutions of 1989–91', pp. 159–176, in Moira Donald and Tim Rees, eds., *Reinterpreting Revolution in Twentieth Century Europe*. Basingstoke: Macmillan, 2001.

28. Donatella Della Porta, *Mobilizing for Democracy: Comparing 1989 and 2011*. Oxford: Oxford University Press, 2014.

29. Charles Tilly, *European Revolutions 1492–1992*. Oxford: Blackwell, 1993.

30. Della Porta, *Mobilizing for Democracy*.

31. Thomson also notes the pertinence of the term 'democratic revolutions' to evaluate recent political changes in Eastern Europe and Asia, but he also posits that a successful institutionalization of democratic practices is a necessary component of this process. Mark R. Thompson, *Democratic Revolutions: Asia and Eastern Europe*. New York: Routledge, 2004.

32. See John Chalcraft, 'The Arab Uprisings of 2011 in Historical Perspective', in Amal Ghazal and Jens Hanssen, eds., *The Oxford Handbook of Contemporary Middle-Eastern and North African History*. Oxford: Oxford University Press, 2015.

33. Doug McAdam, Sidney Tarrow and Charles Tilly, 'Toward an Integrated

Perspective on Social Movements and Revolution', pp. 142–172, at pp. 164–165, in Mark Irving Lichbach and Alan S. Zuckerman, eds., *Comparative Politics: Rationality, Culture, and Structure*. Cambridge: Cambridge University Press, 1997.

34. Doug McAdam, Sidney Tarrow and Charles Tilly, 'To Map Contentious Politics', *Mobilization: An International Quarterly* 1 (1) 1996, pp. 17–34, at p. 24.

35. Goldstone's alternative to this linear approach is a model based on a 'family' of parallel pathways of mobilization distinguished by the type of interaction developing between protest movements and their opponents that produces analytically distinct sub-categories of contentions. Jack Goldstone, 'Social Movements or Revolutions? On the Evolution and Outcomes of Collective Action', pp.125–47, in Marco Giugni, Doug McAdam and Charles Tilly, eds., *From Contention to Democracy*. Lanham: Rowman & Littlefield, 1998.

36. Arthur L. Stinchcombe, 'Ending Revolutions and Building New Governments', *Annual Review of Political Science* 2, 1999, pp. 49–73.

37. At this stage, the usual dilemmas of democratic consolidation become entrenched. See Adam Przeworski, *Democracy and the Market*. Cambridge: Cambridge University Press, 1991.

38. Tilly, *European Revolutions*, p. 8.

39. Jeff Goodwin, *No Other Way Out: States and Revolutionary Movements, 1945–1991*. Cambridge: Cambridge University Press, 2001, p. 9.

40. Charles Kurzman, *The Unthinkable Revolution in Iran*. Cambridge: Harvard University Press, 2004.

41. For Sewell, structures 'are sets of mutually sustaining schemas and resources that empower and constrain social action and that tend to be reproduced by that social action. But their reproduction is never automatic. Structures are at risk, at least to some extent, in all of the social encounters they shape because structures are multiple and intersecting, because schemas are transposable, and because resources are polysemic and accumulate unpredictably.' William H. Sewell, Jr., 'A Theory of Structure: Duality, Agency, and Transformation', *American Journal of Sociology* 98 (1) 1992, pp. 1–29, at p. 19. For a practical illustration, see William H. Sewell, Jr., 'Historical Events as Transformations of Structures: Inventing Revolution at the Bastille', *Theory and Society* 25 (6) 1996, pp. 841–881.

42. Timur Kuran, 'Sparks and Prairie Fires: A Theory of Unanticipated Political Revolution', *Public Choice* 61 (4) 1989, pp. 41–74, at p. 41.

43. Timur Kuran, 'The Inevitability of Future Revolutionary Surprises', *American Journal of Sociology* 100 (6) 1995, pp. 1528–1551, at p. 1538.

44. Kuran, 'Sparks and Prairie Fires', p. 42.

45. Kurzman, *The Unthinkable Revolution*, p. 170.
46. Even in more structured episodes of democratic transitions, Guillermo O'Donnell and Philippe Schmitter argued that 'confusion about motives and interests, plasticity, and even indefinition of political identities' have a significant impact in the reshaping the political system. Guillermo O'Donnell and Philippe C. Schmitter, *Transitions from Authoritarian Rule: Tentative Conclusions about Uncertain Transitions*. Baltimore: Johns Hopkins University Press, 1986, p. 5.
47. Weyland stressed that the usual strategy for analysts using rational choice analysis has been to argue that subjective variations at the level of the individual could be approximated by averaged means when there was a large number of participants in protest events. However, this approach faltered when idiosyncratic deviations 'fail to cancel out in the aggregate and the law of large numbers cannot distil rationality out of a welter of accidental mistakes'. Kurt Weyland, 'The Diffusion of Revolution: "1848" in Europe and Latin America', *International Organization* 63 (3) 2009, pp. 391–423, at p. 400.
48. Jeff Goodwin, 'Why We Were Surprised (Again) by the Arab Spring', *Swiss Political Science Review* 17 (4) 2011, pp. 452–456, at p. 454.
49. Barbara Geddes, 'What Do We Know about Democratization after Twenty Years?', *Annual Review of Political Science* 2, 1999, pp. 115–144.
50. Eva Bellin, 'Reconsidering the Robustness of Authoritarianism in the Middle East: Lessons from the Arab Spring', *Comparative Politics* 44 (2) 2012, pp. 127–49, at p. 134. Her earlier account of the role of the security apparatus is in Eva Bellin, 'The Robustness of Authoritarianism in the Middle East: Exceptionalism in Comparative Perspective', *Comparative Politics* 36 (2) 2004, pp. 139–157.
51. Goodwin, 'Why We Were Surprised', p. 455.
52. Steven Levitsky and Lucan A. Way, *Competitive Authoritarianism: Hybrid Regimes after the Cold War*. Cambridge: Cambridge University Press, 2010. In an earlier working paper, they state this even more clearly when they point out that 'One cannot know for certain how cohesive an organization is until it is seriously tested'. Steven Levitsky and Lucan A. Way, 'Competitive Authoritarianism: The Origins and Dynamics of Hybrid Regimes in the Post-Cold War Era', L Freeman Spogli Institute for International Studies, Stanford University, May 2006, p. 54, http://iis-db.stanford.edu/pubs/24290/Levitsky-Way-Stanford.pdf.
53. In the MENA, from the 1980s onwards, professionalization of the security apparatus commonly meant the routinization of the modalities of containment of the threat of military coups, and the development of shadow economic systems and patronage networks designed

to buy off the military from direct involvement in politics. See Mehran Kamrava, 'Military Professionalization and Civil-Military Relations in the Middle East', *Political Science Quarterly* 115 (1) 2000, pp. 67–92; Philippe Droz-Vincent, 'From Political to Economic Actors: The Changing Role of Middle Eastern Armies', pp. 195–213, in Schlumberger, *Debating Arab Authoritarianism*; Steven A. Cook. *Ruling but Not Governing: The Military and Political Development in Egypt, Algeria, and Turkey*. Baltimore: Johns Hopkins University Press, 2007.

54. For a critique, see the contributors to Jeff Goodwin, James M. Jasper and Francesca Polletta, eds., *Passionate Politics: Emotions and Social Movements*. Chicago: University of Chicago Press, 2001.

55. Sharon Erickson Nepstad, *Nonviolent Revolutions: Civil Resistance in the Late 20th Century*. New York: Oxford University Press, 2011.

56. Goodwin, *No Other Way Out*, p. 25.

57. Weyland, 'The Diffusion of Revolution', p. 401.

58. See Daniel Brinks and Michael Coppedge, 'Diffusion Is No Illusion: Neighbor Emulation in the Third Wave of Democracy', *Comparative Political Studies* 39 (4) 2006, pp. 463–89; Mark N. Katz, *Revolutions and Revolutionary Waves*. New York: St Martin's Press, 1999; John Markoff, *Waves of Democracy: Social Movements and Political Change*. London: Sage Publications, 1996.

59. David Patel, Valerie Bunce and Sharon Wolchik, 'Diffusion et demonstration', pp. 57–76, in Marc Lynch, ed., *The Arab Uprisings Explained: New Contentious Politics in the Middle East*. New York: Columbia University Press, 2014; Marc Lynch, 'Media, Old and New', pp. 93–109, in Lynch, *The Arab Uprisings Explained*.

60. A rich literature has been produced over the last decades in comparative politics and democratization studies proposing typologies of regimes and sectoral analyses of factors contributing to resilience or change. These debates are most concerned with explaining trends in regime changes or resilience and not with the actual processes of deinstitutionalization/reinstitutionalization. They give therefore limited attention to the changing interpretations of state and society, regime and opposition, repression and contestation, that shape political causality in particular instances of mobilization. See Geddes, 'What Do We Know about Democratization'; Axel Hadenius and Jan Teorell, 'Pathways from Authoritarianism', *Journal of Democracy* 18 (1) 2007, pp. 143–157.

61. See Raymond A. Hinnebusch and Anoushiravan Ehteshami, *The Foreign Policies of Middle East States*, 2nd edn. Boulder: Lynne Rienner Publishers, 2014.

62. Sidney Tarrow, 'Cycles of Collective Action: Between Moments of

Madness and the Repertoire of Contention', *Social Science History* 17 (2) 1993, pp. 281–307; Aristide R. Zolberg, 'Moments of Madness', *Politics and Society* 2 (2) 1972, pp. 183–207.

63. Tarrow, 'Cycles of Collective Action ', p. 302.

64. Dan Slater, 'Revolutions, Crackdowns, and Quiescence: Communal Elites and Democratic Mobilization in Southeast Asia', *American Journal of Sociology* 115 (1) 2009, pp. 203–254, at p. 206.

65. As Gandhi and Lust noted, 'parties are weakened by their inability to form stable coalitions and overcome collective action problems. These divisions result from real differences in their policy preferences, their expected benefits from regime change, and institutional rules that make coordination unlikely or reward some opposition elites while punishing others.' Jennifer Gandhi and Ellen Lust-Okar, 'Elections under Authoritarianism', *Annual Review of Political Science* 12, 2009, pp. 403–422, at p. 412.

66. Jack Goldstone, 'Cross-class Coalitions and the Making of the Arab Revolts of 2011', *Swiss Political Science Review* 17 (4) 2011, pp. 457–463.

67. Merouan Mekouar, 'No Political Agents, No Diffusion: Evidence from North Africa', *International Studies Review* 16 (2) 2014, pp. 206–216.

68. Sidney Tarrow. *Power in movement: Social Movements, Collective Action and Mass Politics in the Modern State*. Cambridge: Cambridge University Press, 1998.

69. Doug McAdam, John D. McCarthy and Mayer N. Zald, 'Introduction: Opportunities, Mobilizing Structures and Framing Processes—Toward a Synthetic, Comparative Perspective on Social Movements', pp. 1–21, at p. 16, in Doug McAdam, John D. McCarthy and Mayer N. Zald, eds., *Comparative Perspectives on Social Movements: Political Opportunities, Mobilizing Structures and Cultural Framings*. Cambridge: Cambridge University Press, 1996.

70. Charles Tilly, 'Social Movements and National Politics', pp. 297–317, at p. 304, in Charles Bright and Susan Harding, eds., *State Making and Social Movements: Essays in History and Theory*. Ann Arbor: University of Michigan Press, 1984.

71. Ruud Koopmans, 'Political Opportunity Structure: Some Splitting to Balance the Lumping', *Sociological Forum* 14 (1) 1999, pp. 93–105, at p. 100.

72. For Koopmans, 'cross-national differences in political opportunity structures often concern the most stable and deeply rooted aspects of political systems, and are thus structures beyond reasonable doubt. In within-country analyses these most structural aspects of political opportunity structure will be constants and therefore generally less

helpful in explaining variations over time'. Koopmans, 'Political. Opportunity Structure', p. 100.

73. See Jeff Goodwin and James M. Jasper, eds., *Rethinking Social Movements: Structure, Meaning, and Emotion*. Lanham: Rowman & Littlefield, 2004.

74. William A. Gamson and David S. Meyer, 'Framing Political Opportunity', pp. 275–90, at p. 283, in McAdam, McCarthy and Zald, *Comparative Perspectives on Social Movements*.

75. Robert D. Benford and David A. Snow, 'Framing Processes and Social Movements: An Overview and Assessment', *Annual Review of Sociology* 26, 2000, pp. 611–639, at p. 631.

76. McAdam, McCarthy and Zald, 'Introduction', p. 2.

77. John A. Noakes and Hank Johnston, 'Frames of Protest: A Road Map to a Perspective', pp. 1–29, at pp. 21 and 22, in Hank Johnston and John A. Noakes, eds., *Frames of Protest: Social Movements and the Framing Perspective*. Lanham: Rowman & Littlefield, 2005.

78. Gamson and Meyer, 'Framing Political Opportunity', p. 290.

79. Bayat, *Life as Politics*, p. 2.

80. Jason Brownlee, Tarek Masoud and Andrew Reynolds, *The Arab Spring: Pathways of Repression and Reform*. Oxford: Oxford University Press, 2015, p. 62.

81. James M. Jasper, 'Social Movement Theory Today: Toward a Theory of Action?', *Sociology Compass* 4 (11) 2010, pp. 965–976, at p. 966. See also Charles Kurzman, 'Meaning-Making in Social Movements', *Anthropological Quarterly* 81 (1) 2008, pp. 5–15.

82. Vincent Boudreau, *Resisting Dictatorship: Repression and Protest in Southeast Asia*. Cambridge: Cambridge University Press, 2004.

83. Mark Irving Lichbach, 'Deterrence or Escalation? The Puzzle of Aggregate Studies of Repression and Dissent', *Journal of Conflict Resolution* 31 (2) 1987, pp. 266–297.

84. Goodwin, *No Other Way Out*, p. 26.

85. Ronald A. Francisco, 'The Dictator's Dilemma', pp. 58–81, in Christian Davenport, Hank Johnston, and Carol Mueller, eds., *Repression and Mobilization*. Minneapolis: University of Minnesota Press, 2004.

86. Generically, Kalyvas had argued earlier on that counterproductive indiscriminate violence by the state could occur when regimes saw this as a cheaper option than its alternatives when resources and information were in short supply. Stathis N. Kalyvas, 'The Paradox of Terrorism in Civil War', *Journal of Ethics* 8, 2004, pp. 97–138. In the MENA region, Hafez and Wiktorowicz already illustrated in the 2000s how indiscriminate repression directly provided clear incentives for people to mobilize against the security forces and the regime more generally. Mohammed M. Hafez and Quintan Wiktorowicz, 'Violence

as Contention in the Egyptian Islamic Movement', pp. 61–87, in Quintan Wiktorowicz, ed., *Islamic Activism: A Social Movement Theory Approach.* Bloomington: Indiana University Press, 2004.

87. This applies equally to non-violent resistance. See Nepstad, *Nonviolent Revolutions*; Maria J. Stephan, ed., *Civilian Jihad: Nonviolent Struggle, Democratization, and Governance in the Middle East.* New York: Palgrave Macmillan, 2010.

88. In the context of the Egyptian revolution, see Gunning and Baron, *Why Occupy a Square?*

89. For the importance of reading history forward, as actors must do, and not backward, see Amel Ahmed and Giovanni Capoccia, 'The Study of Democratization and the Arab Spring', *Middle East Law and Governance* 6 (1) 2014, pp. 1–39.

3. ROUTINE AUTHORITARIAN GOVERNANCE BEFORE THE ARAB UPRISINGS: STRUCTURING THE OPTIONS FOR CHANGE

1. Nassim Nicholas Taleb and Mark Blyth, 'The Black Swan of Cairo: How Suppressing Volatility Makes the World Less Predictable and More Dangerous', *Foreign Affairs* 90 (3) 2011, pp. 33–39.

2. F. Gregory Gause III, 'Why Middle East Studies Missed the Arab Spring: The Myth of Authoritarian Stability', *Foreign Affairs* 90 (4) 2011, pp. 81–90; 'The Middle East Academic Community and the "Winter of Arab Discontent"', pp. 11–27, in Ellen Laipson, ed., *Seismic Shift: Understanding Change in the Middle East.* Washington, DC: The Henry L. Stimson Center, 2011.

3. In the Tunisian case, see Frédéric Volpi, Fabio Merone and Chiara Loschi, 'Local (R)evolutions in Times of Democratic Transition: Reconstructing Political Authority in Tunisian Municipalities (2011–2014)', *Middle East Journal* 70 (3) 2016.

4. Jason Brownlee, Tarek Masoud and Andrew Reynolds, *The Arab Spring: Pathways of Repression and Reform.* Oxford: Oxford University Press, 2015.

5. Michael Willis, *Politics and Power in the Maghreb: Algeria, Tunisia and Morocco from Independence to the Arab Spring.* New York: Oxford University Press, 2012.

6. Marsha Pripstein Posusney and Michele Penner Angrist, eds., *Authoritarianism in the Middle East: Regimes and Resistance.* Boulder: Lynne Rienner, 2005.

7. Barbara Geddes, *Paradigms and Sand Castles: Theory Building and Research Design in Comparative Politics.* Ann Arbor: University of Michigan Press, 2003; 'What Do We Know about Democratization after Twenty Years?' *Annual Review of Political Science* 2, 1999, pp. 115–144.

8. I am downplaying here those explanations where the 'regime' signi-
    fies those individuals that have appropriated for themselves the insti-
    tutions and functions of the state.

9. That the Algerian democratic transition did not result in the institution-
    alization of political reformers within a more democratic system, as hap-
    pened with many communist elites in Eastern Europe at the same time,
    but ended in a military takeover, does not invalidate the point.

10. Steven Levitsky and Lucan A. Way, *Competitive Authoritarianism Hybrid
    Regimes after the Cold War*. Cambridge: Cambridge University Press,
    2010; Steven Heydemann, 'Upgrading Authoritarianism in the Arab
    World', Analysis Paper no. 13, Brookings Institution, 2007.

11. Michael C. Hudson, *Arab Politics: The Search for Legitimacy*. New Haven:
    Yale University Press, 1977. Included in these debates are Orientalist
    readings of the region, such as Hudson's suggestion that 'the Arabs are
    a difficult people to govern' (p. 103).

12. Philip S. Khoury and Joseph Kostiner, eds., *Tribes and State Formation
    in the Middle East*. Berkeley: University of California Press, 1990;
    Terence Ranger, 'The Invention of Tradition in Colonial Africa',
    pp. 211–261, in Eric Hobsbawm and Terence Ranger, eds., *The
    Invention of Tradition*. Cambridge: Cambridge University Press, 1983.

13. Willis, *Politics and Power in the Maghreb*; Lisa Anderson, *The State and
    Social Transformation in Tunisia and Libya, 1830–1980*. Princeton:
    Princeton University Press, 1986; Elbaki Hermassi, *Leadership and
    National Development in North Africa: A Comparative Study*. Berkeley:
    University of California Press, 1972.

14. Clifford Geertz, *Islam Observed: Religious Development in Morocco and
    Indonesia*. Chicago: University of Chicago Press, 1971, p. 81.

15. See Abdellah Hammoudi, *Master and Disciple: The Cultural Foundations of
    Moroccan Authoritarianism*. Chicago: University of Chicago Press, 1997.

16. A most useful analysis of the power shifts in Moroccan politics in the
    1960s remains John Waterbury, *The Commander of the Faithful: The
    Moroccan Political Elite—A Study in Segmented Politics*. New York,
    Columbia University Press, 1970.

17. Rémy Leveau, *Le Fellah marocain: Défenseur du trône*. Paris: Presses de
    la Fondation Nationale des Sciences Politiques, 1985; George Joffe,
    'Morocco: Monarchy, Legitimacy and Succession', *Third World Quarterly*
    10 (1) 1988, pp. 201–228.

18. Lisa Anderson, 'Tribe and State: The Libyan Anomalies', in Khoury
    and Kostiner, *Tribes and State Formation*.

19. Dirk J. Vandewalle, *A History of Modern Libya*. Cambridge: Cambridge
    University Press, 2006; Ronald Bruce St John, *Libya: From Colony to
    Revolution*. Oxford: Oneworld, 2008.

20. Dirk Vanderwalle, *Libya Since Independence: Oil and State-Building*. London: I.B. Tauris, 1998.

21. Lisa Anderson, 'Qadhdhafi and His Opposition', *Middle East Journal* 40 (2) 1986, pp. 225–237; George Joffe, 'Islamic Opposition in Libya', *Third World Quarterly* 10 (2) 1988, pp. 615–631. For neo-sultanism, see H.E. Chehabi and Juan J. Linz, 'A Theory of Sultanism 1: A Type of Nondemocratic Rule', pp. 3–25, in H.E. Chehabi and Juan J. Linz, eds., *Sultanistic Regimes*. Baltimore: John Hopkins University Press, 1998.

22. John P. Entelis, *Algeria: The Revolution Institutionalized*. Boulder: Westview Press, 1986.

23. For an analysis of autocratic institutionalization that is far less sanguine than Entelis's, see Rachid Tlemcani, *State and Revolution in Algeria*. Boulder: Westview Press, 1986.

24. William B. Quandt, *Revolution and Political Leadership: Algeria 1954–1968*. Cambridge: MIT Press, 1970.

25. Martinez remarked in the context of the civil conflict of the 1990s that the Algerian war of independence and the ensuing reorganization of power entrenched the notion of the legitimacy of armed struggles to acquire state power. Luis Martinez, *The Algerian Civil War 1990–1998*. Trans. J. Derrick. New York: Columbia University Press, 2000.

26. I am using the term praetorianism here mainly to describe the ideational and organizational entrenchment of the role of the military at the core of the political system. See Amos Perlmutter, 'The Praetorian State and the Praetorian Army: Toward a Taxonomy of Civil-Military Relations in Developing Polities', *Comparative Politics* 1 (3) 1969, pp. 382–404.

27. Jean-François Daguzan, 'Maghreb: Les armées en politique—des trajectoires divergentes', *Confluences Méditerranée* No. 29, 1999, pp. 21–38; L.B. Ware, 'The Role of the Tunisian Military in the Post-Bourguiba Era', *Middle East Journal* 39 (1) 1985, pp. 27–47.

28. Hudson, *Arab Politics*, p. 377.

29. Emma Murphy, *Economic and Political Change in Tunisia: From Bourguiba to Ben Ali*. New York: Palgrave Macmillan, 1999; Michel Camau and Vincent Geisser, *Le Syndrome autoritaire: Politique en Tunisie de Bourguiba à Ben Ali*. Paris: Presse de Sciences Po, 2003.

30. Gilles Kepel, *The Revenge of God: The Resurgence of Islam, Christianity, and Judaism in the Modern World*. Cambridge: Polity Press, 1994.

31. In 1976, Mahfoud Nahnah was even imprisoned for four years for sabotaging a telephone substation in protest against the new national charter imposed by the FLN that emphasised a historical Islamic trajectory leading to a socialist revolution. Omar Carlier, *Entre nation et*

jihad: Histoire sociale des radicalismes algériens. Paris: Presses de Sciences Po, 1995.

32. The Moroccan publication *Tel Quel* cites police sources from 2006 estimating the active membership of this association at over 100,000 members. Abdellatif El Azizi, 'Al Adl vs la monarchie: La guerre secrète', *Tel Quel* No. 234, July 2006. See also Francesco Cavatorta, 'Neither Participation nor Revolution: The Strategy of the Moroccan Jamiat al-Adl wal-Ihsan', *Mediterranean Politics* 12 (3) 2007, pp. 381–397.

33. Ghassan Salamé, ed., *Democracy Without Democrats? The Renewal of Politics in the Muslim World*. London: I.B. Tauris, 1994.

34. About North Africa, see John P. Entelis, ed., *Islam, Democracy, and the State in North Africa*. Bloomington: Indiana University Press, 1997; François Burgat, *The Islamic Movement in North Africa*. Trans. W. Dowell. Austin: University of Texas Press, 1997.

35. Mohammed Elbaki Hermassi, 'La société tunisienne au miroir islamiste', *Maghreb-Machrek* No. 103, 1984; Susan Walz, 'Islamist Appeal in Tunisia', *Middle East Journal* 40 (4) 1986, pp. 651–670; Michael Collins Dunn, 'The Al-Nahda Movement in Tunisia: From Rennaissance to Revolution', pp. 149–165, in John Ruedy, ed., *Islamism and Secularism in North Africa*. New York: Palgrave Macmillan, 1996. For a well-informed if sometimes hagiographic account of Ghannouchi's views, see Azzam Tamimi, *Rachid Ghannouchi: A Democrat Within Islamism*. New York: Oxford University Press, 2001.

36. Murphy, *Economic and Political Change in Tunisia*; Camau and Geisser, *Le syndrome autoritaire*.

37. Burgat, *The Islamic Movement in North Africa*; Alaya Allani, 'The Islamists in Tunisia between Confrontation and Participation: 1980–2008', *Journal of North African Studies* 14 (2) 2009, pp. 257–272; John P. Entelis, 'Political Islam in the Maghreb: The Nonviolent Dimension', in Entelis, *Islam, Democracy, and the State*.

38. Lisa Anderson, 'Political Pacts, Liberalism, and Democracy: The Tunisian National Pact of 1988', *Government and Opposition* 26 (2) 1991, pp. 244–260; L.B. Ware, 'Ben Ali's Constitutional Coup in Tunisia', *Middle East Journal* 42 (4) 1988, pp. 587–601.

39. Michele Penner Angrist, 'Parties, Parliament and Political Dissent in Tunisia', *Journal of North African Studies* 4 (4) 1999, pp. 89–104, at p. 89.

40. Hugh Roberts, 'Radical Islamism and the Dilemma of Algerian Nationalism: The Embattled Arians of Algiers', *Third World Quarterly* 10 (2) 1988, pp. 556–589.

41. Ahmed Rouadjia, *Les frères et la mosquée: Enquête sur le mouvement islamiste en Algérie*. Paris: Karthala, 1990.

42. Frédéric Volpi, *Islam and Democracy: The Failure of Dialogue in Algeria*. London: Pluto Press, 2003.

43. Entelis, 'Political Islam in the Maghreb'; M. Al-Ahnaf, Bernard Botiveau and Franck Frégosi, *L'Algérie par ses islamistes*. Paris: Karthala, 1991.

44. Frédéric Volpi, 'Algeria's Pseudo-democratic Politics: Lessons for Democratization in the Middle East', *Democratization* 13 (3) 2006, pp. 442–455; Robert Mortimer, 'Islamists, Soldiers, and Democrats: The Second Algerian War', *Middle East Journal* 50 (1) 1996, pp. 18–39.

45. Willis, *Politics and Power in the Maghreb*; Entelis, 'Political Islam in the Maghreb'.

46. The roots of the MUR in the 1980s are in the social activism of former members of the Chabiba Islamiya who had renounced political violence. Violent spinoffs of the Chabiba, the 'fighting group' and the 'Moroccan fighters' organization', failed to have a significant impact on the Moroccan scene during that decade. Jamal Benomar, 'The Monarchy, the Islamist Movement and Religious Discourse in Morocco', *Third World Quarterly* 10 (2) 1988, pp. 539–555.

47. Michael McFaul and Tamara Cofman Wittes, 'The Limits of Limited Reform', *Journal of Democracy* 19 (1) 2008, pp. 19–33.

48. Anderson, 'Qadhdhafi and His Opposition'.

49. Luis Martinez, 'Libya: The Conversion of a "Terrorist State"', *Mediterranean Politics* 11 (2) 2006, pp. 151–165.

50. Yahia Zoubir, 'Contestation islamiste et lutte antiterroriste en Libye, 1990–2007', *L'Année du Maghreb* 4, 2008, pp. 267–277.

51. Luis Martinez, *The Libyan Paradox*. New York: Columbia University Press, 2007.

52. Olivier Roy, *The Failure of Political Islam*. Cambridge, MA: Harvard University Press, 1996.

53. Frédéric Volpi, *Political Islam Observed: Disciplinary Perspectives*. New York: Oxford University Press, 2010.

54. Thomas Carothers and Marina Ottaway, eds., *Uncharted Journey: Promoting Democracy in the Middle East*. Washington, DC: Carnegie Endowment for International Peace, 2005.

55. Saad Eddin Ibrahim, 'Toward Muslim Democracies', *Journal of Democracy* 18 (2) 2007, pp. 5–13, at p. 8.

56. Ambassador Robert F. Godec, US Embassy in Tunisia, 'Troubled Tunisia: What Should We Do?', 17 July 2009, https://wikileaks.ch/cable/2009/07/09TUNIS492.html.

57. Tamara Cofman Wittes, *Freedom's Unsteady March: America's Role in Building Arab Democracy*. Washington, DC: Brookings Institution Press, 2008.

58. Eberhard Kienle, 'Democracy Promotion and the Renewal of Authoritarian Rule', pp. 231–249, at p. 247, in Oliver Schlumberger, ed.,

Debating Arab Authoritarianism: Dynamics and Durability in Nondemocratic Regimes. Stanford: Stanford University Press, 2007.

59. Zoubir, 'Contestation islamiste'; Yehudit Ronen, 'Libya's Rising Star: Saif al-Islam and Succession', *Middle East Policy* 12 (3) 2005, pp. 136–144.

60. This is a kind of reverse leverage to the one analysed by Levitsky and Way—i.e. the ability of authoritarian regimes to spread an acceptance of authoritarianism. Steven Levitsky and Lucan A. Way, 'Linkage versus Leverage: Rethinking the International Dimension of Regime Change', *Comparative Politics* 38 (4) 2006, pp. 379–400.

61. Derek Lutterbeck, 'Migrants, Weapons and Oil: Europe and Libya after the Sanctions', *Journal of North African Studies* 14 (2) 2009, pp. 169–184; Yahia Zoubir, 'Libya and Europe: Economic Realism at the Rescue of the Qaddafi Authoritarian Regime', *Journal of Contemporary European Studies* 17 (3) 2009, pp. 401–415.

62. Quoted in Jean-Philippe Bras, 'Le Maghreb dans la "guerre contre le terrorisme": Enjeux juridiques et politiques des legislations "anti-terroristes"', *L'Année du Maghreb* No. 2, 2005–2006, pp. 447–467, at p. 449.

63. Brieg Tomos Powel, 'The Stability Syndrome: US and EU Democracy Promotion in Tunisia', *Journal of North African Studies* 14 (1) 2009, pp. 57–73.

64. Amin Allal, 'Réformes néolibérales, clientélismes et protestations en situation autoritaire', *Politique Africaine* No. 117, 2010, pp. 107–125; Larbi Chouikha and Eric Gobe, 'La Tunisie entre la "Révolte du Bassin Minier de Gafsa" et l'échéance électorale de 2009', *L'Année du Maghreb* No. 5, 2009, pp. 387–420; Vincent Geisser and Éric Gobe, 'Des fissures dans la « Maison Tunisie »? Le Régime de Ben Ali face aux mobilisations protestataires', *L'Année du Maghreb* No. 2, 2005–2006, pp. 353–414.

65. Quoted in José Garçon, 'Droits de l'homme en Tunisie: Chirac blanchit Ben Ali', *Libération*, 5 December 2003.

66. In relation to 'human rights' in Morocco, see Susan Slyomovics, *The Performance of Human Rights in Morocco*. Philadelphia: University of Pennsylvania Press, 2005.

67. Volpi, 'Algeria's Pseudo-democratic Politics'.

68. Paul Holtom, Mark Bromley, Pieter D. Wezeman and Siemon T. Wezeman, 'International Arms Transfers', pp. 285–332, in *SIPRI Yearbook 2010*, Stockholm International Peace Research Institute.

69. Ayşe Aslıhan Çelenk, 'Promoting Democracy in Algeria: The EU Factor and the Preferences of the Political Elite', *Democratization* 16 (1) 2009, pp. 176–192.

70. James N. Sater, 'Parliamentary Elections and Authoritarian Rule in Morocco', *Middle East Journal* 63 (3) 2009, pp. 381–400; Lise Storm, 'Testing Morocco: The Parliamentary Elections of September 2007', *Journal of North African Studies* 13 (1) 2008, pp. 37–54; Michael J. Willis, 'Morocco's Islamists and the Legislative Elections of 2002: The Strange Case of the Party That Did Not Want to Win', *Mediterranean Politics* 9 (1) 2004, pp. 53–81.

71. Malika Zeghal, *Islamism in Morocco: Religion, Authoritarianism, and Electoral Politics*. Princeton: Markus Wiener, 2008.

72. Eva Wegner, *Islamist Opposition in Authoritarian Regimes: The Party of Justice and Development in Morocco*. Syracuse: Syracuse University Press, 2011.

73. Clement M. Henry, *The Mediterranean Debt Crescent: Money and Power in Algeria, Egypt, Morocco, Tunisia, and Turkey*. Gainesville: University Press of Florida, 1996.

74. See Giacomo Luciani, 'Resources, Revenues, and Authoritarianism in the Arab World: Beyond the Rentier State', pp. 211–228, in Rex Brynen, Bahgat Korany and Paul Noble, eds., *Political Liberalization and Democratization in the Arab World, Vol. 1*. Boulder: Lynne Rienner, 1995; Hazem Beblawi, 'The Rentier State in the Arab World', pp. 85–98, in Giacomo Luciani, ed., *The Arab State*. Berkeley: University of California Press, 1990.

75. Clement M. Henry and Robert Springborg, *Globalization and the Politics of Development in the Middle East*. 2nd edn. Cambridge: Cambridge University Press, 2010.

76. Volker Perthes, ed., *Arab Elites: Negotiating the Politics of Change*. Boulder: Lynne Rienner, 2004.

77. Raymond Hinnebusch, 'Authoritarian Persistence, Democratization Theory and the Middle East: An Overview and Critique', *Democratization* 13 (3) 2006, pp. 373–395; 'Liberalization without Democratization in "Post-populist" Authoritarian States', pp. 123–145, in Nils Butenschon, Uri Davis and Manuel Hassassian, eds., *Citizenship and State in the Middle East*. Syracuse: Syracuse University Press, 2000.

78. About the king of Morocco and the Ben Ali family, see Nicolas Beau and Catherine Graciet, *La régente de Carthage: Main basse sur la Tunisie*. Paris: La Découverte, 2009; Catherine Graciet and Eric Laurent, *Le roi prédateur*. Paris: Editions du Seuil, 2012.

79. Melani C. Cammett, *Globalization and Business Politics in Arab North Africa: A Comparative Perspective*. Cambridge: Cambridge University Press, 2006; 'Business–Government Relations and Industrial Change: The Politics of Upgrading in Morocco and Tunisia', *World Development* 35 (11) 2007, pp. 1889–1903.

80. Henry, *The Mediterranean Debt Crescent*; Azzedine Layachi, ed., *Economic Crisis and Political Change in North Africa*. Westport: Praeger, 1998.

81. Cited in Myriam Catusse, 'Maroc: Un fragile état social dans la réforme néolibérale', pp. 121–148, in Myriam Catusse, Blandine Destremau and Eric Verdier, eds., *L'Etat face aux "débordements" du social au Maghreb: Formation, travail et protection*. Paris: Karthala, 2009.

82. John Walton and David Seddon, *Free Markets and Food Riots: The Politics of Global Adjustment*. Oxford: Blackwell, 1994.

83. James Liddell, 'Notables, Clientelism and the Politics of Change in Morocco', *Journal of North African Studies* 15 (3) 2010, pp. 315–331; Abdeslam Maghraoui, 'Depoliticization in Morocco', *Journal of Democracy* 13 (4) 2002, pp. 24–32; Rémy Leveau, 'Morocco at the Crossroads', *Mediterranean Politics* 2 (2) 1997, pp. 93–113.

84. Tom P. Najem, 'Privatization and the State in Morocco: Nominal Objectives and Problematic Realities', *Mediterranean Politics* 6 (2) 2001, pp. 51–67; Sami Zemni and Koenraad Bogaert, 'Trade, Security and Neoliberal Politics: Whither Arab Reform? Evidence from the Moroccan Case', *Journal of North African Studies* 14 (1) 2009, pp. 91–107.

85. Ferdinand Eibl, 'The Party of Authenticity and Modernity (PAM): Trajectory of a Political *Deus ex Machina*', *Journal of North African Studies* 17 (1) 2012, pp. 45–66; Andrew Barwig, 'The "New Palace Guards": Elections and Elites in Morocco and Jordan', *Middle East Journal* 66 (3) 2012, pp. 425–439.

86. Cammett, *Globalization and Business Politics*; Murphy, *Economic and Political Change in Tunisia*.

87. Dirk Vandewalle, 'From the New State to the New Era: Toward a Second Republic in Tunisia', *Middle East Journal* 42 (4) 1988, pp. 602–620; Bradford Dillman, 'The Political Economy of Structural Adjustment in Tunisia and Algeria', *Journal of North African Studies* 3 (3) 1998, pp. 1–24.

88. Christopher Alexander, 'Opportunities, Organizations, and Ideas: Islamists and Workers in Tunisia and Algeria', *International Journal of Middle East Studies* 32 (4) 2000, pp. 465–490.

89. Stephen J. King, *Liberalization Against Democracy: The Local Politics of Economic Reform in Tunisia*. Bloomington: Indiana University Press, 1997.

90. Béatrice Hibou, *The Force of Obedience: The Political Economy of Repression in Tunisia*. Cambridge: Polity Press, 2011.

91. Steffen Erdle, 'Tunisia: Economic Transformation and Political Restoration', pp. 207–236, in Perthes, *Arab Elites*.

92. Béatrice Hibou, 'Domination and Control in Tunisia: Economic Levers

for the Exercise of Authoritarian Power', *Review of African Political Economy*, 33 (108) 2006, pp. 185–206; Béatrice Hibou, Hamza Meddeb and Mohamed Hamdi, 'Tunisia after 14 January and Its Social and Political Economy: The Issues at Stake in a Reconfiguration of European Policy', Copenhagen: Euro-Mediterranean Human Rights Network, June 2011. For a focus on local dynamics, see King, *Liberalization Against Democracy*.

93. Amin Allal, 'Avant on tenait le mur, maintenant on tient le quartier!', *Politique Africaine* No. 121, 2011, pp. 53–67.

94. For an insider's perspective, see Mahfoud Bennoune, *The Making of Contemporary Algeria, 1830–1987*. Cambridge: Cambridge University Press, 1988.

95. Volpi, *Islam and Democracy*; Bradford Dillman, *State and Private Sector in Algeria: The Politics of Rent-Seeking and Failed Development*. Boulder: Westview, 2000; Isabelle Werenfels, 'Obstacles to Privatisation of State-Owned Industries in Algeria: The Political Economy of Distributive Conflict', *Journal of North African Studies* 7 (1) 2002, pp. 1–28.

96. Laabas, Belkacem and Ammar Bouhouche, 'Algeria: Democracy and Development under the Aegis of the "Authoritarian Bargain"', in Ibrahim Elbadawi and Samir Makdisi, eds., *Democracy in the Arab World: Explaining the Deficit*. New York: Routledge, 2010; Clement M. Henry, 'Algeria's Agonies: Oil Rent Effects in a Bunker State', *Journal of North African Studies* 9 (2) 2004, pp. 68–81.

97. Dirk Vandewalle, 'Qadhafi's "Perestroika": Economic and Political Liberalization in Libya', *Middle East Journal* 45 (2) 1991, pp. 216–231; Patrick Haimzadeh, *Au cœur de la Libye de Kadhafi*. Paris: J.C. Lattès, 2011.

98. Ronald Bruce St John, 'The Libyan Economy in Transition', pp. 127–151, in Dirk Vandewalle, ed., *Libya since 1969: Qadhafi's Revolution Revisited*. New York: Palgrave Macmillan, 2008; Alison Pargeter, 'Libya: Reforming the Impossible?', *Review of African Political Economy* 33 (108) 2006, pp. 219–235; Saïd Haddad, 'La Libye et l'Occident depuis 1999: Entre tropisme américain et ancrage euroméditerranéen', *Afrique Contemporaine* No. 209, 2004, pp. 179–196.

99. See in comparative perspective Andreas Schedler, ed., *Electoral Authoritarianism: The Dynamics of Unfree Competition*. Boulder: Lynne Rienner, 2006.

100. Burhan Ghalioun, 'The Persistence of Arab Authoritarianism', *Journal of Democracy* 15 (4) 2004, pp. 126–132, at p. 126.

101. On the predatory role of military elites in particular, see Steven A. Cook, *Ruling but Not Governing: The Military and Political Development in Egypt, Algeria and Turkey*. Baltimore: Johns Hopkins University Press, 2007.

102. Ellen Lust, 'Competitive Clientelism in the Middle East', *Journal of Democracy* 20 (3) 2009, pp. 122–135.

103. Rémy Leveau, 'Morocco at the Crossroads', *Mediterranean Politics* 2 (2) 1997, pp. 95–113; George Joffé, 'The Moroccan Political System after the Elections', *Mediterranean Politics* 3 (3) 1998, pp. 106–125; Jean-Noël Ferrié, 'Succession monarchique et désenchantement de l'alternance partisane: Maroc', *Annuaire de l'Afrique du Nord 1999*, No. 38, 2002, pp. 215–231.

104. Guilain Denoeux and Abdeslam Maghraoui, 'King Hassan's Strategy of Political Dualism', *Middle East Policy* 5 (4) 1998, pp. 104–130; Catherine Sweet, 'Democratization without Democracy: Political Openings and Closures in Modern Morocco', *Middle East Report*, No. 218, Spring 2001, pp. 22–25; Saloua Zerhouni, 'Morocco: Reconciling Continuity and Change', pp. 61–85, in Perthes, *Arab Elites*.

105. Michael J. Willis, 'Between Alternance and the Makhzen: At–Tawhid wa Al–Islah's Entry into Moroccan Politics', *Journal of North African Studies*, 4 (3) 1999, pp. 45–80; Thierry Desrues and Eduardo Moyano, 'Social Change and Political Transition in Morocco', *Mediterranean Politics* 6 (1) 2001, pp. 21–47; Zeghal, *Islamism in Morocco*.

106. McFaul and Cofman Wittes, 'The Limits of Limited Reform'; Ellen Lust-Okar, *Structuring Conflict in the Arab World: Incumbents, Opponents, and Institutions*. Cambridge: Cambridge University Press, 2005.

107. Volpi, 'Algeria's Pseudo-democratic Politics'; Isabelle Werenfels, *Managing Instability in Algeria: Elites and Political Change since 1995*. Abingdon: Routledge, 2007.

108. Louisa Dris-Aït-Hamadouche, 'The 2007 Legislative Elections in Algeria: Political Reckonings', *Mediterranean Politics* 13 (1) 2008, pp. 87–94.

109. Christopher Alexander, *Tunisia: Stability and Reform in the Modern Maghreb*. New York: Routledge, 2010.

110. Larbi Sadiki, 'Bin Ali's Tunisia: Democracy by Non-Democratic Means', *British Journal of Middle Eastern Studies* 29 (1) 2002, pp. 57–78; Camau and Geisser, *Le syndrome autoritaire*.

111. Hibou, 'Domination and Control in Tunisia'; Camau and Geisser, *Le Syndrome autoritaire*.

112. Beau and Graciet, *La régente de Carthage*; Camau and Geisser, *Le syndrome autoritaire*.

113. Martinez, *The Libyan Paradox*; Vandewalle, *Libya since 1969*.

114. Thomas Hüsken, 'The Neotribal Competitive Order in the Borderland of Egypt and Libya', in Ulf Engel and Paul Nugent, eds., *Respacing Africa*. Amsterdam: Brill, 2009; John Davis, *Libyan Politics: Tribe and Revolution*. London: I.B. Tauris, 1987.

115. Pargeter, 'Libya'; Larbi Sadiki, 'Whither Arab "Republicanism"? The Rise of Family Rule and the "End of Democratization" in Egypt, Libya and Yemen', *Mediterranean Politics*, 15 (1) 2010, pp. 99–107; Yehudit Ronen, 'Libya's Rising Star: Saif al-Islam and Succession', *Middle East Policy*, 12 (3) 2005, pp. 136–144.

116. In *States and Social Revolutions*, Skocpol defines a conjuncture as 'the coming together of separately determined and not consciously coordinated (or deliberately revolutionary) processes and group efforts'. Theda Skocpol, *States and Social Revolutions: A Comparative Analysis of France, Russia, and China*. Cambridge: Cambridge University Press, 1979, p. 288.

117. See Jean-Pierre Filiu, *The Arab Revolution: Ten Lessons from the Democratic Uprising*. New York: Oxford University Press, 2011.

4. CONSTRUCTING IMPOSSIBLE UPRISINGS

1. Beatrice Hibou, *The Force of Obedience: The Political Economy of Repression in Tunisia*. Cambridge: Polity Press, 2011.

2. See Larbi Chouikha and Éric Gobe. 'La Tunisie entre la "Révolte du Bassin Minier de Gafsa" et l'écheance électorale de 2009', *L'Annee du Maghreb* No. 5, 2009, pp. 387–420.

3. See Katerina Dalacoura, 'The 2011 Uprisings in the Arab Middle East: Political Change and Geopolitical Implications', *International Affairs* 88 (1) 2012, pp. 63–79.

4. See F. Gregory Gause III, 'Why Middle East Studies Missed the Arab Spring: The Myth of Authoritarian Stability', *Foreign Affairs* 90 (4) 2011, pp. 81–90; Jack A. Goldstone, 'Understanding the Revolutions of 2011: Weakness and Resilience in Middle Eastern Autocracies', *Foreign Affairs* 90 (3) 2011, pp. 8–16.

5. Joffé rightly downplays the pertinence of socio-economically and ideologically construed explanations. George Joffé, 'The Arab Spring in North Africa: Origins and Prospects', *Journal of North African Studies*, 16 (4) 2011, pp. 507–532. Unfortunately, his suggestion that 'the real driver for the insurgencies in Egypt, Tunisia and Libya has been the contempt and repressiveness with which the Mubarak, Ben Ali and Qadhafi regimes treated the people over whom they ruled' (p. 508) reintroduces these structural tropes in a different guise.

6. Peter J. Schraeder and Hamadi Redissi, 'Ben Ali's Fall', *Journal of Democracy*, 22 (3) 2011, pp. 5–19, at p. 10.

7. Charles Kurzman, *The Unthinkable Revolution in Iran*. Cambridge: Harvard University Press, 2004.

8. William H. Sewell, *Logics of History: Social Theory and Social Transformation*.

Chicago: University of Chicago Press, 2005 (particularly chapter 8); Doug McAdam and William H. Sewell, Jr., 'Temporality in the Study of Social Movements and Revolutions', pp. 89–125, in Ronald R. Aminzade et al., eds., *Silence and Voice in the Study of Contentious Politics*. Cambridge: Cambridge University Press, 2001.

9. A sense of the heterogeneity of these interpretations in Tunisia in the early days of the revolt can be obtained from the online material gathered by the Library of Congress and the Bibliothèque Nationale de France at https://archive-it.org/collections/2323;JSESSIONID@ archive-it.org=03E45B2FE0AFCC693D68249C071EECC3. For an early narrative of revolution in the international press, see Brian Whitaker, 'How a man setting fire to himself sparked an uprising in Tunisia', *The Guardian*, 28 December 2010.

10. See Schraeder and Redissi, 'Ben Ali's Fall'.

11. Playing up the 'new media' dimension of the initial revolt, Al Jazeera journalist Yasmine Ryan noted that the key difference in Sidi Bouzid was that locals got news of what was happening out. She quoted a relative of Bouazizi saying that 'we could protest for two years here, but without videos no one would take any notice of us'. Yasmine Ryan, 'How Tunisia's revolution began', *Al Jazeera*, 26 January 2011, http://www.aljazeera.com/indepth/features/2011/01/201112612181598 5483.html.

12. The notion of a 'revolution' only began to emerge distinctly and publicly in the first week of January 2011. For all the subsequent talk of an 'Internet revolution' in relation to the Arab uprisings, it is noteworthy that the first Wikipedia entry for a 'Tunisian revolution' only appeared on 3 January 2011, http://en.wikipedia.org/w/index.php? title=Tunisian_revolution&oldid=405779912.

13. Tunisvisions, 'Un homme essaye de se suicider à Metlaoui', *Tunivisions. net*, http://www.tunivisions.net/27137/152/149/un-homme-essaye-de-se-suicider-a-metlaoui.html. Tunisvisions, 'Tunisie: Le suicide par le fcu cn tant que nouveau rituel contestataire', *Tunisvisions.net*, http://www.tunivisions.net/27411/152/149/tunisie-le-suicide-par-le-feu-en-tant-que-nouveau-rituel-contestataire.html.

14. International Monetary Fund, 'Tunisia: 2010 Article IV Consultation— Staff Report', IMF Country Report No. 10/282, Washington, DC, September 2010, http://www.imf.org/external/pubs/ft/scr/2010/ cr10282.pdf.

15. In the Tunisian case, see Béatrice Hibou, 'Fiscal Trajectories in Morocco and Tunisia', in Steven Heydemann, ed., *Networks of Privilege in the Middle East: The Politics of Economic Reform Revisited*. New York: Palgrave MacMillan, 2004; Amnesty International, 'Behind Tunisia's "Economic

Miracle": Inequality and Criminalization of Protest', Amnesty International Report MDE 30/003/2009, London, June 2009, http://www.amnesty.org/en/library/asset/MDE30/003/2009/en/2e1d33e2–55da-45a3–895f-656db85b7aed/mde300032009en.pdf.

16. Larbi Sadiki, 'Popular Uprisings and Arab Democratization', *International Journal of Middle East Studies* 32 (1) 2000, pp. 71–95, at p. 71.

17. Schraeder and Redissi, 'Ben Ali's Fall', p. 7.

18. About the Sidi Bouzid region, see Union Générale Tunisienne du Travail (UGTT), 'Le Développement régional au gouvernorat de Sidi-Bouzid: Entre la réalité accablante et les moyens prometteurs', UGTT, Tunis, August 2010.

19. Common portrayals of the incident that emerged at the time depicted a scene in which Bouazizi went to the mayor's office to complain about the way he had been treated by the police and to recover his goods. As the mayor refused to see him, Bouazizi threatened to set himself on fire if he was not granted an audience. The mayor still refused, and Bouazizi doused himself with petrol outside the mayor's office and set himself on fire.

20. The following day, a Friday, a sit-in was organized in front of the governorate office. The police brutally dispersed the demonstration using truncheons and tear gas. As a result, there were clashes between police and (young) demonstrators throughout the weekend that led to the first arrests of protesters. For a post hoc account of these events by the participants, see http://www.youtube.com/watch?v=kUtECoRX_P8.

21. Nawaat, 'Tunisie: Un rassemblement de jeune diplomes chomeurs de la ville de Skhira tourne à l'affrontement avec les forces de l'ordre', *Nawaat.org*, 4 February 2010, http://nawaat.org/portail/2010/02/04/tunisie-un-rassemblement-de-jeune-diplomes-chomeurs-de-la-ville-de-skhira-tourne-a-laffrontement-avec-les-forces-de-lordre/; Luiza Toscane, 'En Tunisie, travailler est un droit, le revendiquer est un crime', *Nawaat.org*, 5 April 2010, http://nawaat.org/portail/2010/04/05/en-tunisie-travailler-est-un-droit-le-revendiquer-est-un-crime/; Sadri Khiari (interviewed by Beatrice Hibou), 'La revolution tunisienne ne vient pas de nulle part', *Politique Africaine* No. 121, March 2011, pp. 23–34.

22. See Chouikha and Gobe, 'La Tunisie'.

23. Sofiene Chourabi, 'Special from Tunisia: Self-immolation by desperate youth sets off rare wave of protests', *Egypt Independent*, 26 December 2010, http://www.egyptindependent.com/news/special-tunisia-self-immolation-desperate-youth-sets-rare-wave-protests.

24. Heba Saleh, 'High Unemployment Sparks Tunisian Riot', *Financial Times*, 21 December 2010.

25. Christophe Ayad, 'Face au gâchis social, la Tunisie ose s'insurger', *Libération*, 21 December 2010.
26. While not as prominent as other tribal structures in the region, the tribe/clan affiliation retains some relevance in articulating solidarity networks in Tunisia, particularly in the hinterland. In an interview with the family of Bouazizi conducted after the fall of the regime, there is an explicit identification with this tribal group when justifying the reaction of Bouazizi to the purported slap in the face by the police-woman: 'for us the Hamama this is simply not acceptable'. Quoted in Christophe Ayad, 'Sidi Bouzid, l'étincelle', *Libération* 5, February 2011.
27. Cited in Christophe Ayad, 'Tunisie, la colère est dans la rue', *Libération*, 5 January 2011.
28. On police repression during the protests, see Amnesty International, 'Tunisia in Revolt: State Violence during Anti-Government Protests', Amnesty International Report MDE 30/011/2011, London, February 2011, http://www.amnesty.org/en/library/asset/MDE30/011/2011/en/e991941e-ccee-498b-a7ce-39e594c9d10a/mde300112011en.pdf; Human Rights Watch, 'Tunisia: Hold Police Accountable for Shootings', Human Rights Watch, 29 January 2011, http://www.hrw.org/en/news/2011/01/29/tunisia-hold-police-accountable-shootings; US Department of State, 2010 Human Rights Report: Tunisia, Bureau of Democracy, Human Rights, and Labor, Washington 8 April 2011, http://www.state.gov/j/drl/rls/hrrpt/2010/nea/154474.htm.
29. Al Jazeera, 'Job protests escalate in Tunisia', *Al Jazeera*, 28 December 2010, http://www.aljazeera.com/news/africa/2010/12/20101227204853391930.html.
30. 'Un mort et plusieurs blesses dans des emeutes en Tunisie', *Le Matin* (Algeria), 25 December 2010; Gnet, 'Tunisie, un rassemblement syndical en soutien à Sidi Bouzid', *GlobalNet* (Tunisia), 25 December 2010, http://www.gnet.tn/temps-fort/tunisie-lugtt-solidaire-de-sidi-bouzid-et-menzel-bouzaiene/id-menu-325.html; Perrine Mouterde, 'Le syndicat UGTT se cherche une nouvelle légitimité', *France24*, 5 April 2011, http://www.france24.com/fr/20110304-tunisie-syndicat-ugtt-corruption-revolution-legitimite-jrad-ben-ali
31. See Jeff Goodwin, *No Other Way Out: States and Revolutionary Movements, 1945–1991*. Cambridge: Cambridge University Press, 2001.
32. Full text of the speech available at: http://www.babnet.net/cadre-detail-31652.asp. Extracts are in Le Monde, 'Ben Ali regrette les troubles en Tunisie et accuse les médias étrangers', *Le Monde*, 5 January 2011.
33. A live TV debate addressing openly the flaws of the regime was thus aired the day after the presidential intervention. See https://www.facebook.com/video/video.php?v=129048513826647.

34. See Gilad Lotan, Erhardt Graeff, Mike Ananny, Devin Gaffney, Ian Pearce and Danah Boyd, 'The Revolutions Were Tweeted: Information Flows during the 2011Tunisian and Egyptian Revolutions', *International Journal of Communication* 5, 2011, pp. 1375–1405.
35. As Hofheinz noted, 'the debate between "cyber-skeptics" and "cyber-utopians" reflects the yo-yo pattern of alternating hope and disappointment that appears to be a characteristic thread in how we have come to look at media impact in the Middle East'. Albrecht Hofheinz, 'Nextopia? Beyond Revolution 2.0', *International Journal of Communication* 5, 2011, pp. 1417–1434, at p. 1422.
36. Ryan, 'How Tunisia's revolution began'.
37. Claire Bonnichon and Florence Villeminot, 'La jeunesse défie le président Zine el-Abidine Ben Ali', *France24*, 28 December 2010, http://www.france24.com/fr/20101227-jeunesse-defie-ben-ali-contre-chomage-precarite-tunisie-police-manifestations-sidi-bouzid.
38. Anita Breuer, Todd Landman and Dorothea Farquhar, 'Social Media and Protest Mobilization: Evidence from the Tunisian Revolution', *Democratization* 22 (4) 2015, pp. 764–792.
39. Ayad, 'Tunisie, la colère est dans la rue'; 'Un mort et plusieurs blessés dans des émeutes en Tunisie', *Le Matin* (Algeria), 25 December 2010.
40. In the Egyptian uprising, Miriyam Aouragh and Anne Alexander highlighted the importance of the distinction between 'the use of the Internet as a *tool* by those seeking to bring about change from below, and the Internet's role as a *space* where collective dissent can be articulated'. Miriyam Aouragh and Anne Alexander, 'The Egyptian Experience: Sense and Nonsense of the Internet Revolution', *International Journal of Communication* 5, 2011, pp. 1344–1358.
41. Author's interview with activists having participated in this demonstration, Tunis, December 2012; Gnet, 'Tunisie, un rassemblement syndical en soutien à Sidi Bouzid'.
42. Cited in AFP, 'Tunisie: Le gouverneur de Sidi Bouzid limogé, l'opposition veut des réformes', *Le Point*, 30 December 2010. The Alliance included notably the Democratic Forum for Labour and Liberties (Ettakatol), the Ettajdid Movement, the Patriotic and Democratic Labour Party, as well as independents.
43. Clement M. Henry and Robert Springborg, *Globalization and the Politics of Development in the Middle East*, 2nd edn. Cambridge University, Press, 2010; Mohammed Hachemaoui, 'La corruption politique en Algérie: L'Envers de l'autoritarisme', *Esprit*, June 2011, pp. 111–134.
44. Jean-Pierre Filiu, 'The Local and Global Jihad of al-Qa'ida in the Islamic Maghrib', *Middle East Journal* 63 (2) 2009, pp. 213–226; Mohammad-

Mahmoud Ould Mohamedou, 'The Many Faces of Al Qaeda in the Islamic Maghreb', GCSP Policy Paper No. 15, May 2011.

45. International Crisis Group, 'Algeria: Unrest and Impasse in Kabylia', ICG Middle East/North Africa Report No. 15, June 2003.

46. Ambassador Robert Ford, 'Scene Setter for A/S Welch Visit to Algeria', US Algiers Embassy, 28 February 2008, http://wikileaks.ch/cable/2008/02/08ALGIERS198.html#.

47. The *El Watan* data are cited in Jack Brown, 'Algeria's Midwinter Uproar', *Middle East Report Online*, 20 January 2011, http://www.merip.org/mero/mero012011; the *Liberté* data are cited in Isabelle Mandraud, 'L'Algérie confrontée à ses multiples paradoxes', *Le Monde*, 31 December 2010.

48. See Ahmed Aghrout and Yahia Zoubir, 'Introducing Algeria's President-for-Life', *Middle East Report Online*, 1 April 2009, http://www.merip.org/mero/mero040109.

49. Nouria Bourihane, 'Hausse généralisée des prix des produits alimentaires', *Le Temps d'Algérie*, 1 January 2011.

50. See Mehdia Belkadi, 'Tunisie: Révolte ou révolution?', *El Watan Magazine*, 31 December 2010.

51. See Djamel Khiat, 'De violentes émeutes éclatent dans plusieurs quartiers d'Oran, deuxième ville d'Algérie', *DNA: Dernières Nouvelles d'Algérie*, 5 January 2011; B. Mehdi, 'Douaouda et l'ouest d'Alger en ébullition', *Le Temps d'Algérie*, 5 January 2011.

52. Cited in AFP/NouvelObs, 'Algérie/émeutes: "De cette vie sans lendemain, nous n'en pouvons plus"', *NouvelObs.com*, 7 January 2011, http://tempsreel.nouvelobs.com/monde/20110107.OBS5891/reportage-algerie-emeutes-de-cette-vie-sans-lendemain-nous-n-en-pouvons-plus.html.

53. Wahib Ait Ouakli, 'Oran: Plusieurs quartiers en proie à la protestation', *L'Expression*, 6 January 2011; M. Aziza, Z. Mehdaoui and M. Mehdi, 'Alger: Scènes de pillage et une capitale paralysée', *Le Quotidien d'Oran*, 8 January 2011.

54. 'Urgent: Des coups de feu à Alger, l'embrasement à Oran: les premières vidéos', *Le Matin dz*, 5 January 2011, http://www.lematindz.net/news/3578-urgent-des-coups-de-feu-a-alger-lembrasement-a-oran.htm.

55. Assiya Hamza, 'L'Algérie s'embrase aussi sur le net', *Europe1.fr*, 7 January 2011, http://www.europe1.fr/international/l-algerie-s-embrase-aussi-sur-le-net-364197.

56. Karim Aimeur, 'Paradoxe algérien: Des protestations sans slogans politiques', *L'Expression*, 10 January 2011.

57. See Salim Mesbah, 'Émeutes: L'embrasement', *El Watan*, 7 January 2011.

58. Cited in Djamel Belayachi, 'Nouvelle vague d'émeutes sur l'Algérie', *Afrik.com*, 7 January 2011, http://www.afrik.com/article21672.html

59. 'Batailles rangées et édifices détruits et brûlés: Les deux folles nuits d'Alger', *Le Soir d'Algérie*, 8 January 2011.

60. Cited in AFP/NouvelObs, 'Algérie/émeutes'. See also Brown, 'Algeria's Midwinter Uproar'.

61. Omar Berbiche, 'Pertes et profits', *El Watan*, 10 January 2011; Beatrice Khadige, 'Unrest eases in Algeria as prices drop', *AFP*, 10 January 2011, http://www.middle-east-online.com/english/?id=43557.

62. See Myriam Berber, 'La situation tunisienne préoccupe le monde arabe', *Radio France International*, 19 January 2011, http://www.rfi.fr/economie/20110119-situation-tunisienne-preoccupe-le-monde-arabe.

63. The first suggestion was voiced by Mohamed Larbi Zitout on Al Jazeera. Al Jazeera, 'Algeria set for crisis talks', *Al Jazeera*, 8 January 2011, http://www.aljazeera.com/news/africa/2011/01/2011187476 735721.html. The second comment was in a communiqué of the national council of the FFS. FFS, 'Le pouvoir ne peut pas acheter le silence des Algériens', *DNA: Dernières Nouvelles d'Algérie*, 8 January 2011.

64. Djamel Khiat, 'Des centaines de manifestants en instance de jugement, leurs familles réclament leurs libérations', *DNA: Dernières Nouvelles d'Algérie*, 9 January 2011.

65. Tayeb Belmadi, 'Censure, filtrage, connexion lente: Pourquoi Facebook n'est pas accessible en Algérie', *DNA: Dernières Nouvelles d'Algérie*, 10 January 2011.

66. Jeune Afrique, 'Vague de tentatives de suicide par le feu en Algérie', *Jeune Afrique*, 17 January 2011; Chawki Amari, Mélanie Matarese, Ramdane Koubabi and Ghellab Smail, 'Je brûle, donc je suis', *Courrier International*, 21 January 2011.

67. Frédéric Volpi, *Islam and Democracy: The Failure of Dialogue in Algeria*. London: Pluto Press, 2003.

68. A critical report by an independent Algerian commission of inquiry led by Mohand Issad concluded that the violence in Kabylia was provoked and kept going by the gendarmes who repeatedly exceeded their authority by firing live rounds at rioters, and that the gendarmes' behaviour could not be explained away as individual excesses. International Crisis Group, 'Algeria: Unrest and Impasse in Kabylia', ICG Middle East/North Africa Report No. 15, London, June 2003.

69. Cited in Rabah Beldjenna, 'Ould Kablia: "La situation est contenue"', *El Watan*, 9 January 2011.

70. Cited in Mohamed Boufatah, 'Le ministre de l'intérieur à l'APS: "La Page est tournée"', *L'Expression*, 10 January 2011.

71. Even when the state of emergency restrictions would be lifted at the end of February 2011, a new raft of anti-terrorism measures brought in by the government ensured that the security forces still had extensive freedom of action regarding any matter that was deemed to be 'a threat to the nation'. Réseau Euro-Méditerranéen des Droits de l'Homme (REMDH), 'La levée de l'état d'urgence: Un trompe-l'oeil', 24 February 2012, http://euromedrights.org/fr/publication/rapport-du-remdh-sur-la-levee-de-letat-durgence-en-algerie-des-reformes-en-trompe-loeil/.

72. By 10 January, when the situation was much calmer, it emerged that 'only' five people had died during this week of nation-wide unrest. See Z. Mehdaoui, 'Après plusieurs jours de violence: La capitale renoue avec le calme', *Le Quotidien d'Oran*, 10 January 2011; R.N., 'Le calme se dessine à l'Ouest', *Le Quotidien d'Oran*, 10 January 2011.

73. Dirk Vandewalle, ed., *Libya since 1969: Qadhafi's Revolution Revisited*. Basingstoke: Palgrave Macmillan, 2008.

74. International Crisis Group (ICG), 'Popular Protest in North Africa and the Middle East (V): Making Sense of Libya', Middle East/North Africa Report No. 107, 6 June 2011, http://www.crisisgroup.org/en/regions/middle-east-north-africa/north-africa/libya/107-popular-protest-in-north-africa-and-the-middle-east-v-making-sense-of-libya.aspx

75. See Society for Threatened Peoples (STP), 'Libyan Arab Jamahiriya', Göttingen, 12 April 2010, http://lib.ohchr.org/HRBodies/UPR/Documents/Session9/LY/STP_SocietyforThreatenedPeoples.pdf; Bruce Maddy-Weitzman, *The Berber Identity Movement and the Challenge to North African States*. Austin: University of Texas Press, 2011.

76. Luis Martinez, *The Libyan Paradox*. London: Hurst, 2007.

77. ICG, 'Popular Protest in North Africa'; Mohamed Abdel-Baky, 'Libya Protest over Housing Enters its Third Day', *Ahramonline*, 16 January 2011, http://english.ahram.org.eg/NewsContent/2/8/4032/World/Region/Libya-protest-over-housing-enters-its-third-day.aspx.

78. See Khaled Mahmoud, 'Gaddafi Ready for Libya's "Day of Rage"', *Asharq al-Awsat*, 9 February 2011, http://www.aawsat.net/2011/02/article55247591; Al Jazeera, '"Day of rage" kicks off in Libya', *Al Jazeera*, 17 February 2011, http://www.aljazeera.com/news/africa/2011/02/201121755057219793.html

79. Leela Jacinto, 'Libyans Hope their Revolution will also be Tweeted', *France24* 16 February 2011, http://www.france24.com/en/20110216-libya-hope-revolution-will-also-be-tweeted-uprising-facebook-internet-gaddafi/.

80. BBC News, 'Libya Protests: Second City Benghazi Hit by Violence',

BBC, 16 February 2011, http://www.bbc.co.uk/news/world-africa-12477275. Many videos uploaded on YouTube at around that time also purport to show these demonstrations. See http://www.youtube.com/watch?v=rk_Ys3rfGFE.

81. Al Jazeera, 'Libyan Police Stations Torched', *Al Jazeera*, 16 February 2011, http://www.aljazeera.com/news/africa/2011/02/2011216705 1422444.html.

82. Associated Press, 'Anti-Government Protesters Killed in Libyan Clash', *Washington Post*, 17 February 2011, http://www.washingtontimes.com/news/2011/feb/17/anti-government-protesters-killed-libyan-clash/?page=all. See also the many videos uploaded on YouTube at the time, for example, http://www.youtube.com/user/enoughgaddafi/videos.

83. Frank Gardner, 'Libya not Immune to Winds of Change', *BBC*, 16 February 2011, http://www.bbc.co.uk/news/world-africa-12484186.

84. The Muslim Brotherhood, 'Muslim Leaders Urge for the End of Massacre in Libya', *Ikhwanweb*, 20 February 2011, http://www.ikhwanweb.com/article.php?id=28066; Human Rights Watch, 'Libya: Security Forces Fire on 'Day of Anger' Demonstrations', Human Rights Watch, 18 February 2011, http://www.hrw.org/news/2011/02/17/libya-security-forces-fire-day-anger-demonstrations.

85. Cited in Jean-Pierre Perrin, 'Benghazi, la liberté au prix du sang', *Libération*, 25 February 2011.

86. Martinez, *The Libyan Paradox*.

87. Nick Meo, 'Libya protests: 140 "Massacred" as Gaddafi Sends in Snipers to Crush Dissent', *The Telegraph*, 20 February 2011; Al Jazeera, 'Libya Clashes Spread to Tripoli', *Al Jazeera*, 20 February 2011, http://www.aljazeera.com/news/africa/2011/02/20112202148108558.html.

88. Saif Gaddafi's televised speech of 20 February 2011 is available on YouTube at http://www.youtube.com/watch?v=Pp6DFM9_NuU. Translated extracts are available from Channel 4 news, 'Libya: Gadaffi "Last Man Standing" Vow as Protests Spread', Channel 4 News, 21 February 2011, http://www.channel4.com/news/libya-regime-vow-to-fight-until-last-man-standing.

89. Al Jazeera, 'Uprising Flares in Libyan City', *Al Jazeera*, 20 February 2011, http://www.aljazeera.com/news/africa/2011/02/20112201425 9976293.html; Reuters, 'L'Est de la Libye échappe au contrôle du régime Kadhafi', *L'Express*, 22 February 2011, http://www.lexpress.fr/actualites/2/monde/l-est-de-la-libye-echappe-au-controle-du-regime-kadhafi_965142.html.

90. Arthur Quesnay, 'L'Insurrection libyenne: Un movement revolutionaire decentralisé', pp. 113–132, in Amin Allal and Thomas Pierret, eds., *Au cœur des révoltes arabes: Devenir revolutionaires*. Paris: Armand

Colin, 2013; Lourdes Garcia-Navarro, 'Provisional Government Forming in Eastern Libya', *National Public Radio*, 23 February 2011, http://www.npr.org/2011/02/23/134003954/New-Government-Forms-In-Eastern-Libya

91. Cited in Jean-Pierre Perrin, 'Benghazi fait table rase de Kadhafi', *Libération*, 26 February 2011.

92. The resignation statement of Younis on 22 February is available on YouTube at http://www.youtube.com/watch?v=-yaagShCKaU. Translated transcripts are available from Al Jazeera at http://blogs.aljazeera.com/blog/africa/live-blog-libya-feb-22.

93. Those actors having started the uprising in Benghazi were well aware of the risk of being perceived in the west of the country as a secessionist movement and of the regime's propaganda in portraying them at such. In this context, a local council member stressed that they should 'avoid forming a government until the west of the country was conquered'. Cited in Jean-Pierre Perrin, 'Benghazi fait table rase de Kadhafi'.

94. Gaddafi's televised speech on 22 February is available on YouTube at http://www.youtube.com/watch?v=FMDplUrXvAw. Translated sections are available at http://www.liberation.fr/monde/2011/02/22/kadhafi-nous-n-avons-pas-encore-utilise-la-force_716664.

95. This is well illustrated in the many videos uploaded by protesters on YouTube at the time. See http://www.youtube.com/user/enough-gaddafi/videos.

96. US President Ronald Reagan famously called Gaddafi the 'mad dog of the Middle East' in the mid-1980s after a series of bombings in Europe deemed to be orchestrated by Libya. Ronald Reagan, 'The President's News Conference', 9 April 1986, The American Presidency Project, ed. By John T. Woolley and Gerhard Peters, available at www.presidency.ucsb.edu/ws/?pid=37105.

97. See Sudarsan Raghavan and Leila Fadel, 'Military Helicopters Reportedly Fire on Protesters in Libya', *Washington Post*, 21 February 2011, http://www.washingtonpost.com/wp-dyn/content/article/2011/02/20/AR2011022004185.html.

98. Kurt Weyland, 'The Diffusion of Revolution: "1848" in Europe and Latin America', *International Organization* 63 (3) 2009, pp. 391–423.

99. Cited in AFP, 'Sarkozy juge que "Kadhafi doit partir"', *Le Point*, 25 February 2011, http://www.lepoint.fr/monde/sarkozy-juge-que-kadhafi-doit-partir-25-02-2011-1299638_24.php.

100. Transcript of the statement available at http://www.whitehouse.gov/the-press-office/2011/02/26/readout-president-obamas-call-chancellor-angela-merkel-germany.

101. Christiane Amanpour interview with Gaddafi, *ABC News*, 28 February

2011, http://abcnews.go.com/International/christiane-amanpour-interviews-libyas-moammar-gadhafi/story?id=13019942&singlePage=true.

102. The movement's initial webpage was: https://www.facebook.com/Movement20?v=wall.

103. Regarding the common limitations on freedom of expression at that time, see Moshe Gershovich, 'The "New Press" and Free Speech under Mohammed VI', pp. 93–108, in Bruce Maddy-Weitzman and Daniel Zisenwine, eds., *Contemporary Morocco: State, Politics and Society under Mohammed VI*. New York: Routledge, 2013.

104. Ahmed Benchemsi, 'Feb20's Rise and Fall: A Moroccan Story', *Le Blog de Ahmed Benchemsi*, 17 July 2012, http://ahmedbenchemsi.com/feb20s-rise-and-fall-a-moroccan-story/.

105. See Abdelmajid Hannoum, 'Tangier in the Time of Arab Revolutions: An Ethnopolitical Diary', *Journal of North African Studies* 18 (2) 2013, pp. 272–290; Koenraad Bogaert, 'The Revolt of Small Towns: The Meaning of Morocco's History and the Geography of Social Protests', *Review of African Political Economy* 42 (143) 2015, pp. 124–140.

106. The call for participation issued by al-Adl wal-Ihsane on 16 February was published on the organization's website at http://www.aljamaa.net/fr/document/2484.shtml.

107. Sélim Smaoui and Mohamed Wazif, 'Étandard de lutte ou pavillon de complaisance', in Allal and Pierret, *Au cœur des révoltes arabes*.

108. The interior minister, Taib Cherkaoui, announced on 21 February that 120 people had been arrested throughout the country during these demonstrations, and that several public buildings, banks and properties had been vandalized. The troubles that erupted in some locations after the demonstrations were attributed by activists to the Moroccan security services seeking to undermine the peaceful character of the protests. See, for example, http://voxmaroc.blog.lemonde.fr/2011/02.

109. Smaoui and Wazif, 'Étandard de lutte'.

110. See PJD, Mustapha Ramid et al., Open letter, 17 February 2011; PJD, 'Statement about the changes that we want', Rabat, 23 March 2011.

111. Author's interview with Abdellah Bouanou, leader of the PJD parliamentary group, Rabat, Morocco, 3 July 2013.

112. Oumar Baldé and Ghita Ismaili, 'Interview exclusive avec Mustapha Rami du PJD', *Yabiladi*, 22 February 2011, http://www.yabiladi.com/articles/details/4668/interview-exclusive-avec-mustapha-ramid.html.

113. Thierry Desrues, 'Le mouvement du 20 février et le régime

marocain: Contestation, révision constitutionnelle et élections', *L'Année du Maghreb* 8, 2012, pp. 359–389.

114. Desrues, 'Le mouvement du 20 février'.

115. There were more radical forms of process inspired by the protest events in the region, such as the self-immolation of a young woman in a small provincial town who had been refused social housing; but this event did not draw particular attention at the time. Souhaïl Karam and Marc Deltei, 'Une jeune marocaine, mère célibataire, s'immole par le feu', *Lexpress.fr*, 23 January 2011, http://www.lexpress.fr/actualites/2/monde/une-jeune-marocaine-mere-celibataire-s-immole-par-le-feu_965662.html.

116. Abdelilah Benkirane interview in 'Mais encore?', Channel 2M, 28 February 2011, http://www.dailymotion.com/video/xhb0zp_mais-encore-avec-abdelilah-benkirane_tv.

117. Mohammed VI, 'Discours adressé, mercredi 09 mars 2011, à la nation par SM le Roi Mohammed VI', Royaume du Maroc, http://www.maroc.ma/fr/discours-royaux/texte-int%C3%A9gral-du-discours-adress%C3%A9-par-sm-le-roi-la-nation#.

118. In his speech, the king declared that because of his 'commitment to create optimal conditions for the decentralization process to be as efficient as possible, we have decided to inscribe this process within the framework of a global constitutional reform designed to modernize and upgrade the state structures'. Mohammed VI, 'Discours'.

5. REDRAWING CONTENTION AND AUTHORITARIAN PRACTICES

1. The first Wikipedia entry for a 'Tunisian revolution' only appeared on 3 January 2011. See: http://en.wikipedia.org/w/index.php?title=Tunisian_revolution&oldid=405779912.

2. Cited in AFP, 'At Least Four Killed in Tunisia Unrest', *Ahram Online*, 9 January 2011, http://english.ahram.org.eg/NewsContent/2/8/3460/World/Region/At-least-four-killed-in-Tunisia-unrest-witnesses.aspx.

3. Elodie Auffray, 'A Kasserine, le "chaos" relaté par les internautes tunisiens', *Libération*, 11 January 2011.

4. Cited in Marion Solletty, 'C'est bien un mouvement sans précédent que nous vivons là pour la Tunisie', *Le Monde*, 5 January 2011.

5. David Hess and Brian Martin, 'Repression, Backfire, and the Theory of Transformative Events', *Mobilization* 11 (1) 2006, pp. 249–267.

6. AFP, 'Manifestations mortelles en Tunisie', *Libération*, 9 January 2011.

7. See Arnaud Vaulerin, 'Le régime dépassé par la cyberrésistance', *Libération*, 11 January 2011; Elodie Auffray, 'Nawaat.org, le site de la contestation sociale tunisienne', *Libération*, 12 January 2011.

8. Ben Wagner, '"I Have Understood You": The Co-evolution of Expression

and Control on the Internet, Television and Mobile Phones during the Jasmine Revolution in Tunisia', *International Journal of Communication* No. 5, 2011, pp. 1295–1302.

9. Mehdi Mabrouk, 'A Revolution for Dignity and Freedom: Preliminary Observations on the Social and Cultural Background to the Tunisian Revolution', *Journal of North African Studies* 16 (4) 2011, pp. 625–635, at p. 632.

10. See Marion Solletty, 'C'est bien un mouvement sans précédent que nous vivons là pour la Tunisie'.

11. Ben Ali, Speech of 10 January 2011. The text of the discourse is available (in French) at: http://www.liberation.fr/monde/01012313672-l-integralite-de-l-allocution-du-president-tunisien-ben-ali.

12. Ben Ali, Speech of 10 January 2011.

13. Cited in AFP/NouvelObs, 'Tunisie: Couvre-feu décrété à Tunis et sa banlieue', NouvelObs.com, 12 January 2011, http://tempsreel.nouvelobs.com/monde/20110112.OBS6073/tunisie-couvre-feu-decrete-a-tunis-et-sa-banlieue.html.

14. The headquarters of the Progressive Democratic Party, the main opposition party calling for a demonstration, had been surrounded by police forces, and so was the building of the National Union of Journalists. José Douglas, 'Le régime Ben Ali réprime, la rue tunisienne continue d'y croire', *Libération*, 12 January 2011.

15. AFP, 'Tunisie: Couvre-feu décrété à Tunis et sa banlieue', *Le Nouvel Observateur*, 12 January 2011.

16. Douglas, 'Le régime Ben Ali'.

17. See Informations Ouvrières, 'Tunisie: La révolution en marche 1', No. 132, 20 January 2011, http://parti-ouvrier-independant.fr/2011/03/06/tunisie-la-revolution-en-marche-1/; Informations Ouvrières, 'Tunisie: La révolution en marche 2', No. 133, 27 January 2011, http://parti-ouvrier-independant.fr/2011/03/06/tunisie-la-revolution-en-marche-2/.

18. He added, 'We are all saying that repression and the firing of live ammunition have to end, and that a national commission of investigation needs to be set up'. Cited in Douglas, 'Le régime Ben Ali'.

19. AFP, 'Tunisie: Couvre-feu décrété'.

20. Cited in Douglas, 'Le Régime Ben Ali'.

21. Ben Ali, Speech of 13 January 2011. The full text is available (in French) at: http://www.businessnews.com.tn/details_article.php?t=520&a=22999&temp=1&lang.

22. AFP, 'Tunisie: Les promesses de Ben Ali plutôt bien accueillies par l'opposition, *Libération*, 14 January 2011.

23. Mabrouk, 'A Revolution for Dignity and Freedom', p. 631.

24. The head of the army, General Rachid Ammar, had been sidelined for failing to carry out orders, and was replaced by Ahmad Shabir, head of the secret service. Abdelaziz Barrouhi, 'Tunisie: Que mijotait Ali Seriati?', *Jeune Afrique*, 28 March 2011.

25. See Reuters, 'Ben Ali Says He Was Deceived Into Leaving Tunisia', *The Guardian*, 20 June 2011; Pierre Puchot, 'Ce qu'il s'est vraiment passé le 14 janvier à Tunis', Mediapart, 9 August 2011, http://nawaat.org/portail/2011/08/09/tunisie-ce-qu%E2%80%99il-s%E2%80%99est-vraiment-passe-le-14-janvier-a-tunis-mediatpart/.

26. Barrouhi, 'Tunisie: Que mijotait Ali Seriati?'

27. According to Lanxade, the former French ambassador to Tunisia, one of the first regime actors to make this point was General Ammar, who told Ben Ali that he was 'finished' and he should go when the president removed him from his post. Le Point, 'Tunisie: Jacques Lanxade estime que l'armé peut jouer un rôle modérateur', *Le Point*, 16 January 2011.

28. Le Monde, 'Tunisie: Les propos "effrayants" d'Alliot-Marie suscitent la polémique', *Le Monde*, 14 January 2011.

29. AFP, 'Tunisie: Fillon inquiet de "l'utilisation disproportionnée de la violence"', *Le Monde*, 13 January 2011.

30. Le Parisien, 'Tunisie: Ben Ali chasse du pouvoir, la France "ne souhaite pas" l'accueillir', *Le Parisien*, 14 January 2011.

31. Arthur Quesnay, 'L'Insurrection libyenne: Un mouvement révolutionnaire décentralisé', in A. Allal and T. Pierret, eds., *Au cœur des révoltes arabes: Devenir révolutionnaires*. Paris: Armand Colin, pp. 113–135; Nicole Dupont, Eric Faye and Reuters, 'L'Est de la Libye échappe au contrôle du régime Kadhafi', *L'Express*, 22 February 2011, http://www.lexpress.fr/actualites/2/monde/l-est-de-la-libye-echappe-au-controle-du-regime-kadhafi_965142.html.

32. Brian McQuinn, *After the Fall: Libya's Evolving Armed Groups*. Small Arms Survey, Graduate Institute of International and Development Studies, Geneva, 2012.

33. National Transition Council, Founding Statement, published on the original website of the NTC, www.ntclibya.org, which is now offline. A copy of the statement is available at the Cambridge University Lauterpacht Centre for international law: http://www.lcil.cam.ac.uk/sites/default/files/LCIL/documents/arabspring/libya/Libya_12_Founding_Statement_TNC.pdf.

34. Derek Henry Flood, 'Special Commentary from Inside Western Libya—On the Precipice: Libya's Amazigh in Revolt', The Jamestown Foundation, 25 July 2011, http://www.jamestown.org/single/?no_cache=1&tx_ttnews[tt_news]=38225&tx_ttnews[backPid]=61&cHash=c53ae0ca337b5dca9b36d87f3c1423a0#.UlmEVlM7Z9U.

35. National Transition Council, Founding Statement.

36. Cited in Nicholas Watt, 'US Defence Secretary Robert Gates Sams "Loose Talk" about No-Fly Zones', *The Guardian*, 3 March 2011.

37. See Adrian Blomfield, 'Libya: Warplanes Bomb Rebels in Show of Air Power', *The Telegraph*, 1 March 2011; Christian Peregin, 'Two Libyan fighter pilots defect to Malta', *Times of Malta*, 22 February 2011.

38. The only situation that showed some similarities was the Saudi-led military intervention in Bahrain on 14 March 2011, albeit in support of the regime in this case.

39. Cited in Anthony Shadid, 'Qaddafi Forces Bear Down on Strategic Town as Rebels Flee', *New York Times*, 10 March 2011.

40. Jason Pack, 'The Two Faces of Libya's Rebels', *Foreign Policy*, 5 April 2011; David Zucchino, 'Mistakes Costing Libyan Rebels', *Los Angeles Times*, 8 March 2011.

41. Ben Farmer, 'Libya: Military Instructor Attempts to Turn Youthful Volunteers into Fearsome Fghting Force', *The Telegraph*, 5 April 2011; Rod Nordland, 'Libyan rebels say they're being sent weapons', *New York Times*, 16 April 2011.

42. This grassroots war economy and the bottom-up organization of a supply chain for armed resistance were most visible in besieged Misrata. See C.J. Chivers, 'Hidden Workshops add to Libyan Rebels' Arsenal', *New York Times*, 4 May 2011.

43. https://www.facebook.com/notes/national-transitional-council-of-libya/introducing-the-council/203658689673270.

44. The full list of the CNCD members can be found in the communiqué of the LADDH available at http://www.la-laddh.org/spip.php?article568. In Tunisia, the January 14 Front was a coalition of leftist organizations that sought to ensure the substantive transformation of the system of governance inherited from Ben Ali. See http://reveil-communiste.over-blog.fr/article-tunisie-formation-du-front-du-14-jan-vier-65774529.html/.

45. See the Rachad documents at http://www.rachad.org/.

46. The FFS communiqué can be found at http://ffs1963.unblog.fr/2011/01/22/le-ffs-estime-que-la-concertation-doit-sapprofondir-et-eventuellement-selargir-a-lavenir/.

47. Salima Tlemçani, 'Après les mises en garde de la wilaya contre la marche à Alger: Bras de fer entre le RCD et les autorités', *El Watan*, 22 January 2011.

48. Rabah Beldjenna, 'Empechement de la marche du RCD: Des blessés devant le siège du parti à Alger et de nombreuses arrestations', *El Watan*, 22 January 2011.

49. See the declaration of Karim Tabbou, general secretary of the FFS, in Zineb Dryef, 'Manifestations en Algérie: "Le pays est miné de toute

part"', *Rue89.com*, 22 January 2011, http://www.rue89.com/2011/01/22/manifestations-en-algerie-le-pays-est-mine-de-toute-part-186938.

50. El Moudjahid, 'Communiqué du conseil des ministres', *El Moudjahid*, 3 February 2011.

51. The official declaration of the end of the state of emergency came on 24 February. See Arezki Ait Larbi, 'Bouteflika restaure l'état de droit en Algérie', *Le Figaro*, 24 February 2011.

52. Christian Lowe and Lamine Chikhi, 'Algeria Police Stifle Egypt-inspired Protest', *Reuters*, 12 February 2011, http://in.reuters.com/article/2011/02/12/idINIndia-54845720110212. A detailed chronology of the protest that day can be found in *Le Monde* at http://www.lemonde.fr/afrique/article/2011/02/12/suivez-en-direct-les-manifestations-en-algerie_1479002_3212.html#ens_id=1461890.

53. Cited in Mustapha Benfodil, 'La manifestation de la CNCD s'est tenue à Alger: Un premier pas pour le changement', *El Watan*, 13 February 2011; Karima Bennoune, 'Yesterday Egypt, Today Algeria', *The Guardian*, 12 February 2011.

54. Karima Bennoune, 'Hopes and Fears: An Algiers Diary', *The Guardian*, 17 February 2011.

55. In Tahrir Square, the focal point of the Egyptian revolution of 2011, tens of thousands of demonstrators managed to occupy the square on the first day of protest, on 25 January. A few days later, their numbers had increased to over 100,000 according to the BBC and over 200,000 according to Al Jazeera. On 1 February, Al Jazeera even suggested that the total number of demonstrators may have reached 1 million, though other analysts put the maximum number of protesters at a more conservative 300,000 mark. See BBC, 'Egypt Protesters Step up Pressure on Hosni Mubarak', *BBC*, 31 January 2011, http://www.bbc.co.uk/news/world-middle-east-12320959. Al Jazeera, 'Protesters flood Egypt streets', *Al Jazeera*, 1 February 2011, http://www.aljazeera.com/news/middleeast/2011/02/2011215827193882.html. For an analysis of mobilization at the square, see Jeroen Gunning and Ilan Zvi Baron, *Why Occupy a Square?: People, Protests and Movements in the Egyptian Revolution*. London: Hurst, 2014.

56. Adam Nossiter and Timothy Williams, 'Security Forces Halt Protest in Algeria', *New York Times*, 12 February 2011.

57. Some news report pointing to Internet restrictions—especially access to Twitter and Facebook—at that time further illustrated the government's reliance on security options, even though an information blackout did not constitute a key element of the regime's strategy of control. Nabila Ramdani, 'Algeria Tried to Block Internet and Facebook as Protest Mounted', *The Telegraph*, 12 February 2011.

58. Indicative of these tensions were the declarations of Louisa Hanoune, the leader of the Workers Party, once a vocal opponent of the regime, who was co-opted by Bouteflika and who defended the president, saying he was no Ben Ali or Mubarak, and condemned the march as right-wing. Sonia Lyes, 'Louisa Hanoune: "Bouteflika n'est ni Ben Ali, ni Moubarak"', *Tout sur l'Algérie*, 13 February 2011, http://www.tsaalgerie.com/politique/louisa-hanoune-bouteflika-n-est-ni-ben-ali-ni-moubarak_14280.html

59. Cited in Peggy Bruguière, 'La "marche pour la démocratie" du 12 février divise les Algériens', *France24.com*, 10 February 2011, http://observers.france24.com/fr/20110210-algerie-marche-manifestations-etudiants-abdelaziz-bouteflika-alger.

60. AFP, 'Algérie: L'opposition CNCD annonce une marche le 19 février à Alger', *Le Point*, 13 February 2011, http://www.lepoint.fr/monde/algerie-l-opposition-cncd-annonce-une-marche-le-19-fevrier-a-alger-13–02–2011–1294952_24.php.

61. *El Watan*, 'Malgré l'imposant dispositif policier: Ils étaient là', *El Watan*, 20 February 2011. A detailed chronology of the events of the day compiled by Al Jazeera is available at http://blogs.aljazeera.net/africa/2011/02/15/live-blog-eye-algeria.

62. N.B., 'CNCD: C'est la division', *Le Temps d'Algérie*, 22 February 2011.

63. For a critical analysis of the limited security implications of the end of the state of emergency, see Réseau Euro-Méditerranéen des Droits de l'Homme (REMDH), 'La levée de l'état d'urgence: un trompe-l'oeil. L'Exercice des libertés d'association, de réunion et de manifestation en Algérie', Rapport du Réseau Euro-Méditerranéen des Droits de l'Homme, Copenhagen, December 2011.

64. Madjid Makedhi, 'La CNCD appelle à une marche à partir de la place des martyrs: Le "mur de l'interdit" sera-t-il abattu?', *El Watan*, 26 February 2011.

65. Mehdi Benslimane, 'Said Sadi agressé à Alger: "Dégage sale kabyle, retourne chez toi à Tizi Ouzou"', *DNA: Dernières Nouvelles d'Algérie*, 5 March 2011.

66. Cited in Al Jazeera, 'Youths Attack Algerian Protesters', *Al Jazeera*, 5 March 2011, http://www.aljazeera.com/news/africa/2011/03/20113512417540287.html.

67. See AFP, 'Le gouvernement désormais confronté à la grogne des gardes communaux', *France24*, 7 March 2011, http://www.france24.com/fr/20110307-algerie-gardes-communaux-alger-bravent-interdiction-marche-police-gendarmerie-manifestations; Mohamed Boufatah, 'Garde communale: Le Directeur Général limogé', *L'Expression*, 2 April 2011.

68. Brown, 'Algeria's Midwinter Uproar'.

69. Karima Direche-Slimani, 'Le mouvement des âarch en Algérie: Pour une alternative démocratique autonome?' *Revue des Mondes Musulmans et de la Mediterranée* No. 111–112, 2006, pp. 183–196.

70. Oudasou Bida, 'Le lynchage raciste de Said Sadi: Peut-on se taire?', *Le Matin d'Algérie*, 7 March 2011.

71. Eva Bellin, 'The Robustness of Authoritarianism in the Middle East: Exceptionalism in Comparative Perspective', *Comparative Politics* 36 (2) 2004, pp. 139–157.

72. Volpi, *Islam and Democracy*; Robert Mortimer, 'Islamists, Soldiers, and Democrats: The Second Algerian War', *Middle East Journal* 50 (1) 1996, pp. 18–39.

73. See Isabelle Werenfels, *Managing Instability in Algeria: Elites and Political Change since 1995*. New York: Routledge, 2007; Robert Mortimer, 'State and Army in Algeria: The "Bouteflika effect"', *Journal of North African Studies* 11 (2) 2006, pp. 155–171.

74. See Bruguière, 'La "marche pour la démocratie" du 12 février divise les Algériens'.

75. The Moroccan Ministry of Foreign Affairs duly compiled a selection of all the positive endorsements by foreign governments of the 9 March discourse, available at: http://www.diplomatie.ma/Portals/0/Discours%20Royal%20du%209%20mars,%20R%C3%A9actions%20%C3%A0%20l%27%C3%A9tranger.pdf.

76. Statement of Alain Juppé, Foreign Affairs Minister, 11 March 2011, http://www.ambafrance-ma.org/Entretien-du-ministre-d-Etat-avec.

77. Alain Juppé, 'Entretien avec la coalition des jeunes pour la révolution', Cairo, 6 March 2011, http://www.diplomatie.gouv.fr/fr/pays-zones-geo/egypte/la-france-et-l-egypte/visites-8493/article/entretien-d-alain-juppe-avec-la-90364 (accessed 2 March 2012).

78. European Council, Declaration: Extraordinary European Council, 11 March 2011, EUCO 7/1/11 REV 1, Brussels, 20 April 2011, http://www.consilium.europa.eu/ucdocs/cms_data/docs/pressdata/en/ec/119780.pdf.

79. Statement by Mr Alain Juppé, Minister of Foreign and European Affairs, Security Council—Libya, 17 March 2011, http://www.franceonu.org/17-March-2011-Security-Council.

80. For an illustration of these networking activities, see: http://solidmar.blogspot.fr/2011/03/le-comite-marocain-de-suivi-du-20_31.html; https://www.facebook.com/notes/collectif-des-amazighs-de-france-pour-le-changement-d%C3%A9mocratique-au-maroc/communiqu%C3%A9-du-collectif-des-amazighs-de-france-pour-le-changement-d%C3%A9mocratique-a/153811794680462.

81. Sélim Smaoui and Mohamed Wazif, 'Étendard de lutte ou pavillon de complaisance?', pp. 55–79, in Allal and Pierret, *Au cœur des révoltes arabes*.

82. See F. Iraki and M. Boudharam, 'Ils n'ont rien compris!', *Tel Quel*, 9–15 April 2011, http://www.atlasinfo.fr/Reforme-constitutionnelle-les-propositions-des-partis-politiques-sur-la-table_a15372.html; Lahcen Daoudi, Nabila Mounib and Nabil Benabdellah, 'Le Matin Forum', *Le Matin*, 6 April 2011.

83. The communiqué is available at http://www.bladi.net/constitution-parti-socialiste-unifie.html; http://www.maghress.com/fr/lakomefr/257.

84. Isabelle Mandraud, 'Maroc: Un "Mouvement du 9 mars" favorable au roi s'oppose au "Mouvement du 20 février"', *Le Monde*, 26 Mars 2011; Allan Popelard and Paul Vannier, 'A Marrakech, le mouvement du 20 février se poursuit', *Les Blogs du Monde Diplomatique*, 5 May 2011, http://blog.mondediplo.net/2011-05-05-A-Marrakech-le-mouvement-du-20-fevrier-se.

85. AFP, 'Maroc: Manifestations le 20 mars, un test après le discours du roi', *L'Express*, 18 March 2011, http://www.lexpress.fr/actualites/1/monde/maroc-manifestations-le-20-mars-un-test-apres-le-discours-du-roi_973959.html.

86. Souleiman Bencheikh, 'Maroc: Pas de consensus sur la réforme de la constitution', *L'Express*, 10 May 2011, http://www.lexpress.fr/actualite/monde/maroc-pas-de-consensus-sur-la-reforme-de-la-constitution_990820.html.

87. AFP, 'Maroc: Manifestations le 20 mars, un test après le discours du roi'.

88. Smaoui and Wazif, 'Étendard de lutte'.

89. See Montserrat Emperador, 'Les manifestations des diplômés chômeurs au Maroc: La rue comme espace de négociation du tolérable', *Genèses* 77 (4) 2009, pp. 30–50; Myriam Catusse and Frederic Vairel, 'Question sociale et développement: Les territoires de l'action publique et de la contestation au Maroc', *Politique Africaine* 120 (4) 2010, pp. 5–23.

90. RFI, 'Au Maroc, la violente répression d'une manifestation à Casablanca fait plusieurs blessés graves', *Radio France Internationale*, 14 March 2011, http://www.rfi.fr/afrique/20110314-maroc-violente-repression.

91. Cited in AFP/L'Express, 'Maroc: Dizaines de blessés après une manifestation à Casablanca', LEXPRESS.COM, 13 March 2011, http://www.lexpress.fr/actualites/1/actualite/maroc-dizaines-de-blesses-apres-une-manifestation-a-casablanca_971720.html.

92. See Bennani, 'Manifs: Tabassage, mutinerie et vidéos', *Tel Quel*, 28 May—3 June 2011. See also the *Tel Quel* special section, 'Le Makhzen contre-attaque' in the same issue.

93. Amnesty International, *Au Maroc, les personnes soupçonnées d'activités liées au terrorisme continuent d'être victimes d'atteintes aux droits humains*, Synthèse, MDE 29/013/2010, 16 June 2010, http://www.amnesty. org/en/library/asset/MDE29/013/2010/en/ceaa7630-50a5-4618-bd4c-47e75caf3718/mde290132010fra.pdf.

94. See M. Jaabouk, 'La marche tourne à la bastonnade', *Le Soir*, 17 May 2011; M. Jaabouk, 'Ça cogne le dimanche', *Le Soir*, 24 May 2011; L. Hallaoui, 'Marches cauchemars', *Le Soir*, 27 May 2011; M. Boudharam, 'Un après-midi en enfer', *Tel Quel*, 28 May—3 June 2011.

95. See Thierry Desrues, 'Le mouvement du 20 février et le régime marocain: Contestation, révision constitutionnelle et élections', *L'Année du Maghreb* No. 8, 2012, pp. 359–389.

96. AFP/Le Monde, 'Le roi du Maroc gracie 190 détenus, dont des prisonniers politiques', *Le Monde*, 14 April 2011.

6. DEMOBILIZATION AND RECONSTRUCTION OF THE ACTORS OF THE UPRISINGS

1. Donatella Della Porta, *Mobilizing for Democracy: Comparing 1989 and 2011*. Oxford: Oxford University Press, 2014.

2. The 'beacon of hope' expression is from US Secretary of State John Kerry in relation to the Tunisian parliamentary elections of 2014. Secretary of State John Kerry, 'Statement about the Parliamentary Elections in Tunisia', October 27, 2014, http://tunisia.usembassy.gov/tunisias-democratic-transition/statement-by-secretary-kerry-on-parliamentary-elections-in-tunisia-october-27-2014.html. For a scholarly illustration of this view, see Eva Bellin, 'Reconsidering the Robustness of Authoritarianism in the Middle East: Lessons from the Arab Spring', *Comparative Politics* 44 (2) 2012, pp. 127–149.

3. Such potentialities were illustrated by the spectacular rise of the Salafists of Ansar al-Sharia in 2011–13. See Stefano M. Torelli, Fabio Merone and Francesco Cavatorta, 'Salafism in Tunisia: Challenges and Opportunities for Democratization', *Middle East Policy* 19 (4) 2012, pp. 140–154.

4. This issue is on a par with the debate over who 'owns' the revolution and, reciprocally, who can 'steal' it. Regarding the debates about 'ending' the French Revolution, see François Furet, *Interpreting the French Revolution*. Trans. E. Forster. Cambridge: Cambridge University Press, 1981.

5. See Arthur L. Stinchcombe, 'Ending Revolutions and Building New Governments', *Annual Review of Political Science* No. 2, 1999, pp. 49–73.

6. Fears of a military takeover were voiced in the press at the time. See David Kirkpatrick, 'Military Backs New Leaders in Tunisia', *New York*

Times, 16 January 2011; Pierre Robert Baduel, 'Tunisie: Le rôle complexe et déterminant de l'armée', *Le Monde*, 20 February 2011.

7. See Hélène Sallon, 'Les jeunes de la Kasbah reprennent la révolution tunisienne en main', *Le Monde*, 4 March 2011; Karim M, 'Tunisie: Le rôle de la Casbah et l'avenir de la Révolution', *Nawaat*, 4 March 2011, http://nawaat.org/portail/2011/03/04/tunisie-le-role-de-la-casbah-et-lavenir-de-la-revolution; Éric Gobe, 'Tunisie an I: Les Chantiers de la transition', *L'Année du Maghreb* 8, 2012, pp. 433–454.

8. Cited in Delphine Minoui, 'Tunisie: Les écoles ne rouvrent pas, l'armée promet la paix', *Le Figaro*, 24 January 2011.

9. Tellingly, two days after the flight of the president, army units had to launch an assault on the presidential palace still controlled by loyalist forces. Catherine Boullay and Damien Gourlet, 'Tunisie: L'armée donne l'assaut', *Europe1*, 16 January 2011, http://www.europe1.fr/International/Tunisie-l-armee-donne-l-assaut-373831.

10. Cited in Minoui, 'Tunisie: Les écoles ne rouvrent pas, l'armée promet la paix'.

11. Jeune Afrique, 'Ben Ali fuit la Tunisie, Mohamed Ghannouchi prend le pouvoir', *Jeune Afrique*, 15 January 2011.

12. Jean-Denis Renard, 'Tunis aux mains de l'armée et des habitants', *Sud-Ouest*, 16 January 2011.

13. AFP, 'La Tunisie entre pillages et ordre nouveau', *L'Express*, 16 January 2011.

14. Le Figaro, 'Les vivres commencent à manquer à Tunis', *Le Figaro*, 16 January 2011.

15. Catherine Boullay, 'Tunisie: Un gouvernement de transition', *Europe1*, 17 January 2011, http://www.europe1.fr/International/Tunisie-un-gouvernement-de-transition-375637; Europe1, 'Tunisie: Le parti de Ben Ali conspué', *Europe1*, 17 January 2011, http://www.europe1.fr/International/Tunisie-le-parti-de-Ben-Ali-conspue-375647.

16. AFP, 'Tunisie: Amnistie générale en vigueur', *Le Figaro*, 19 January 2011.

17. See AFP, 'Tunisie: Trente-trois membres du clan Ben Ali arrêtés', *Le Nouvel Observateur*, 20 January 2011; AFP, 'Tunisie: Le gouvernement d'union nationale explose déjà', *Le Nouvel Observateur*, 19 January 2011.

18. Cited in Minoui, 'Tunisie: Les écoles ne rouvrent pas, l'armée promet la paix'.

19. A court validated the dissolution of the RCD on 9 March. Al Jazeera, 'Tunisia Bans Ruling Party Oficials from Vote', *Al Jazeera*, 27 April 2011, http://www.aljazeera.com/news/africa/2011/04/2011427185824517250.html.

20. See Bellin, 'Reconsidering the Robustness of Authoritarianism in the Middle East'.

21. Robert Springborg and Clement M. Henry, 'Army Guys', *The American Interest*, May/June 2011.

22. Amy Kallander, 'Tunisia's post-Ben Ali Challenge', *Middle East Report Online*, 26 January 2011, http://www.merip.org/mero/mero012611.

23. For probing queries about the 'virtuous' role of the military, see Alejandro Pachon, 'Loyalty and Defection: Misunderstanding Civil-Military Relations in Tunisia During the "Arab Spring"', *Journal of Strategic Studies* 37 (4) 2014, pp. 508–531.

24. It was after these riots that then Brigadier-General Zine el-Abidine Ben Ali was appointed director of national security at the Interior Ministry.

25. L.B. Ware, 'The Role of the Tunisian Military in the Post-Bourgiba Era', *Middle East Journal* 39 (1) 1985, pp. 27–47, at p. 39.

26. About tensions between different branches of the Tunisian security apparatus, see Hicham Bou Nassif, 'A Military Besieged: The Armed Forces, the Police, and the Party in Bin Ali's Tunisia, 1987–2011', *International Journal of Middle East Studies* 47 (1) 2015, pp. 65–87.

27. Looking at the Egyptian case, it could also be said that initially General Sisi was not seen to have a strong political agenda that clashed with the Muslim Brotherhood when he emerged as a leading military figure of the post-Mubarak period. Yet he would soon engineer the end of the Egyptian democratic transition. See Robert Springborg, 'Sisi's Islamist Agenda for Egypt: The General's Radical Political Vision', *Foreign Affairs*, 25 July 2013.

28. See Francis Ghiles, 'Viewpoint: Military Coup Would Harm Tunisia's Interests', *BBC News*, 6 March 2011, http://www.bbc.co.uk/news/world-africa-12623237.

29. Boullay and Gourlet, 'Tunisie: L'armée donne l'assaut'.

30. Monia Ghanmi, 'Tunisia Offers Concessions to Security Forces', *Magharebia*, 2 February 2011, http://www.magharebia.com/cocoon/awi/xhtml1/en_GB/features/awi/features/2011/02/02/feature-01.

31. Cited in Catherine Simon, 'A Bizerte, la population se méfie d'un ennemi invisible', *Le Monde*, 18 January 2011.

32. Cited in David Kirkpatrick 'Chief of Tunisian army pledges his support for "the revolution"', *New York Times*, 24 January 2011.

33. See Samy Ghorbal, 'L'armée peut-elle intervenir dans la crise politique en Tunisie?', *Rue89.Nouvelobs*, 3 March 2011, http://rue89.nouvelobs.com/2011/03/03/l-armee-peut-elle-intervenir-dans-la-crise-politique-en-tunisie-193291.

34. Dominique Lagarde 'Tunisie: Touche pas à ma révolution!', *L'Express*,

1 March 2011; AFP, 'La Tunisie change de premier ministre', *Le Nouvel Observateur*, 27 February 2011.

35. His resignation was followed by that of five of his ministers in a matter of days.

36. In an interview, Ben Achour detailed the tensions between the transitional government and the National Council. He noted that the Council wanted to supervise the actions of the government and vet the people nominated by it. As the government did not want to have such a supra-institutional process, they initiated negotiations to create a new institutional body which merged together the two previous bodies. Pierre Barbancey, 'Tunisie: Yadh ben Achour "une révolution de type moderne"', *L'Humanité*, 6 September 2011.

37. By then it was composed of 12 political parties and 19 unions and professional or civil associations, as well as several independent personalities.

38. Stepan even commented that the Tunisian High Commission was 'one of the most effective consensus-building bodies in the history of "crafted" democratic transitions'. Alfred Stepan, 'Tunisia's Transition and the Twin Tolerations', *Journal of Democracy* 23 (2) 2012, pp. 89–103, at p. 92.

39. See Emna el-Hammi, 'Le Bourguibisme de Béji Caid Essebsi contre la menace islamiste', *Tunisie Blogs Liberation*, 18 April 2011, http://tunisie.blogs.liberation.fr/2011/04/18/le-bourguibisme-de-beji-caid-essebsi-contre-la-menace-islamiste. For the full list of the members of the government, see AFP, 'Un nouveau gouvernement provisoire en Tunisie', *Radio France Internationale*, 7 March 2011, http://www.rfi.fr/afrique/20110307-nouveau-gouvernement-provisoire-tunisie.

40. AFP/L'Express, 'Tunisie: La majorité silencieuse défend son droit à se remettre au travail', LEXPRESS.fr, 5 April 2011, http://www.lexpress.fr/actualites/1/monde/tunisie-la-majorite-silencieuse-defend-son-droit-a-se-remettre-au-travail_969129.html.

41. See Laryssa Chomiak, 'The Making of a Revolution in Tunisia', *Middle East Law and Governance* 3 (1–2), pp. 68–83; Amin Allal and Vincent Geisser, 'La Tunisie de l'après-Ben Ali', *Cultures and Conflicts* 83, 2011, pp. 118–125; Gobe, 'Tunisie an I'.

42. See Jean-Pierre Filiu, 'The First Year of the Tunisian Revolution', in Saïd Amir Arjomand, ed., *The Arab Revolution of 2011: A Comparative Perspective*. Albany: SUNY Press, 2015.

43. AFP/Le Monde, 'L'élection d'une assemblée constituante en Tunisie repoussée au 23 octobre', *Le Monde*, 6 June 2011.

44. AFP, 'Tunisie: L'instance des réformes clôt l'acte I de la révolution', *L'Express*, 13 October 2011.

45. See Élodie Auffray, 'En Tunisie, la jeune démocratie compte plus de

100 partis', *Sud-Ouest*, 2 October 2011; Tarek Amara, 'Tunisia Opens First Election Campaign Since Uprising', *Reuters*, 2 October 2011, http://www.reuters.com/article/2011/10/02/us-tunisia-poll-id USTRE7901TX20111002.

46. The first anniversary of the fall of Ben Ali brought to Tunis an array of Arab leaders, from Qatar to Algeria, who were keen to be seen congratulating the Tunisian people for their revolution. President Bouteflika of Algeria even declared on that occasion that 'Algerians are optimistic after your victory'. AFP, 'Moncef Marzouki: "La Tunisie va poursuivre sa marche vers la liberté"', *Jeune Afrique*, 14 January 2012, http://www.jeuneafrique.com/152929/politique/moncef-marzouki-la-tunisie-va-poursuivre-sa-marche-vers-la-libert/.

47. The NTC declared that Libya was officially 'liberated' on 23 October 2011.

48. Frederic Wehrey, 'NATO's Intervention', in Peter Cole and Brian McQuinn, eds., *The Libyan Revolution and Its Aftermath*. New York: Oxford University Press, 2015.

49. International Crisis Group (ICG), 'Holding Libya Together: Security Challenges after Gadhafi', Middle East/North Africa Report No. 115, 14 December 2011.

50. Brian McQuinn, 'History's Warriors: The Emergence of Revolutionary Brigades in Misrata', in Cole and McQuinn, *The Libyan Revolution*.

51. Cited in Adrian Blomfield and Richard Spencer, 'Libya: Confusion in the Mountains, Mixed Messages from the West', *The Telegraph*, 16 July 2011.

52. In May 2011 already, the NTC declared on its official Facebook page that 'the Council derives its legitimacy from the decisions of local councils set up by the revolutionary people of Libya on the 17th of February. These local councils facilitated a mechanism to manage daily life in the liberated cities and villages.' See https://www.facebook.com/notes/national-transitional-council-of-libya/introducing-the-council/203658689673270.

53. Wolfram Lacher and Ahmed Labnouj, 'Factionalism Resurgent: The War in the Jabal Nafusa', in Cole and McQuinn, *The Libyan Revolution*.

54. The text of the interim constitution is available at the Max Planck Institute website, http://www.mpil.de/en/pub/archive/projekte_2010_11/globaler_wissenstransfer/constitutional_reform_in_arab_/libyen.cfm.

55. Frederic Wehrey, 'Ending Libya's Civil War: Reconciling Politics, Rebuilding Security', Carnegie Endowment for International Peace, September 2014.

56. Peter Cole and Umar Khan, 'The Fall of Tripoli: Part 2', in Cole and McQuinn, *The Libyan Revolution*;

57. Cited in David Kirkpatrick and Rod Nordland, 'Tripoli Divided as Rebels Jostle to Fill Power Vacuum', *New York Times*, 30 August 2011.

58. Brian McQuinn, *After the Fall: Libya's Evolving Armed Groups*, Geneva: Small Arms Survey, 2012; International Crisis Group (ICG), 'Holding Libya Together'.

59. Cited in Nick Meo, 'Libya Dispatch: As Lawlessness Spreads, are the Rebel "Good Guys" Turning Bad?', *The Telegraph*, 5 November 2011.

60. Regarding the resistance of the eastern provinces vis-à-vis the new central government, see Frederic Wehrey, 'The Struggle for Security in Eastern Libya', Carnegie Endowment for International Peace, September 2012, http://carnegieendowment.org/files/libya_security_2.pdf.

61. See Saïd Haddad, 'Insécurité, exclusion et blocage politiques dans une Libye fragmentée', *L'Année du Maghreb* 9, 2014, pp. 231–249; Hanspeter Mattes, 'Rebuilding the National-Security Forces in Libya', *Middle East Policy* 21 (2) 2014, pp. 85–99.

62. Cited in Gabriel Gatehouse, 'Misrata Votes for Brighter Libyan Future', BBC News, 20 February 2012. http://www.bbc.co.uk/news/world-africa-17107048

63. See Mahmoud Habboush, 'Battle Between Tripoli, Misrata Militias Kills 4', *Reuters*, 3 January 2012, http://www.reuters.com/article/2012/01/03/us-libya-rebels-clash-idUSTRE8021FP20120103; Libya Herald, 'Misrata ports now handed over; Tripoli airport still in Zintan hands', *Libya Herald*, 18 March 2012, http://www.libyaherald.com/2012/03/18/misrata-ports-now-handed-over-tripoli-airport-still-in-zintan-hands/#axzz2i47WrcvT.

64. Wehrey, 'Ending Libya's Civil War'.

65. Cited in AP, 'Libya: Western Militias Unite, Posing Challenge to Transitional Government', *New York Times*, 14 February 2012.

66. Paul Salem and Amanda Kadlec, 'Libya's Troubled Transition', Carnegie Middle East Centre, June 2012, http://carnegie-mec.org/2012/06/14/libya-s-troubled-transition/c057#.

67. Lacher and Labnouj, 'Factionalism Resurgent'.

68. Salem and Kadlec, 'Libya's Troubled Transition'; Wehrey, 'The Struggle for Security in Eastern Libya'.

69. See Kim Sengupta, 'Armed Federalists Shut Down Libya Oil Terminals Ahead of Vote', *The Independent*, 6 July 2012; AFP, 'Oil terminals in east Libya forced shut', *Al-Arabiya*, 6 July 2012, http://english.alarabiya.net/articles/2012/07/06/224769.html.

70. Wehrey, 'The Struggle for Security in Eastern Libya'.

71. See Rebecca Murray, 'Libya's Tebu: Living in the Margins', in Cole and McQuinn, *The Libyan Revolution*; Yvan Guichaoua, 'Tuareg Militancy

and the Sahelian Shock Waves of the Civil War in Libya', in Cole and McQuinn, *The Libyan Revolution*.

72. Rana Jawad, 'Gunmen Occupy Libyan Parliament', *BBC*, 1 November 2012, http://www.bbc.com/news/world-africa-20170826.

73. Roman David and Houda Mzioudet, 'Personnel Change or Personal Change? Rethinking Libya's Political Isolation Law', Stanford Paper, Brookings Doha Center, 2014, http://www.brookings.edu/~/media/research/files/papers/2014/03/17%20libya%20lustration%20david%20mzioudet/lustration%20in%20libya%20english.pdf.

74. See Lamine Chikhi and Christian Lowe, 'Algeria Police use Tear Gas on Protest in Capital', Reuters, 16 March 2011, http://af.reuters.com/article/commoditiesNews/idAFLDE72F1VJ20110316; Larbi Louafi and Christian Lowe, 'Algerian police clash with rioters in housing row', Reuters, 23 March 2011, http://af.reuters.com/article/algeriaNews/idAFLDE72M1W620110323.

75. Cited in RFI, 'Algérie: Tension palpable après les émeutes du logement à Alger', *Radio France Internationale*, 25 April 2011, http://www.rfi.fr/afrique/20110325-apres-emeutes-contre-destruction-logements-alger-tension-est-toujours-palpable.

76. Ali Chibani, 'En Algérie, répression et opportunismes', *Le Monde Diplomatique*, 8 April 2011.

77. Chibani, 'En Algérie, répression et opportunismes'. Chibani noted that this strategy had already been used by the regime ahead of the 2009 presidential election when Bouteflika undermined the opposition by offering better pay conditions.

78. Farid Aïchoune, 'Algérie: Comment Bouteflika maintient le statu quo', *Le Nouvel Obs*, 17 March 2011.

79. See Le Matin d'Algérie, 'L'Incroyable marche des étudiants à Alger', *Le Matin d'Algérie*, 13 April 2011.

80. Luiz Martinez, *The Violence of Petrodollar Regimes: Algeria, Iraq and Libya*. New York: Columbia University Press, 2012.

81. See Fidet Mansour, 'Algeria Finances Strained by Strife', *Magharebia*, 7 July 2011, http://www.magharebia.com/cocoon/awi/xhtml1/en_GB/features/awi/features/2011/07/07/feature-02; Hamoud Salhi, 'Is Algeria immune from the Arab spring?' *BBC*, 27 July 2011, http://www.bbc.co.uk/news/world-africa-14167481.

82. See World Bank, 'Algeria: Country Brief', Washington, DC: World Bank, April 2011, http://go.worldbank.org/T2K4PW3270; Hakim Darbouche, 'Algeria's Failed Transitions to a Sustainable Polity: Coming to Yet Another Crossroads', MEDPRO Technical Report No. 7, Brussels, October 2011.

83. Algeria's Finance Minister, Karim Djoudi, estimated that Algeria's bud-

get would be able to sustain these increases until 2014–15. Cited in Mansour, 'Algeria Finances Strained by Strife'.

84. The IMF estimated at the time that for the country to absorb the growing number of yearly entries into the job market, its non-hydro-carbon sector had to grow by at least 5 per cent annually. IMF, 'Algeria Should Reduce Reliance on Oil, Create More Jobs, Says IMF', *IMF Survey Magazine*, 26 January 2011, http://www.imf.org/external/pubs/ft/survey/so/2011/int012611a.htm.

85. Steven A. Cook, *Ruling but Not Governing: The Military and Political Development in Egypt, Algeria, and Turkey*. Baltimore: Johns Hopkins University Press, 2007, p. 45.

86. John P. Entelis, 'Algeria, Revolutionary in Name Only', *Foreign Policy*, 7 September 2011.

87. SIPRI Military Expenditure Database, 'Algeria', Stockholm International Peace Research Institute, Stockholm, 2012, http://milexdata.sipri.org/.

88. See L.O., 'DGSN: Hausse de salaire de 50% pour les policiers', *Le Jour d'Algérie*, 28 December 2010; Ali Graichi, 'Malaise dans l'armée: Soudaine augmentation de 40% des salaires sur fond de guerre des clans', *Le Quotidien d'Algérie*, 6 January 2011.

89. President Abdelaziz Bouteflika, 'Discours du Président de la République à la Nation', Présidence de la République, Algiers, 15 April 2011, http://www.elmouradia.dz/francais/president/activites/PresidentActi.htm.

90. These included the Future Front led by Abdelaziz Belaid, the Youth Party led by Hamana Boucharma, the Party of Dignity led by Mohamed Ben Hammou, the Front of Rightly-Guided Governance led by Aissa Bel-Hadi, the Movement of Free Citizens led by Mustapha Boudina, and the New Dawn led by Tahar Benbaibeche.

91. Cited in Ali Chibani, 'Algérie: Des élections jouées d'avance', *SlateAfrique.com*, 10 May 2012, http://www.slateafrique.com/86975/des-elections-legislatives-algerie-bouteflika-abstention-10-mai.

92. See Yahia H. Zoubir and Ahmed Aghrout, 'Algeria's Path to Reform: Authentic Change?', *Middle East Policy* 19 (2) 2012, pp 66–83; Frédéric Volpi, 'Algeria versus the Arab Spring', *Journal of Democracy* 24 (3) 2013, pp. 104–115.

93. US Secretary of State Hillary Clinton judged at the time that these elections were 'a welcome step in Algeria's progress toward democratic reform'. Hillary Rodham Clinton, Press Statement, Algerian Elections, Washington, DC, 12 May 2012, http://www.state.gov/secretary/rm/2012/05/189811.htm.

94. See Mohamed Jaabouk, 'La matraque tient toujours la vedette', *Le Soir*

Echos, 31 May 2011; Ilhem Rachidi, 'Au Maroc, le pouvoir a signifié la fin de la récré', *Rue 89-Nouvel Obs*, 29 May 2011, http://www.rue89.com/2011/05/29/repression-au-maroc-le-pouvoir-signifie-la-fin-de-la-recre-206438.

95. Human Rights Watch, 'Maroc: Les violences policières sont un test pour la nouvelle constitution', *Human Rights Watch*, 11 July 2011, https://www.hrw.org/fr/news/2011/07/11/maroc-les-violences-policieres-sont-un-test-pour-la-nouvelle-constitution.

96. See Souad Mekhennet and Steven Erlanger, 'Fatal Bomb in Morocco Shows Signs of Al Qaeda', *New York Times*, 29 April 2011; Irene Fernández Molina, 'The Monarchy vs. the 20 February Movement: Who Holds the Reins of Political Change in Morocco?', *Mediterranean Politics* 16 (3) 2011, pp. 435–441.

97. On the interactions between the regime and the workers' unions in this context, see Matt Buehler, 'Labour Demands, Regime Concessions: Moroccan Unions and the Arab Uprising', *British Journal of Middle Eastern Studies* 42 (1) 2015, pp. 88–103.

98. The text of the referendum was published in Royaume du Maroc, *Bulletin Officiel* No. 5952, Rabat, 17 June 2011.

99. AFP, 'Référendum au Maroc: Partisans et opposants par milliers dans la rue', *L'Express*, 26 June 2011. On the activities of the Boutchichia more generally, see Abdelilah Bouasria, 'La Tarîqa Qadiria Boutchichi au Maroc: La genèse d'un soufisme de marché?', *Mamfakinch.com*, 22 February 2012, https://www.mamfakinch.com/la-tariqa-qadiria-boutchichi-au-maroc-la-genese-dun-soufisme-de-marche.

100. Cited in Souhail Karam, 'Rival Groups March over King's Reforms in Morocco', *Reuters*, 26 June 2011, http://www.reuters.com/article/us-morocco-idUSTRE75P1UB20110626.

101. Mamfakinch, 'Communiqué sur les atteintes à l'intégrité du scrutin référendaire', *Mamfakinch*, 28 June 2011, https://www.mamfakinch.com/communique-de-mamfakinch-sur-les-atteintes-a-lintegrite-du-scrutin referendaire.

102. Mamfakinch, 'Communiqué sur les atteintes'.

103. Rickard Lagervall, 'The King's Two Bodies: The New Moroccan Constitution', *Jadaliyya*, 23 April 2012, http://www.jadaliyya.com/pages/TME1/5240/the-king%E2%80%99s-two-bodies_the-new-moroccan-constitutio.

104. See Mustapha Ajbaili, 'In Morocco, "Vote Early and Vote Often" even if the Results are Preordained', *Al Arabiya*, 2 July 2011, http://english.alarabiya.net/articles/2011/07/02/155708.html; Adam Kouider, 'Maroc: Où est le changement?', *Eplume*, 2 July 2011, http://eplume.wordpress.com/2011/07/02/maroc-ou-est-le-changement.

105. See Leïla Slimani, 'Maroc: Trop de contestation tue la contestation', *Jeune Afrique*, 4 October 2011, http://www.jeuneafrique.com/ Article/ARTJAJA2646p050–051.xml0/islamistes-islamisme-manifestation-mohammed-vimaroc-trop-de-contestation-tue-la-contestation. html; Pierre-François Naudé, 'Maroc: Le Mouvement du 20 février fête son premier anniversaire', *Jeune Afrique*, 20 February 2012, http://www.jeuneafrique.com/Article/ARTJAWEB2012022008 2133/maroc-pjd-pauvrete-corruptionmaroc-le-mouvement-du-20-fevrier-fete-son-premier-anniversaire.html.

106. James N. Sater, 'Parliamentary Elections and Authoritarian Rule in Morocco', *Middle East Journal* 63 (3) 2009, pp. 381–400.

107. See Hélene Salllon, 'Boycotter les élections législatives au Maroc?', *Blogs Le Monde*, 25 November 2011, http://printempsarabe.blog.lemonde.fr/2011/11/25/boycotter-les-elections-legislatives-au-maroc; Oussama Elkhlifi interviewed by Ilhem Rachidi, 'Au Maroc, le Mouvement du 20 Février maintient la pression', *Rue 89-Nouvel Obs*, 11 September 2011, http://www.rue89.com/2011/09/11/au-maroc-le-mouvement-du-20-fevrier-maintient-la-pression-221483.

108. Cited in Souhail Karam, 'Thousands of Moroccans Protest for Reform, Violence in the Capital', *Al Arabiya News*, 24 October 2011, https://www.alarabiya.net/articles/2011/10/24/173494.html.

109. Mouvement 20 Février, 'Appel au boycott des élections', *YouTube*, http://www.youtube.com/watch?v=P1LQU_dI7MA&feature= player_embedded.

110. Al-Adl wal-Ihsane Secrétariat Général du Cercle Politique, 'Al-Adl wal-Ihsane décide la suspension de sa participation au Mouvement 20 Février', Al-Adl wal-Ihsane, 18 December 2012, http://www. aljamaa.net/fr/document/4134.shtml; Au Fait Maroc, 'Al-Adl wal-Ihsane annonce son retrait du Mouvement du 20 Février: La Fin de la lune de miel', *Au Fait Maroc*, 18 December 2012, http://www. aufaitmaroc.com/actualites/maroc/2011/12/18/la-fin-de-la-lune-de-miel#.UiIkFn87bN4.

111. Fathallah Arsalane interviewed by Noureddine Jouhariin, *Maroc Hebdo*, No. 959, 23–29 December 2011.

112. Ashraf Nabih El Sherif, 'Institutional and Ideological Re-construction of the Justice and Development Party (PJD): The Question of Democratic Islamism in Morocco', *Middle East Journal* 66 (4) 2012, pp. 660–682. Eva Wegner, *Islamist Opposition in Authoritarian Regimes: The Party of Justice and Development in Morocco*. Syracuse: Syracuse University Press, 2011.

113. AFP, 'Au Maroc, des négociations ont débuté en vue de former un gouvernement', *Le Monde*, 29 November 2011.

114. See Paul Schemm, 'Morocco: Islamist Justice and Development Party

leads government', *World Post*, 3 January 2012, http://www.huffing-tonpost.com/2012/01/03/morocco-islamist-justice-and-development_n_1181086.html.

115. See Reporters sans Frontières, 'Après un an de prison, Rachid Nini retrouve la liberté', *Reporters sans Frontières*, 30 April 2012, http://fr.rsf.org/maroc-apres-un-an-de-prison-rachid-nini-30-04-2012,42396.html.

116. AP/Al Jazeera, 'Moroccans burn selves in unemployment protest', *Al Jazeera*, 20 January 2012, http://www.aljazeera.com/news/afr ica/2012/01/20121192320413900.html.

117. At a local level, see Janine A. Clark and Emanuela Dalmasso, 'State Actor-Social Movement Coalitions and Policy-making under Authoritarianism: The Moroccan Party of Justice and Development in the Urban Municipality of Kenitra', *Middle East Law and Governance*, 7 (2) 2015, pp.185–211.

118. Author's interview with Abdellah Bouanou, leader of the PJD parliamentary group, Rabat, Morocco, 3 July 2013.

119. See Frédéric Vairel, *Politique et mouvements sociaux au Maroc: La révolution désamorcée?*, Paris: Presses de Sciences Po, 2014.

120. Cited in AFP, 'Les Marocains fêtent l'anniversaire du Mouvement du 20-Février', France24.com, 20 February 2012, http://www.france24.com/fr/20120220-marocains-fetent-anniversaire-mouvement-20-fevrier-m20-casablanca-contestation-manifestation.

7. CONCLUSION: MOBILIZATION AND DEMOBILIZATION IN THE NORTH AFRICAN UPRISINGS

1. Charles Kurzman, *The Unthinkable Revolution in Iran*. Cambridge: Harvard University Press, 2004.

2. Jason Brownlee, Tarek Masoud and Andrew Reynolds, *The Arab Spring: Pathways of Repression and Reform*. Oxford: Oxford University Press, 2015.

3. Brownlee, Masoud and Reynolds, *The Arab Spring*, p. 62.

4. Sidney Tarrow, 'Cycles of Collective Action: Between Moments of Madness and the Repertoire of Contention', *Social Science History* 17 (2) 1993, pp. 281–307.

5. Charles Kurzman, 'Can Understanding Undermine Explanation? The Confused Experience of Revolution', *Philosophy of the Social Sciences* 34 (3) 2004, pp. 328–351, p. 347.

6. Dobry described these changing logics in protest situations well before the Arab uprisings. See Michel Dobry, 'Critical Processes and Political Fluidity: A Theoretical Appraisal', *International Political Anthropology* 2 (1) 2009, pp. 74–90.

7. See Wendy Pearlman, 'Emotions and the Microfoundations of the Arab Uprisings', *Perspectives on Politics* 11 (2) 2013, pp. 387–409.

8. See Kurt Weyland, 'The Arab Spring: Why the Surprising Similarities with the Revolutionary Wave of 1848?', *Perspectives on Politics* 10 (4) 2012, pp. 917–934.

9. These dynamics were already visible during the 2008 Gafsa protest. See Amin Allal, 'Réformes néolibérales, clientélismes et protestations en situation autoritaire: Les mouvements contestataires dans le bassin minier de Gafsa en Tunisie (2008)', *Politique Africaine* No.117, 2010, pp. 107–126.

10. Anja Hoffmann and Christoph König, 'Scratching the Democratic Façade: Framing Strategies of the 20 February Movement', *Mediterranean Politics* 18 (1) 2013, pp. 1–22.

11. Tocqueville's observation about the reassessment of one's plight once the perspective of change appears on the horizon remains most pertinent in this situation: 'A sovereign who seeks to relieve his subjects after a long period of oppression is lost, unless he be a man of great genius. Evils which are patiently endured when they seem inevitable, become intolerable when once the idea of escape from them is suggested.' Alexis de Tocqueville, *The Old Regime and the French Revolution*. Trans. J. Bonner. New York: Dover Publications, 2010 [1856], p. 214.

12. Alain Juppé, 'Entretien d'Alain Juppé avec la coalition des jeunes pour la révolution', Cairo, 6 March 2011, Ministère des Affaires Étrangères, http://www.diplomatie.gouv.fr/fr/pays-zones-geo/egypte/la-france-et-l-egypte/visites-8493/article/entretien-d-alain-juppe-avec-la-90364.

13. See Jeroen Gunning and Ilan Zvi Baron, *Why Occupy a Square?: People, Protests and Movements in the Egyptian Revolution*. New York: Oxford University Press, 2014.

14. See Steven Heydemann and Reinoud Leenders, 'Authoritarian Learning and Authoritarian Resilience: Regime Responses to the "Arab Awakening"', *Globalizations* 8 (5) 2011, pp. 647–653.

15. Quoted in Alain Gresh, 'Tunisia: compromise versus chaos', *Al-Ahram Weekly* No. 1144, 18 April 2013, http://weekly.ahram.org.eg/News/2295/21/Tunisia—compromise versus chaos.aspx. The leader of the FIS at the time of the 1991 elections to the Algerian parliament, Abdelkader Hachani, recognized afterwards that the fears of the FIS leadership were misplaced, and they ought to have been worried about doing too well, as their victory could trigger an authoritarian reversal. Frédéric Volpi, *Islam and Democracy: The Failure of Dialogue in Algeria*. London: Pluto Press, 2003.

16. See Roman David and Houda Mzioudet, 'Personnel Change or Personal Change? Rethinking Libya's Political Isolation Law', Brookings Doha

Center-Stanford Paper, 17 March 2014, http://www.brookings.edu/research/papers/2014/03/17-libya-lustration-david-mzioudet; Florence Gaub, 'A Libyan Recipe for Disaster', *Survival: Global Politics and Strategy* 56 (1) 2014, pp. 101–120.

17. See Hanspeter Mattes, 'Rebuilding the National-Security Forces in Libya', *Middle East Policy* 21 (2) 2014, pp. 85–99; Marc R. DeVore, 'Exploiting Anarchy: Violent Entrepreneurs and the Collapse of Libya's Post-Qadhafi Settlement', *Mediterranean Politics* 19 (3) 2014, pp. 463–470.

18. See Carmen Geha, *Civil Society and Political Reform in Lebanon and Libya: Transition and Constraint*. New York: Routledge, 2016; Carmen Geha and Frédéric Volpi, 'Constitutionalism and Political Order in Libya 2011–2014: Three Myths about the Past and a New Constitution', *Journal of North African Studies* 21 (4) 2016.

19. See Stefano M. Torelli, Fabio Merone and Francesco Cavatorta, 'Salafism in Tunisia: Challenges and Opportunities for Democratization', *Middle East Policy* 19 (4) 2012, pp. 140–154.

20. Kayla Branson, 'Islamist Cyber-activism: Contesting the Message, Redefining the Public', *Journal of North African Studies* 19 (5) 2014, pp. 713–732.

21. See Thierry Desrues, 'Mobilizations in a Hybrid Regime: The 20th February Movement and the Moroccan Regime', *Current Sociology* 61 (4) 2013, pp. 409–423; Samia Errazzouki, 'Morocco's 20 February Movement: Two Years Later', *Jadaliyya*, 7 March 2013, http://www.jadaliyya.com/pages/index/10514/moroccos-20-february-movement_two-years-later.

22. Emma C. Murphy, 'The Tunisian Elections of October 2011: A Democratic Consensus', *Journal of North African Studies* 18 (2) 2013, pp. 231–247.

23. Francesco Cavatorta, 'Salafism, Liberalism, and Democratic Learning in Tunisia', *Journal of North African Studies* 20, 2015.

24. Inmaculada Szmolka, 'Inter- and Intra-party Relations in the Formation of the Benkirane Coalition Governments in Morocco', *Journal of North African Studies* 20 (4) 2015, pp. 654–674.

25. Similar limitations and caveats to the use of counterfactuals in critical junctures also apply in this context. See Giovanni Capoccia and R. Daniel Kelemen, 'The Study of Critical Junctures: Theory, Narrative, and Counterfactuals in Historical Institutionalism', *World Politics* 59 (3) 2007, pp. 341–369.

INDEX